The Virtual University

Open and Distance Learning Series

Series Editor: Fred Lockwood

OPEN AND DISTANCE LEARNING SERIES

The Virtual University

The Internet and Resource-Based Learning

STEVE RYAN, BERNARD SCOTT, HOWARD FREEMAN & DAXA PATEL

KOGAN PAGE

London • Sterling (USA)

First published in 2000
Reprinted 2001

Kogan Page Limited
120 Pentonville Road
London N1 9JN
UK

Stylus Publishing Inc.
22883 Quicksilver Drive
Sterling VA 20166-2012
USA

British Library Cataloguing in Publication Data

A CIP record for this book is available from the British Library.

ISBN 0 7494 2508 3

Typeset by JS Typesetting, Wellingborough, Northants
Printed and bound in Great Britain by Biddles Ltd, *www.biddles.co.uk*

Contents

About the authors

Steve Ryan is Head of the Centre for Educational Technology and Development (CETD), Department of Learning Technologies at De Montfort University, Leicester, UK. Steve is particularly interested in the application of CIT to education and training.

Steve has been responsible for the development of a number of open and distance learning packages and is currently developing Internet-based courses, running workshops and researching conferencing systems.

His research interests relate to ways in which CIT can support teaching and learning.

Bernard Scott is a Senior Lecturer in De Montfort University's CETD. During the 1970s Bernard worked with Gordon Pask studying styles and strategies of learning and helped develop conversation theory as a framework for understanding learning and teaching. Bernard went on to train and practise as an educational psychologist. In 1990 he returned to full-time research and consultancy in higher education and worked at the Liverpool John Moores University and the Open University's Institute for Educational Technology before joining the CETD in 1996.

His research interests include theories of learning and teaching, knowledge and task analysis, learning styles and strategies and reading skills.

Howard Freeman is a Senior Lecturer in educational media in the CETD. He was a chartered biologist and member of the Institute of Biology. Howard has supported academics in the production of a wide range of CAL and multimedia learning materials and has developed his own sophisticated authoring support software.

Current interests include research and development in the use of concept mapping software (Conceptmapper, Webmapper) as part of the analysis, specification and delivery of multimedia, network and Web-based learning materials.

Daxa Patel was a principal lecturer in operational research in the School of Computing and Mathematical Sciences before becoming IT in Teaching and Learning Manager, in the Division of Learning Development in De Montfort University.

Daxa developed De Montfort University's first IT in Teaching and Learning Strategy in 1994. Since then she has been responsible for a number of major research and development initiatives in this area. She initiated (with Steve Ryan) an institution-wide project to facilitate the embedding of resource-based learning into the curriculum She has been involved in several national (TLTP) and European projects related to the use of CIT for resource-based learning.

Her work in the last two years has focused on a major review of university processes. Her research interests include the impact of CIT on the teaching and learning process, re-engineering and the management of change in HE.

Series editor's foreword

Teachers and trainers, whether they be in schools or universities, industry or commerce, are faced with a bewildering array of claims about the impact of Communication and Information Technology and the ways in which it can and should be deployed to our advantage. Managers and administrators are battling with the increasing demands to make education and training more widely available and cost effective. All of us want our provision to be of the highest quality; to combine our knowledge of subject content with appropriate pedagogy in meeting the changing needs of our learners in the new millennium. It is in this context that the book *The Virtual University: the Internet and resource-based learning* by Steve Ryan, Bernard Scott, Howard Freeman and Daxa Patel makes a significant contribution.

The book is written by a team of specialist practitioners at De Montfort University, UK; a team that is sharing its considerable insights and experience with all of us. The opening chapter sets the scene – it reviews the developments in education and training with regard to resource-based learning and the Internet. It not only identifies the opportunities and possibilities but also the threats and dangers. Other chapters provide insights into associated systems and provide illustrations of the resources – textual, aural and visual – that are available. Literally dozens of Web sites are identified as possible resources and a whole world suddenly becomes available which can be combined into a learning experience many of us could only dream about a few years ago.

However, the main message in the book is not dominated by the flashing lights of technology but rather the role of the teacher and trainer – or rather the changing role. The book echoes the call of Derek Rowntree, for us to be a 'guide on the side rather than the sage on the stage', as a facilitator rather than guru; for us to become part of a learning culture where we may have more to learn than we have to teach, where we use the most appropriate technology, not merely that which is fashionable. The books stands alone on its merits but also complements other books in the Open and Distance Learning Series.

In *Mega-Universities and Knowledge Media: Technology Strategies for Higher Education* (1996), the Vice-Chancellor of the Open University (OU), Sir John Daniel, comments on the growth in the number of students studying online with the OU. Today the OU has approximately 40,000 students studying part of their course online. In an average day 15,000 computer connections are made, over 5000 computer conferences are operational and 20,000 mail messages are posted – yet this is merely one institution among many in the world today as *The Virtual University: the Internet and resource-based learning* makes clear.

In other books, Marc Eisenstadt and Tom Vincent, authors of *The Knowledge Web: Learning and Collaborating on the Net* (2000), explore and illustrate the impact of the Knowledge Media on education and training, whilst in *Delivering Digitally* (1999) Alistair Inglis, Peter Ling and Vera Joosten provide managers and administrators, teachers and technicians, in fact anyone associated with the move to delivering teaching or training material digitally, with an invaluable resource. These existing books, together with the present one, with its clear focus on teaching and learning and using the new technologies to best effect, will provide you with a resource that will enable you to keep your feet on the ground and your finger on the pulse.

Fred Lockwood
April 2000

Acknowledgements

We wish to thank the following: James Atherton and Steve Wilson, colleagues at DMU, with whom Steve Ryan and Bernard Scott developed the Master's level module on RBL described in Chapter 9. Debates with them helped shape the discussion of RBL and the presentation of the theoretical ideas dealt with in Chapter 2.

Jos Boys, a colleague in the CETD, for reading and commenting on draft chapters for the book.

Tom Routen, a former colleague at DMU, who contributed to the initial planning for this book.

Not least, Fred Lockwood, for suggesting we write this book and for being a constant source of inspiration, advice and support.

Introduction

> Join any group of distance educators today and the chances are you will hear talk of exponential expansion of education when the information super highways come into being within a decade. This might be called the Big Bang theory of distance education. You will hear enthusiastic talk about two way communication (at last) between teacher and student replacing the old one way systems of print, radio and television. At last students everywhere will be able to share massive knowledge stores. You may also hear gloomy comments about limited access, costs and the dangers of technological determinism. You may even hear critics who seriously decry the commodification of knowledge represented by distance education. And, of course, there will be cautious optimists who advocate slow but steady advance, but not at any price. (Hawkridge, 1995a, p.4)

Hawkridge, writing a few years ago, raised many of the issues that are of concern not just to distance educators but to all working in higher education. While we may not have had a 'big bang' (the term refers to the change overnight from paper-based trading to trading using computers that occurred on the London Stock Exchange), there is little doubt that major change is taking place. It may not be happening overnight but the pace is rapid and increasing. A recent report on virtual institutions worldwide concluded that:

> While there are still few examples of virtual institutions in the purest sense, the amount of development activity in all types and levels of educational organizations, both public and private, is considerable in all parts of the world. No one seems to doubt that the development and deployment of information and communication technologies will have a profound impact on access, institutional functioning, and the teaching and learning process. However, teachers and administrators have many questions and concerns. (Farrell, online)

It is with this profound impact on the teaching and learning process that we are most concerned.

What this book is about

This book examines ways in which Communications and Information Technology (CIT) is having a major impact on higher education and, in particular, how the Internet is being (and can be) used to support teaching and learning.

CIT is now enabling the increased deployment of resource-based learning (RBL). A major theme of the book is that of quality. We claim that RBL can only be done well (with or without the extensive use of CIT) if supported by appropriate models of learning and teaching and principles of course design.

Good pedagogy (to use a term commonly used in discussions of RBL) can help to avoid the shortcomings that are apparent in many RBL and Internet-based courses. This argument applies across a wide range of institutions and courses, from the wholly online university seeking a global market, to the 'conventional' campus-based institution, where there is a more moderate but increasing use of RBL and the Internet.

For many of the topics covered the authors are able to draw on their personal experience as professional educational technologists working in a higher education institution (HEI).

A virtual university?

What is a virtual university? Here is one definition:

A Virtual Education Institution may be defined as:

(a) An institution which is involved as a direct provider of learning opportunities to students and is using information and communication technologies to deliver its programmes and courses and provide tuition support. Such institutions are also likely to be using information and communication technologies for such other core activities as:

  – administration (eg, marketing, registration, student records, fee payments, etc);
  – materials development, production, and distribution;
  – delivery and tuition;
  – career counselling/advising, prior learning assessment, and examinations.

(b) An organization that has been created through alliances/partnerships to facilitate teaching and learning to occur without itself being involved as a direct provider of instruction. Examples of such organizations would be the Open Learning Agency of Australia, the emerging Western Governors University in the United States, and the National Technological University. (Farrell, online)

We would accept this definition but in thinking of the 'virtual university' we would also include 'hybrid' or dual mode institutions (Rumble, 1997, p.60). These are 'conventional' campus-based institutions that are seeking to combine the possibilities offered by CIT for RBL with the strengths of face-to-face teaching. They may offer a range of courses, some taught conventionally and others through the use of the World Wide Web and related Internet technologies. The impact of the Internet does of course extend further. Students and staff are, for example, using the Internet to directly access resources and many teachers make available to their students lecture notes and other teaching material through the Web. Such occurrences are now routine, and while we would strongly reject any suggestion that universities are becoming (or should be) 'virtual' in the sense that all their activities are delivered online, the impact of the Internet is being felt by all.

Who this book is for

The book is chiefly for teaching staff in HEIs, typically very busy people, who wish to be informed about the changes happening around them and to reflect on their implications critically and deeply. The book should also be of interest to a number of other individuals in HEIs and other institutions (schools, Further Education (FE) colleges, businesses, and government agencies) where there is a concern with education and training. As well as teaching staff, we have in mind managers and administrators, library staff and other support staff such as those concerned with computing, networking and course design and delivery.

The impact of the Internet

The Internet offers the means to deliver courses to new and different audiences who may be dispersed geographically and who may not have had the opportunity to study in a conventional setting. These audiences may want to study part-time, on full degree or postgraduate programmes or to follow short courses, possibly with a vocational orientation. But these are only some of the possibilities. Students and staff on campus are also feeling the impact of the new technologies. Here are just some of the ways in which this is happening:

- Teaching staff are using the Web to find resources to incorporate into their teaching.
- They are guiding their students to use resources on the Web directly and students are finding resources themselves.
- Whole courses or substantial parts of courses (developed locally or 'bought in' from another institution) are being delivered online.
- Students and staff are using e-mail, bulletin boards and computer conferencing systems for communication and support, both on and off campus.
- The use of computer aided assessment is increasing, much of it delivered online.
- Course management systems are supporting registration and course administration as well as providing feedback on assessments and other performance data.

Students now need a wider set of core study skills. The ability to search effectively and to access a range of resources from the Web is required, as is an understanding of the norms and conventions of computer conferencing. These need to be linked to the more traditional range of study skills, work organization and time management.

Staff too are finding the nature of their work is being redefined. In some instances there is a separation between the original writers and developers of the course and those who teach and support it. An institution may buy in a whole course from an external supplier. In other instances, through the use of 'educational objects', elements of teaching and learning interaction developed in one context are re-used and re-purposed in a different educational setting (see Chapter 8). Bulletin boards and conferencing systems mean that new skills need to be developed to support and guide students in their learning.

HEIs are also changing. A range of pressures, including those towards the globalization of higher education, are leading towards a rethink of where their core markets lie and what are the most appropriate methods of reaching them. Some institutions are seeking to compete directly in that global market, perhaps through strategic alliances with other like-minded institutions. Others have a more regional focus, concentrating on attracting students from a more narrowly defined geographical location, but wishing to make good use of CIT as part of their learning and teaching strategy. Both face competition from non-traditional providers. We are seeing courses being offered by commercial organizations, training providers and 'for profit' educational institutions. Some of these new players offer courses worldwide using the Internet as the prime means of course delivery.

The Internet and RBL

The technological possibilities offered by the Web should not be allowed to obscure one of the fundamental aims of HEIs: to offer high-quality teaching and learning opportunities to students. Putting a course online does not in itself do this. It may address access issues but unless the course is carefully and appropriately designed it is unlikely to prove satisfactory.

It is for this reason that we emphasize the principled use of RBL. RBL may be known by a number of names, including 'open learning', 'distance learning' and 'independent study'. At the core of the concept is the belief that there is a range of strategies and methods that can be applied to the design and development of teaching material in order to ensure the achievement of effective learning. We agree with the National Council for Open and Distance Education (NCODE, online) of Australia that:

> Resource Based Learning (RBL) is defined as an integrated set of strategies to promote student-centred learning in a mass education context, through a combination of specially designed learning resources and interactive media and technologies.

We will return to this theme later in the book.

How the book is organized

The following is an outline of how the book is organized. If you are not familiar with the area, we recommend you read the chapters in order. However, each chapter is relatively self-contained and can be read individually if you are mainly concerned with a particular topic.

Accompanying the book is a Web site at http://westworld.dmu.ac.uk/vu-rbl This contains links to all the Web pages mentioned in the book as well as updates and new links. You will also be able to e-mail the authors from it. We will be very interested in any comments and feedback you may want to give.

We do need to sound a clear note of warning. The impact of the Internet on education is now so rapid and much is changing so fast that material will date quickly. While the general thrust of our arguments will still be relevant, data we quote and examples we give will inevitably be superseded. Major initiatives and developments will undoubtedly occur in the time between writing this and first publication. We will try and offset this through the use of the Web. As this is a jargon-filled subject we have included a glossary at the end of the book, which aims to clarify frequently used words and abbreviations.

When we have had the option of giving a reference to a source that is available in both print form and on the Web, we have given the Web version. This is likely to be more accessible for many of our readers. Web references do not include page numbers.

Chapter 1 offers an overview of current developments in HE and the impact of the Internet both in the UK and elsewhere. This provides a backcloth for future chapters.

Chapter 2 engages more directly with RBL as a concept and presents theories of teaching and learning particularly relevant for understanding how to do RBL well. A framework for course design is developed. This provides a model for thinking about how the Web can be used effectively for teaching and learning.

Chapter 3 introduces the key technologies of delivery and interaction on the Internet, along with the applications that are of most relevance to education. It is necessary to have an overview of the main technologies in order to work effectively with colleagues and contribute to the development of Web-based teaching and learning.

Chapter 4 focuses more closely on the course development and delivery process. Questions such as when faculty staff should be developing RBL, what resources will be required and what are the major constraints staff face are addressed.

Before committing extensive time to course development, it is necessary to examine what resources are available already on the Web. This is the theme of Chapter 5. These resources may be for supporting course development activities or for directly inputting into a course. The Web is an Aladdin's cave of a wide variety of resources. We briefly overview the kinds of resources that are there and how to find them, with some pointers on how to evaluate what you find.

Computer mediated communication (CMC) is a key topic. We address it specifically in Chapter 6. It is easy to think of the Internet in terms of Web pages only, but communication and conferencing systems are often a vital part of learning and teaching delivered online.

Chapter 7 considers computer aided assessment (CAA), which is becoming an increasingly common feature in HEIs. Having a fair and robust assessment strategy is a key ingredient for the effective use of RBL. The Internet has the potential to facilitate CAA by enabling dispersed users to access the assessment system. We describe a number of CAA systems, ranging from those that deliver multiple choice question tests to those that mark essays.

Chapter 8 focuses on virtual learning environments (VLEs). These are course delivery systems that integrate a number of elements dealt with previously as discrete components (CMC, CAA). They provide an environment for the management, delivery and assessment of students studying via the Web. The chapter also describes the Instructional Management System project (IMS) and the impact it is likely to have. IMS is about establishing 'metadata' standards that allow courses and other 'educational objects' to be classified and readily accessed over the Internet.

Under the impact of new technologies, roles, expectations and, potentially, whole cultures are changing, being 're-engineered'. In Chapter 9 we examine these in a little more detail and indicate how these developments are impacting on teachers, students and others in HEIs.

In Chapter 10 we look ahead to the brave new world of education in the 21st century. We speculate about technological developments to come and their likely impact on educational systems. We conclude by highlighting a number of inter-related 'great debates' about the role of HEIs in a global context.

In writing this book we were well aware of our limitations. We work in the UK but are writing about the Internet and education – a worldwide phenomenon. Our knowledge and our examples reflect the educational context and culture in which we work. Many important developments are happening in Africa, Asia, Latin America and elsewhere and these are not covered in this book. We can only plead that we do not attempt to be comprehensive and that others are better equipped to deal with these aspects. We also realize that all our examples are from English language Web sites. English may be dominant on the Web but it is not exclusive. Once again we can only acknowledge our limitations.

Chapter 1

A changing context – education and the Internet

Introduction

The educational world is changing rapidly. We are seeing the use of the Internet and Communications and Information Technology (CIT) becoming an important part of the learning and teaching strategies of many universities. Some are seeking to become global, virtual institutions, others are using the Internet as part of a mixed economy, combining traditional modes of delivery with online teaching. This chapter reviews some of the developments that are influencing the growth of resource-based learning (RBL) and the Internet in order to set the scene for the rest of the book We will be examining the following:

- the growth and development of the Internet;
- some key changes in the world of education;
- an overview of RBL, universities and the Internet.

These themes are explored in more detail in later chapters.

The growth of the Internet

Claims about the Internet revolutionizing our lives are now commonplace. In part they are based on its rapid growth: it is estimated that in the year 2000, 327 million people around the world will have Internet access. There will be 25 countries where over 10 per cent of the population will be Internet users (Cyberatlas, online).

This growth is illustrated graphically by Huber (1997, p.12):

> The Internet's pace of adoption eclipses all other technologies before it. Radio was in existence 38 years before 50 million people tuned in; TV took 13 years to reach that point. Once the Net was opened up to the general public, the Internet crossed that line in four years.

There are limits, but for the Internet these limits are not even close. Projections by Lottor (online) suggest a ten-fold increase over the next five years. The number of individual Web pages has already reached this figure. A recent report (Center for Next Generation Internet, online) describes the current annual growth rate as 63 per cent.

This growth of the Internet from a mainly closed academic network to a common feature in many people's lives is being driven by a number of factors. In particular, the real opportunities for electronic commerce and trade, the integration of television, radio and entertainment systems and the communication opportunities offered by e-mail, audio and video-conferencing are having a major impact. These developments affect education. Tony Blair, the UK Prime Minister, has said:

> Technology has revolutionized the way we work and is now set to transform education. Children cannot be effective in tomorrow's world if they are trained in yesterday's skills. Nor should teachers be denied the tools that other professionals take for granted. (Blair, 1998, p.1)

But the changes occurring are far more significant than those resulting only from the need to train students in new skills. We are now moving into what has been characterized as an information age where the key commodities being traded are not physical goods but data and information.

An information age?

It can be argued that we have always lived in an information age. In humans, our informing is shared through the coordinating and representing functions of language. Sharing information one with another is called 'communication'. Communication affords prediction and control. It took the genius of Norbert Wiener to recognize the ubiquity, the universality, of processes of control and communication throughout the man-made and natural worlds. Wiener coined the name 'cybernetics' for the general transdisciplinary study of control and communication in complex systems (Wiener, 1948).

The development of the first general purpose digital computers brought questions of control and communication to the fore. It was recognized that it should now be possible to automate most if not all of the functions of control and communication being carried out by humans in industrial processes. It is but a short intellectual step to move from the idea of the automation of the industrial processes to consider the implications of automating much of what happens within educational systems.

Digital computers have been around for some 50 years. Their influence has been felt in fits and starts. Early significant applications were in science, engineering and mathematics. In the last 20 years we have seen computing become relatively universal with stand-alone PCs and workstations commonplace in homes, offices and factories. Both computational power and data storage capacity have become relatively cheap. Powerful application packages for word-processing, numerical processing and graphical work are readily available. Data of all kinds can now be represented and manipulated digitally, including photographs, video and audio tracks. Increasingly all of this is possible not just on stand-alone computers but over networks and in particular the Internet.

The growth of networks

The Internet is a global communications network. Its origins lie in the 1970s with the development of the US military's Arpanet for scientific communication and the parallel development of time-shared computing systems where several work stations are linked by a network to one or more central processors. For many years, developments appeared to be very slow. Networks were built up to link scientific and academic communities and used by the few in those communities who took the trouble to find out how to use the systems with their arcane and awkward-to-use protocols.

The use of electronic mail with the development of user-friendly front-end mailing systems was a major step forward. The most recent breakthrough in terms of ease of use and applicability came with the development of the World Wide Web, which supports hypertext linking and full multimedia digital delivery of data. However, the infrastructure of the information age is only partly in place. It is not yet the case that every household with a telephone is connected to the Internet, nor does every household with a television also have a personal computer, but there does seem to be an air of inevitability about these developments. The only question appears to be, when will it happen? Within five years, within ten years?

Visionaries of the information age have predicted and anticipated these developments for some 30 to 40 years. Bush (1945), Pask and Curran (1982), Nelson (1990) and others have considered how global networks will impact on our lives.

Learning for life – the changing context

The relevance of CIT for universities needs to be viewed within the context of an increasing emphasis on lifelong learning and the impact CIT is having on all aspects of education. From this perspective education is not something that only 'happens' during childhood and early adulthood but rather is a continuing process throughout an individual's life. Over time a person's educational needs will change as will the amount and pattern of time that can be committed to it. The level of resource available to support the educational activities may also vary.

The requirement for a workforce with up-to-date skills and the need for continuing professional updating and training mean that the educational and training process needs to be viewed as ongoing. There is also considerable interest now being addressed in older learners, those who have perhaps finished in full-time employment and have the time to pursue educational activities for personal fulfilment.

Universities and other providers are responding to these changing demands by increasing the flexibility of their provision, offering a greater range and variety of courses that can be studied in various modes and by a number of means, including part-time attendance and distance learning.

The role of CIT is critical here. It can provide the flexibility of delivery that many lifelong learners require as well as addressing access issues. Courses can be studied at home, in work, at school or in local centres such as libraries.

Developments in schools – The National Grid for Learning

We can illustrate some of these developments with the example of the National Grid for Learning. In the UK a coherent strategy for networked learning is being developed. This involves the introduction of networks and hardware into schools and a programme of staff development for teachers. This strategy, known as the National Grid for Learning, is quite explicitly part of a move to improve the competitiveness of British business. The grid:

> will provide a national focus and agenda for harnessing new technologies to raise educational standards, and improve quality of life and Britain's international competitiveness, especially the new literacy and numeracy targets. (Blair, 1998, p.3)

Under this initiative all schools, libraries and universities are being connected to the Grid. A major programme of staff development is being undertaken with teachers and other professionals, and appropriate software and resources are being developed. The Grid is being developed as a partnership between business and education, 'bringing together the best of private sector creativity and the highest standards of public service' (Blair, 1998).

Underpinning the conception of the Grid is a belief in the importance of developing and sharing resources so that teachers and students can quickly find and access appropriate materials from within a networked environment far richer and more extensive than the kind of resources traditionally available to schools. We are already seeing the emergence of a number of Web sites providing resources, links, professional development information and the opportunity to conference for teachers. The National Grid For Learning has a Virtual Teachers Centre (http://www.vtc.org.uk/) and other sites have been developed through:

- universities, for example Teachernet (http://www.teachernetuk.org.uk);
- European funding grants, for example European school net (http://www.en. eun.org/front/actual/);
- computer and telecommunications companies with a particular interest in the schools market, for example Research Machines (http://www.eduweb. co.uk/), Campus World, (http://www.campus.bt.com/CampusWorld/pub/);
- the broadcasting companies who are becoming particularly active in the schools market, such as the BBC (http://www.bbc.co.uk/education/home/today/).

These developments are leading to new relationships between commercial organizations and teachers and schools, including financial support and sponsorship. Web sites are being created by organizations that go far beyond the provision of resources, which could be seen as a logical extension of traditional educational publishing, to include online activities and assessment, and conferencing facilities. These organizations, via the Web, are becoming directly involved in teaching.

The above examples from the UK are part of a worldwide development. The British National Grid for Learning is heavily influenced by developments in the United States where school/business links in this area are well established and a vast array of teaching resources are available. A similar pattern can be seen in Australia. The European Commission is funding a European schools network currently involving a number of schools and organizations in 10 countries (http://www.en.eun.org/front/actual/).

Lifelong learning and training

Changes in employment patterns and increased competition in world markets have made governments in all industrialized nations take seriously the need for lifelong training and education. The idea of 'a job for life' was the norm until relatively recently. Now the norm is for skilled and semi-skilled workers to change jobs frequently, every few years, to seek advancement and to respond flexibly as 'old' businesses die or are transformed by new technology and as new businesses come into being. In Europe the influential report *Europe and the Global Information Society* (Bangemann, online) made a number of recommendations for action, including to:

promote distance learning centres providing courseware, training and tuition services tailored for SMEs (small and medium enterprises), large companies and public administrations. Extend advanced distance learning techniques into schools and colleges.

In the UK it is accepted that the government has a role to play in the creation and maintenance of a workforce that has the relevant skills and adaptability to respond flexibly in changing circumstances. Business organizations, in recognition of the same needs, are investing more in training programmes. They – and the government – are looking to new technologies to help deliver that education and training in cost-effective, efficient ways. Somewhat ironically, one of the major forces driving the need for training and re-skilling is the new technologies themselves, as they continue to transform the way jobs are done.

The University for Industry

A major UK initiative is the University for Industry (UfI), envisaged as a three-way partnership between business organizations, government and education providers.

It is expected that one of the main areas to be transformed will be that of 'on the job training'. There will be more of it and it will be done more effectively. UfI would:

- help build a learning society in which people and businesses are able to take control of their own destinies and build their futures;
- encourage lifelong learning to raise business competitiveness;
- help adults to improve their knowledge and skills, from basic literacy and numeracy through to advanced management techniques;
- help promote and support the habit of effective and purposeful lifelong learning for all adults.

According to UfI (online) this will be done by:

- creating a nationwide distributed open and distance learning network for UfI that is capable of meeting a wide variety of learning needs;
- providing a wide range of high-quality learning packages that give maximum flexibility for users, allowing them to learn where, when and how they want, encouraging people to 'own' their learning by making it relevant to their working lives and personal aspirations;
- building learners' confidence in their ability to manage their own learning through access to specialist support and interaction with other learners.

Changes in universities

A round table of high-level educators and administrators focused on the impact of the Internet and education and concluded that:

- new learning technologies can transform the way knowledge is packaged, delivered, accessed, acquired, and measured, altering higher education's core production and delivery processes;
- students will demand flexible, targeted, accessible learning methods, potentially altering higher education's traditional role;
- a huge population of new learners – estimated at millions more students in the next decade – would expand the total market for education and entice new competitors;

- relying on technology rather than bricks and mortar, non-traditional competitors will give colleges and universities a run for their money. (Coopers and Lybrand, online)

The term 'virtual university' is now being used widely, with its suggestion of a university in cyberspace offering courses to remote students working from home or work. But we should not assume that a virtual university is just a new name for a distance-teaching university, where students study remotely, often alone, using the Internet rather than workbooks or videos. While this is undoubtedly one element of the picture, it is likely that the impact will be much greater on more conventional, campus-based universities. Universities are now investing heavily in resource centres (Hertfordshire), library extensions (De Montfort University) or learning centres (John Moores and Sunderland); all are characterized by large numbers of networked workstations and very few, if any, books. (The 'electronic campus' of De Montfort University is shown in Figure 1.1.) The proposed budget of the UK Universities Joint Information Systems Committee (JISC) is projected to rise by approximately one-third over the five years 1996–2001 (JISC, online).

One reason why there is so much interest in using CIT for teaching and learning is that it is regarded as providing a cost-efficient way of expanding higher education, indeed perhaps the only realistic way. This can be seen in some of the studies that informed the Committee of Inquiry into Teaching and Learning in the UK, The Dearing Report. In Appendix 2 of the report various models are shown to illustrate

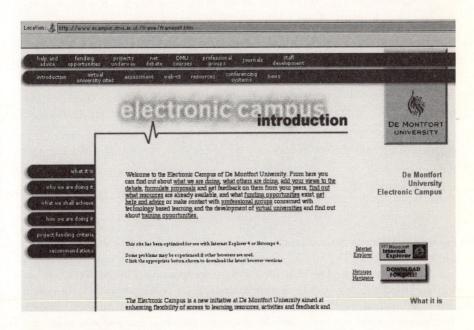

Figure 1.1 *The Electronic Campus home page at De Montfort University (http://www.ecampus.dmu.ac.uk)*

the costs of teaching. The report states, 'If universities are to widen participation and provide access to more students of all ages, they will need to find pedagogically acceptable combinations of teaching methods and cost structures to sustain increased student numbers' (Dearing, online).

So far, the report argues, this expansion has led to a move from small group teaching to large group teaching, and from individual supervision to group supervision, with an 'inevitable loss of quality of learning experience for students'. But perhaps the new technology can avoid this reduction in quality while still being cost-effective. So far, it is argued, these efficiency savings have not yet been achieved.

The report examines a number of scenarios for future expansion. Table 1.1 illustrates some options. A 'traditional' teaching pattern with its heavy emphasis on small group work becomes increasingly expensive and difficult to sustain as numbers rise. This has led to the adoption of patterns closer to those illustrated in the 'current study hours' column. Small group work has been replaced in large measure by lectures, with some increase in RBL. But this 'current' model has led to a reduction in the quality of the students' learning experience and, in the words of the report, 'the price paid in terms of diminished student learning experience makes this unacceptable as a model for the future'. The 'future' model, if it is based on well designed and developed RBL, would provide a richer student learning experience. The costs of producing high-quality RBL in-house across a range of disciplines would be beyond the means of most institutions. Therefore, in the example shown, 50 per cent of the RBL materials are bought in from external sources or have been produced collaboratively.

Table 1.1 *Alternative combinations of teaching methods (Dearing, online)*

Methods	Traditional study hours	Current study hours	Future? study hours
Lectures	30	60	10
Groups	50	5	3
RBL (extended)	15	15	50
RBL (in-house)	5	20	10

Figure 1.2 illustrates the staff time required for the three models as student numbers per course double. The steady increase in costs of the traditional model mean that it is not a practicable basis for continued expansion. The attraction of the 'current' model is that it does appear to contain costs, but as we have seen, this comes at an unacceptable price in terms of the quality of learning experience. The 'future' model not only starts from a lower cost base but also retains its cost advantage as numbers continue to expand.

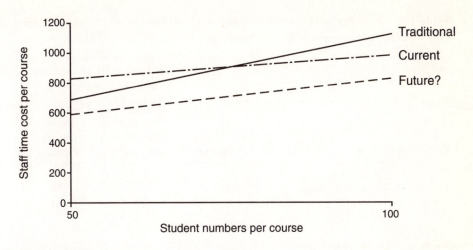

Figure 1.2 *Comparative staff time costs for alternative combinations of teaching methods (Dearing, online)*

The analysis suggests that if access to higher education is to continue to expand within a framework of tightly constrained costs, this might be achieved by an increasing emphasis on RBL and the sharing of resources developed collaboratively.

Economic factors may lead to 'traditional' campus-based universities competing more directly with distance education providers, leading to the emergence of dual mode institutions using both face-to-face and distance teaching. Rumble (1997, p.160) speculates that what will emerge will be:

> a new kind of educational institution using a mix of technologies and face to face teaching to reach students wherever they are – at home, in the workplace, in remote classrooms or in campus classrooms. Perhaps the main lesson from experience is that the only strategy open to educational institutions in a cash strapped mass education system is to adopt open and distance learning methods.

International trends

A similar pattern can be seen in the United States. A National Center for Education Statistics study, *Distance Education in Higher Education Institutions* (Lewis et al, 1995) reported that, 'A third of higher education institutions offered distance education courses in fall 1995, another quarter planned to offer such courses in the next three years.'

Institutions will increasingly exploit technology for this delivery (see Table 1.2):

> About three-quarters of the institutions that currently offer or plan to offer distance education courses plan to start or increase their use of two-way interactive video, two-way online (computer-based) interactions during instruction, and other computer-based technologies to deliver their distance education courses in the next three years. (Lewis et al, 1997)

Table 1.2 *Percentage of HEIs currently offering, and planning to offer, distance education courses that use various types of delivery technologies (source: Lewis et al, 1997)*

Technology	Currently use the technology[1]	Plan to start or increase use of the technology	
		Currently offer distance education courses[1]	Plan to offer distance education courses[2]
Two-way interactive video	57	81	77
Two-way audio, one-way video	24	33	38
One-way live video	9	27	31
One-way prerecorded video	52	52	44
Audiographics	3	9	7
Two-way audio (eg, audio/phone conferencing)	11	18	21
One-way audio (eg, radio, audiotapes)	10	11	11
Two-way (computer-based) interactions during instruction	14	75	64
Other computer-based technology (eg, Internet)	22	84	74

1: Percents are based on institutions that offered distance education courses in fall 1995.
2: Percents are based on institutions that plan to offer distance education courses in the next 3 years.
Note: Data are for higher education institutions in the 50 states, the District of Columbia, and Puerto Rico.
Source: U.S. Department of Education, National Center for Education Statistics, Post-secondary Education Quick Information System, Survey on Distance Education Courses offered by Higher Education Institutions, 1995.

It is clear that the Internet is likely to be a key delivery option for many institutions. The Western Governors initiative (http://www.wgu.edu/wgu/index.html) is a good example, and we can see a similar pattern at work in Australia:

> The issue of resource-based learning (RBL) is engaging an increasing number of Australian universities. By the year 2000, at least 30% of all undergraduate teaching – on and off campus – is likely to involve the use of specially designed learning resources. The factors driving this fundamental change in teaching/learning arrangements include institutional responses to the shift from semi-elite to mass higher education, the advent of new information technologies, political pressures to do more with less, and greater emphasis on the conditions of learning in more flexible, innovative and student-centred teaching. (NCODE, online)

Developments in Africa

Virtual universities are also making an impact in areas with less well developed infrastructures. In Africa, for example, the World Bank-funded African Virtual University (see Figure 1.3) has run a small number of pilot courses. Findings from the project so far suggest that it is possible to:

- set up a virtual university in Africa, using very advanced communication technology;
- obtain collaboration at state level and at university level between different African countries (and also overseas countries);
- use the most advanced technology without losing the students who are not used to the technology;
- use a common language (English) to deliver the lectures without any real communication problems;
- prove that the operation can be financially viable, even in such esoteric subjects as mathematics because of the economy-of-scale effect, summed over the various download sites;
- prove that the technology is stable and that its equipment can be used over long periods in non-industrialized areas of Africa;
- prove that it is one of the ways in which to accelerate the production of graduates in subjects that are difficult to teach at the level of single states because of the lack of suitably qualified staff. (Naido and Schutte, 1999, p.118)

The Internet, of course, breaks down national boundaries and for some the potential market for higher education is truly global. The Web is making reaching this market a reality. The market for higher education through distance learning has been estimated at $300 billion worldwide (Newby, 1999).

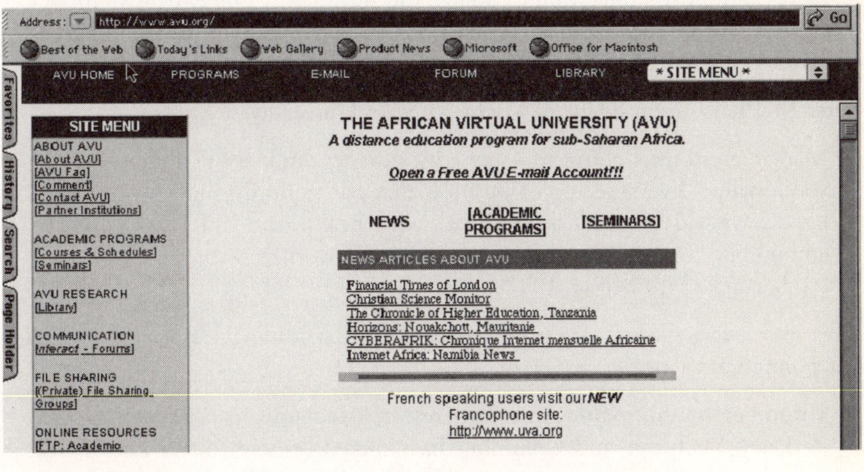

Figure 1.3   *The African Virtual University (http://www.avu.org)*

We may see attempts to produce multinational courses (or rather, courses primarily designed for students in the USA) offered internationally. According to Coopers and Lybrand (online):

> In fact, research indicates that the creation of a mere 25 courses would serve an estimated 80 per cent of total undergraduate enrolment in core undergraduate courses. What type of courses compromise the 'core'? Courses like calculus 101, biology 101 and so on. The software would serve an estimated 50 per cent of the total student enrolment in community colleges as well as an estimated 35 per cent of the total student enrolment in four-year institutions... a 'core' course could be replaced with a high quality, technology-based course. The technology-based course could be supplemented with a 24-hour international help desk, offering eight hours of help in the US, eight hours in Europe, etc. At this scale, it would be conceivable to spend $3 million on a course, and develop a truly effective learning tool – one that would transform education delivery methods.

Commercialization and alliances

Universities are therefore looking towards using the Internet to expand greatly their range and provision of courses. At the same time others are looking at the traditional markets of the universities and suggesting that methods developed in business and commerce may provide a cost-effective option.

The features of the Internet that make it so attractive to universities also provide opportunities for alternative forms of course provision. Forbes magazine graphically describes one change in education – that of the increasing commercialization of the delivery of courses using the Internet and the Web:

> Detroit makes luxury cars and stripped-down economy cars, four wheel drives and sports convertibles. College Inc. makes only one expensive model – with leather seats and air conditioning. Technology is changing that. (Gubernick and Ebeling, 1997)

Peter McPherson, President of Michigan State University, suggests that:

> Market pressure is going to force educators to think about things unconventionally... Every sector of business that has gone through this struggle has always said 'we can't do it'. That's what health care said, that's what the automobile companies said. But the markets do work, and change does come. (Gubernick and Ebeling, 1997)

This may lead to some very potent partnerships. A leading UK Vice Chancellor has pointed out that:

> a number of the major American research-led universities, such as UC Berkeley, Michigan, and Columbia, have linked up with major knowledge providers in the private sector, such as Time Warner, Disney Corporation, Microsoft, and Cisco, to form partnerships which will develop the appropriate

courseware and support needed to attack the global market in higher education in the twenty-first century.

While the universities provide most of the academic expertise – and crucially the 'branding' necessary for market credibility – the partners provide production facilities, distribution, and marketing, as well as much of the underlying technology, in order for the operation to proceed on a truly global basis. (Newby, 1999)

Direct competition is also a reality. This is illustrated by some of the costs quoted in the *Forbes* article:

The University of Phoenix is a for-profit enterprise. It costs Phoenix online $237 to provide one credit hour of cybereducation, against $486 per hour for conventional education at Arizona State. The big difference: teaching salaries and benefits – $247 per credit hour for Arizona State against only $46 for Phoenix. Arizona State professors get an average of $67,000 a year. The typical University of Phoenix online faculty member is part time and earns only $2,000 a course teaching from a standardized curriculum. (Gubernick and Ebeling, 1997)

The University of Phoenix's home page is shown in Figure 1.4.

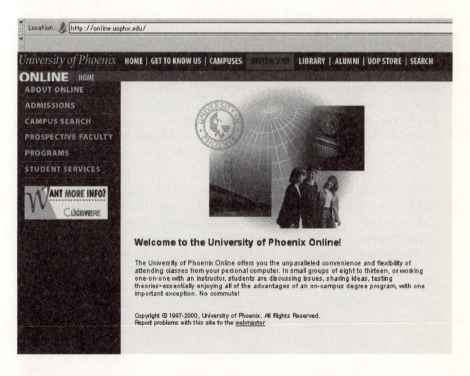

Figure 1.4 *The University of Phoenix (http://online.uophx.edu/)*

The same university has estimated that around 250,000 course assistants (compared with 750,000 fully tenured professors at the present time) could support the entire US higher education system with bought-in presentations from 1000 star performers – the leading researchers and teachers who actually appear in front of camera (Newby, 1999).

The UK Government has responded to such developments by seeking to establish an 'e-University'. At the time of writing this proposal has only just been announced, but the plan is that the Higher Education Funding Council for England (HEFCE) in collaboration with other UK agencies would develop an 'e-University' from a consortium of UK universities which would provide courses and expertise:

> The HEFCE is concerned that UK higher education (HE) should be able to capitalize on its considerable expertise in new technologies and its reputation for quality to secure a significant share in the markets accessed by these virtual/corporate providers, both overseas and in UK. We, with other UK funding bodies, now wish to explore how we can catalyse a virtual learning initiative of a scale and quality that will challenge the best in the world, and the Government has signalled its strong support for this initiative. (HEFCE, online)

These factors have led some commentators to warn of the dangers of this process. Noble (1997), for example, does not see this as part of a progressive trend but quite the opposite: an emphasis on mass-production, standardization and purely commercial interests:

> Once faculty put their course material online, moreover, the knowledge and course design skill embodied in that material is taken out of their possession, transferred to the machinery and placed in the hands of the administration. The administration is now in a position to hire less skilled, and hence cheaper, workers to deliver the technologically pre-packaged course. It also allows the administration, which claims ownership of this commodity, to peddle the course elsewhere without the original designer's involvement or even knowledge.

For Noble it is in the coercion of academics to place their materials on the Web that leads to the difficulties he identifies. When this happens academics lose control and are vulnerable to exploitation. While the issues he raises are real ones and abuses will occur, they should not blind us to the exciting possibilities of what might be achieved. The very real opportunities offered by the Internet for coopera-tion, collaboration and indeed control of content at an individual level present a very different picture. In this scenario we are all potentially publishers and pro-ducers, offering our materials worldwide.

Virtual communities

Others see the traditional university based on a physical grouping of academics and students being challenged by the collaborative nature of the Web. Delong (1997) argues that:

The culture of higher education is likely to be profoundly changed as a result. Development of pedagogical tools and curricular content will move beyond the scope of most individual faculty, who will require the help of a skilled team. Individual departments will be less important as the literal and figurative interconnectedness of information on the Web exposes the artificiality of disciplinary barriers. And individual institutions will learn to share their resources, students, and revenues, inevitably diluting the importance of 'the university as a physical space' in many cases.

The ability to make your course or resources available to anyone appears to offer an attractive way of reaching increasingly diverse groups of potential students regardless of location. But having the potential to deliver courses is not in itself sufficient. It says nothing about their quality in terms of the suitability of their content or pedagogical effectiveness. It is here that an understanding and an application of the strategies and methodologies underpinning RBL can help us.

A note of caution

For universities wishing to expand in a time of constrained resource, the use of the Web appears very attractive. Linking up with externally produced resources offers the possibility of using others' material rather than developing everything 'in-house'. The ability to make your course available to anyone appears to offer a way of reaching increasingly diverse groups of potential students who can access your courses at a time that suits them. This can and should involve far more than students passively reading Web pages on screen. Indeed the Internet is capable of supporting dynamic, creative and exciting educational experiences that may not be possible in other educational contexts. It is the combination of providing the means to access a range and variety of resources located around the world and the ability to communicate, collaborate and interact that gives it its strength.

While we recognize the tremendous potential of the Internet for education, this can be and sometimes is overstated. The perceived educational benefits of the Internet are being marketed not only to educational institutions but also directly to parents of school-age children. Clearly we need to approach all such claims with care, particularly as there are huge commercial interests involved in the development and sale of Internet-based services and products. A highly respected expert on distance education, Börje Holmberg, when discussing the impact of technology on distance education, recently wrote:

> Nethertheless isn't there something pretty naive in today's enthusiasm for new techniques? Do the developments of the last couple of decades really represent such a revolution of methods and media that we have reason to describe their result as a paradigm shift? (Holmberg, 1998)

Perhaps not so far, but changes happening now may well amount to such a shift.

Holmberg is right to urge caution; we do need to disentangle the hyperbole from reality. But we are seeing an investment and commitment, at unparalleled levels, to the introduction of technology into teaching and learning at all phases.

This ranges from schools, colleges and universities, to professional updating and lifelong learning. The investment in British schools, for example, is led by a drive to introduce the Internet and Internet-based technologies into education with the assumption that this will change and improve teaching and learning. The spread of these technologies is leading to an increase in the use of RBL across all sectors of education. This use of RBL, both in a classroom setting and at a distance, raises many issues and requires a consideration of fundamental questions about the most appropriate strategies for learning and teaching in a changing environment. Bates (1995, p.42) argues cogently that educational institutions are under tremendous pressure to change and that institutions need to develop a clear vision and strategy for managing this change process.

The role of RBL

The argument so far has concentrated on technology and the context of its development. We now need to shift the focus away from this to the teaching and learning context. We use the term 'resource-based learning' precisely for this reason – so that the emphasis is placed on the processes of learning through a range of resources rather than any one media form. We would accept the point being made by the Australian National Council of Open and Distance Learning (NCODE, online) that:

> Resource-based Learning (RBL) is defined as an integrated set of strategies to promote student-centred learning in a mass education context, through a combination of specially designed learning resources and interactive media and technologies.

These integrated strategies for RBL should be based on the application of a range of instructional design principles to the development of learning materials and on the development of student support and assessment systems that underpin and promote student learning.

One important element of this strategy relates to the selection and use of appropriate media and technologies. This selection should be based on an understanding of what particular media elements can contribute to teaching and learning. Laurillard (1993) has demonstrated how such an approach may work in practice. She analyses different media forms in terms of the extent to which they do or do not contribute to the model of teaching and learning she outlines. What we are now seeing is the way in which the Internet can incorporate many media elements – video, audio and multimedia as well as the ability to communicate and to collaborate. By so doing it creates a rich educational environment which goes far beyond the possibilities offered by any one media form.

The Internet and RBL

Below are six ways in which the Internet can support RBL:

1. delivering courses;
2. identifying and using resources;
3. communicating and conferencing;
4. activities and assessment;
5. collaborative work;
6. student management and support.

These advantages are not just for the institution. The Internet offers students real chances for pursuing a range and variety of study options that would not otherwise have been possible. Porter (1997, pp.12–16), for example, identifies the following:

*   the ability for students to learn at their own pace;
*   to learn in a convenient location;
*   to learn about topics not covered in their course or programmes offered in their area;
*   to participate in programmes of universities that offer high prestige programmes without having to relocate;
*   to learn according to their preferred mode of learning;
*   to have the opportunity to use a range of different technologies;
*   to direct their own learning.

Delivering courses

An obvious way to use the Internet might be to deliver complete modules or courses. A number of sites now act as clearing houses, listing courses available over the Internet from institutions around the world. The World Lecture Hall (http://www.utexas.edu:80/world/lecture/), for example, now lists hundreds of courses available via the Internet. Another site, Ed/x, serves as a global resource for information on online learning (see Figure 1.5).

In the UK, with the increasing development of modular courses, the possibilities for students to construct programmes of study drawing on a range of modules delivered from different institutions are greatly increased. Equally, institutions can enter into credit sharing and other arrangements to offer courses not taught at a particular campus. The joint development of courses, which reduces costs, is now a reality.

This approach also fits in well with the development of modules designed for professional updating or training and with the general provision of modules as part of courses for lifelong learning. De Montfort University, for example, has developed Master's programmes for professional updating in science and technology specifically aimed at graduates now working in industry. These courses are delivered via the Internet and are available worldwide.

The use of teaching materials developed in one context for other purposes does of course raise many issues. What pedagogical assumptions do the materials make? Do they embody specific cultural assumptions that may be inappropriate

Figure 1.5 *The home page of Ed/x (http://www.ed-x.com)*

or even misleading when used in a different context? Can they be adapted for use at different levels? These questions and many more will need to be addressed by the institution making use of them. It is essential that appropriate quality and validation mechanisms are in place to assess the materials. We return to this theme in Chapters 5 and 9.

Identifying and using resources

The delivery of whole courses is perhaps the exception rather than the rule. A more typical use is to obtain specific resources from the Internet. These resources may be used by individual teachers in the development of courses and modules, just as any other resource material might be used. But of more significance is the exploitation of the ability of the Web to link to other sites so that elements and resources held remotely can be used as part of the course. These resources may be used to supplement parts of the course, much like the 'further reading' in a traditionally taught course, or they can be specific examples of features or processes that others have produced, such as examples of molecular structures. The identification of resources may in itself be part of the learning process whereby students are required to use the Internet to identify and find certain resources. Increasingly tools and collections of links have been produced to help in this process.

We distinguish between resources such as electronic journal articles, information and data held on Web sites, and 'educational objects', specific elements or resources such as a Java applet (Chapter 3) developed to be used within an educational context. These educational objects are becoming increasingly important and, with the development of metadata standards to describe and identify resources on the Internet, their impact is likely to increase. The Instructional Management Systems (IMS) project is setting international metadata standards for the description of objects. We will examine this further in Chapter 8.

Communicating and conferencing

The potential of the Internet for teaching and learning is far greater than simply being able to browse resources. As Pask, Laurillard and others have argued, learning takes place through conversation, the description and re-description of that which is being taught. It is therefore essential that communication between teacher and student, and student and student, takes place. The Internet supports this in a number of ways. Communication may be synchronous or asynchronous, that is, happening in real time or over a period of time. The communication may be one-to-one, or one-to-many. It may be via a video or audio link or through typed messages.

A range of technologies exist to support computer mediated communication (CMC), from simple e-mail systems, bulletin boards and conferencing systems to multi-link video conferencing. These communication systems play a vital role in student progression and support, enabling individual queries and problems to be dealt with and for students to teach, encourage and support each other. These issues are explored in Chapter 6.

Activities and assessment

A fundamental principle of RBL is that the course material should actively engage the student. (We discuss this in some detail in Chapter 2.) It is through this engagement that much of the learning takes place. In traditional paper-based RBL, in-text activities or self-assessment questions serve this purpose. Good Web-based RBL also needs to embody activities. There are a number of ways in which network technology can support this; for example, multiple choice type questions can be incorporated into Web pages. More sophisticated questioning and dialogue styles are also possible, such as identifying areas on a map or matching elements. Student responses can be stored and collated.

The use of Java, JavaScript and other languages enables the construction of objects that can be manipulated on the Web by a user. In the example of a virtual photographic studio shown in Figure 1.6, students can change settings such as the type and angle of the lighting and the position of the model in the studio, and then shoot and 'print' the picture virtually before viewing the result.

The Internet will also assist in the electronic submission of assignments. An example of this is through the use of electronic forms that contain basic student data and upon which the teacher will enter comments. Various tools have also been developed for the online marking of assignments. We will return to these themes in Chapter 7.

Collaborative work

One possibility offered by the ability to communicate and exchange data is undertaking collaborative work between students separated by large distances. This may involve the exchange of documents, images and other resources so that groups of students jointly submit a project. A computer conferencing system can greatly facilitate this process.

Collaborative work may also take advantage of specialist software running over the Internet. An example of this would be an electronic 'whiteboard' on which

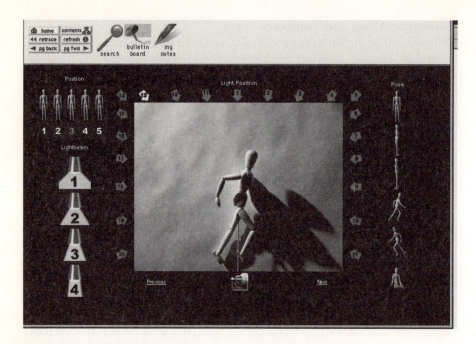

Figure 1.6 *A virtual studio (http://westworld.dmu.ac.uk/vu-rbl)*

participants can write and draw via their computer screens. A teacher, for example, may write part of an equation on the white board and a student at a remote location is asked to complete it.

The last few years have seen the emergence of specialist collaborative work tools, such as Microsoft NetMeeting. These tools are primarily designed for use in business but have considerable applicability in education. Users are connected between remote locations via the Internet and not only do they have facilities such as electronic white boards but also an application being run on one computer can be viewed and controlled by another. A teacher might be using a spreadsheet and students will be able to follow what is happening on screen. At any point the teacher can give control of the spreadsheet to an individual student and that student can then use the package running on the teacher's machine.

Teachers and students can also jointly visit remote Web sites, for example a virtual museum, and when the teacher points to an object, all the students will also see that object being pointed at.

Educators are just beginning to explore the potential of collaborative work tools. They are generating much interest and excitement. The possibility of groups of students collaborating and working together, although separated by considerable distance, is real. It is far removed from the notion of the isolated student passively reading large volumes of text from the computer screen.

Student management and support

We have seen that the Internet can support a range of activities, including the delivery of materials, assessment and student support. A number of systems have been developed to integrate a whole range of activities into one student management and delivery system.

These systems are designed to provide students with a simple interface from which they can access learning materials, check bulletin boards, join conference or discussion groups, submit assignments and receive feedback. The systems also have a number of specific features to help course teachers. Typically these include simplified ways of uploading course material, sometimes using pre-designed templates, as well as a number of administration and monitoring systems. Teachers can view class lists, check whether students have submitted assignments, see whether an individual student has viewed a particular piece of course material, and check on grades.

We examine such systems in detail in Chapter 8. They represent an important development, potentially simplifying and removing some of the barriers and difficulties in delivering courses on the Web.

Towards the development of high-quality courses

In March 1987, the *American Association of Higher Education Bulletin* first published 'Seven principles for good practice in undergraduate education'. The principles, created by Chickering and Gamson, have been very influential and several hundred thousand copies have been distributed. They have recently been updated to take account of the impact of the new technology. The seven principles are:

1. Good Practice Encourages Contacts Between Students and Faculty.
2. Good Practice Develops Reciprocity and Cooperation Among Students.
3. Good Practice Uses Active Learning Techniques.
4. Good Practice Gives Prompt Feedback.
5. Good Practice Emphasizes Time on Task.
6. Good Practice Communicates High Expectations.
7. Good Practice Respects Diverse Talents and Ways of Learning. (Chickering and Ehrmann, online)

The conclusion to the seven principles article, 'Technology is not enough', needs to be considered carefully by anyone planning to develop Web-based courseware:

> The Seven Principles cannot be implemented by technophiles alone, or even by faculty alone. Students need to become familiar with the Principles and be more assertive with respect to their own learning. When confronted with teaching strategies and course requirements that use technologies in ways contrary to the Principles, students should, if possible, move to alternatives that serve them better. If teaching focuses simply on memorizing and regurgitating pre-packaged information, whether delivered by a faculty

lecture or computer, students should reach for a different course, search out additional resources or complementary experiences, establish their own study groups, or go to the professor for more substantial activities and feedback.

Faculty members who already work with students in ways consistent with the Principles need to be tough-minded about the software- and technology-assisted interactions they create and buy into. They need to eschew materials that are simply didactic, and search instead for those that are interactive, problem oriented, relevant to real-world issues, and that evoke student motivation.

Institutional policies concerning learning resources and technology support need to give high priority to user-friendly hardware, software, and communication vehicles that help faculty and students use technologies efficiently and effectively. Investments in professional development for faculty members, plus training and computer lab assistance for students, will be necessary if learning potentials are to be realized.

Finally, it is appropriate for legislators and other benefactors to ask whether institutions are striving to improve educational practice consistent with the Seven Principles. Much depends on the answer. (Chickering and Ehrmann, online)

Conclusion

Chickering and Ehrmann remind us of the importance of taking a principled approach to teaching and learning. This reminder is timely when, as we have seen, competing interests are all striving to gain a foothold or to retain their position in an environment that is rapidly changing. We are only beginning to explore the possibilities offered by the Internet for teaching and learning and coming to recognize its strengths and limitations. But what is clear is that it does not provide quick and easy solutions and that educators need to build on their expertise and experience as teachers and apply them while working with others in the development of Web-based teaching and learning.

We will be examining some of the principles underlying the development of good RBL materials in the next chapter.

Chapter 2

Learning, teaching and course design with resource-based learning

Introduction

In this chapter we discuss RBL in much greater depth and examine its implications for learning, teaching and course design. First, we review:

- what is meant by RBL;
- advantages and disadvantages of RBL;
- different forms of RBL.

Next, we present some theoretical models for understanding learning, teaching and effective pedagogy, and a framework for course design. We do this in the belief that RBL cannot be effectively implemented and evaluated without such explicit frameworks and guiding principles. Without the application of these principles the possibilities offered by the Internet for learning and teaching will not be fully realized.

The problem of the quality of educational materials was highlighted by the Coopers and Lybrand (1996) evaluation and critique of the UK's Teaching and Learning Technology Programme (TLTP), an ongoing £40,000,000-plus national initiative to support the development and dissemination of RBL and CAL materials for higher education. Coopers and Lybrand reported that a 'substantial minority' of TLTP products 'must be deemed *amateur*' (section 259) and 'in only a small number of cases did we encounter projects which had taken account of pedagogic issues in any systematic way' (section 282).

It can also be argued that, with learning technologies, we should be aiming for better, not 'the same for less'. Good quality RBL can enhance and improve learning by the effective use of different media and by individualizing instruction in a variety of ways. The development of 'hypermedia', a term coined by Ted Nelson (1990), presents particular challenges and opportunities. Media-rich, non-linear, interactive environments may lead to effective learning for some individuals on some occasions, sometimes not. We need a principled understanding of why this is so. Therefore it is important to be aware of research findings concerning individual differences in styles and strategies of learning and in attitudes and approaches to learning.

What is RBL?

Over the last two decades or so, a number of phrases have come in to vogue that attempt to capture the ideas behind new approaches to teaching and learning. RBL is one of these. Recently it has become particularly popular, partly because it reflects new trends and developments in the use of learning technologies and also because it serves as an umbrella term for other terms found in the education literature, such as open learning, flexible learning, individualized learning, computer aided learning, project-based learning, problem-based learning, student-centred learning and self-organized learning.

As an umbrella term it is perhaps too general for some purposes in that it blurs important distinctions, such as learner-centred rather than teacher-centred, or the distinction between self-organized learning and learning that follows an instructional system. However, it is useful for explaining the shifts away from traditional forms of learning and teaching. As noted in the Introduction, as a useful summary definition we would accept the emphasis of the Australian National Council of Open and Distance Learning (NCODE, online) that:

> Resource-based Learning (RBL) is defined as an integrated set of strategies
> to promote student-centred learning in a mass education context, through
> a combination of specially designed learning resources and interactive media
> and technologies.

Probably the best way to appreciate the way in which the term RBL has come to be used is to contrast it with what is *not* RBL. We have in mind those traditional approaches where the main resource is a human teacher who delivers lessons, lectures and seminars to groups of students, as few as one or two or as many as two to three hundred at a time.

In traditional approaches, other resources in addition to the teacher may be important, such as textbooks or laboratory equipment. However, the role of the teacher or lecturer is essential. Teachers are expected to have a command of the subject matter to be taught and to be skilled at teaching and expounding that subject matter. They have a major responsibility for deciding lesson content and how to teach it and they are expected to have responsibility for student progress and to know how to assess that progress, both formatively and summatively.

From this perspective, RBL is very much about reducing or otherwise modifying the central role of the human teacher. As an example of the extensive use of RBL, let us consider the teaching methods adopted by the UK's Open University.

Case history: teaching methods at the UK's Open University

Open University courses are designed for students learning at a distance. Face-to-face tuition does take place but at a fairly minimal level and it is optional for students. Most of the learning and teaching takes place in the student's own home or other personal 'learnplace', using materials or 'learning chunks' that may consist of a range of materials using different media, such as specially written course units and study guides, television programmes, video tapes and audio tapes. (The quoted terms are from Ford *et al,* 1996.) Typically, the specially written course units contain activities and self-assessment questions. The objectives of the units may be explicitly spelt out as a list of learning outcomes. The writing style is one where a friendly, personal tone is adopted. As well as information about the structure of the course and the relevance and place of the different learning resources in the learning pack, there is frequently an explicit reference to study skills and suggestions for how to carry out projects and assignments and (not least) how to revise for examinations.

To a very large extent 'learning packs' are self-contained as learning materials. However, important roles are played by the OU's part-time associate lecturers who act as tutors and counsellors. Rather than being direct teachers of the subject matter, the tutor is more of a learning facilitator or learning coach. An associate lecturer acting as a tutor is expected to have a command of the subject matter being taught and, at the optional tutorials, will review, discuss and interpret a selection of the course materials. He or she may also be available at the end of the telephone line to trouble-shoot when individual students are having difficulties with their learning.

Probably the most crucial role of the staff is to play a major part in the OU's machinery for assessing student progress and providing regular feedback to students. As well as assigning a grade or mark to the assignments, the tutor is expected to supply in-depth commentary and feedback to the students about the strengths and weaknesses of their work: where they may have got it wrong and what they must do to achieve a higher grade. Commentary may be aimed at dispersing misconceptions or reinforcing key teaching points from the course units. Tutors are expected to monitor and comment on students' individual progress and to work to establish the idea that there is a personal relationship between tutor and tutee.

Other examples of the use of RBL

Examples of the use of RBL are spread throughout the book. Here we will mention two particular developments that are helping transform traditional teaching: Internet and CD ROM-based resources.

Through the UK's TLTP initiative, a wealth of learning materials have become available, albeit of varying quality. The TLTP central Web site has links to the 75-plus projects that have been funded to date (http://www.ncteam.ac.uk/tltp/). Typically, the materials are distributed to the UK HE sector on CD ROM at low cost or downloaded for free from the Internet. In addition, there are an increasing number of commercially available CD ROM-based learning resources. As discussed in Chapter 5, many resources are available via the Web, often for free.

The process of incorporating such materials into traditional courses is often referred to as 'embedding'. We discuss the embedding process in Chapter 9, with case histories. Here, it is sufficient to note that to embed RBL materials well requires an investment of time and expertise that is often not available to the traditional teacher. As a consequence, many readily available RBL materials are under-used. Typically, they serve only as 'back-up' materials to be used at a student's discretion, augmenting traditional methods rather than replacing them.

Advantages and disadvantages of RBL

RBL, done well, can provide high quality teaching, but there are advantages and disadvantages that need to be taken into account.

Possible advantages include:

- students may work through materials at their own pace;
- formative feedback on progress may be provided, helping to ensure learning is effective;
- the explicit, transparent nature of RBL, which lends itself to thorough evaluation;
- the efficient use of resources, particularly for avoiding duplication of effort in the preparation of course materials.

Possible disadvantages include:

- high initial costs of preparing materials;
- extra costs of maintaining, revising and updating courses;
- the need for students to be well-motivated and self-organizing learners;
- the lack of peer contact and interaction for students working alone;
- the need for flexibly available tutorial support;
- problems of ensuring materials are pedagogically of a high quality.

Rowntree (1990) provides useful additional discussion of these issues. On balance, for the right students, properly prepared RBL may well be the most efficient way of delivering effective learning. High initial development costs are a major inhibiting factor as are ingrained, institutionalized ways of working. We look further at the problems of culture change in Chapter 9.

Major types of RBL

There are many ways of classifying different types of RBL. Here, we will highlight and explore four major aspects, to help appreciate the range of possibilities to which the term may refer:

1. the amount and kind of teacher support;
2. the extent to which the materials are prescribed and structured;
3. the extent to which learning experiences are prescribed and structured;
4. the ways in which different kinds of media are deployed.

1. The amount and kind of teacher support

As already noted, RBL is essentially being contrasted with didactic, teacher-centred learning, in which a human teacher delivers a body of subject matter that is supposed to be understood by the student. RBL moves away from this model of teaching in several ways.

Much more emphasis is put on the learner and the role he or she plays in achieving goals set, such as coming to understand a body of subject matter or mastering a set of skills and procedures. In other words, the orientation towards learning is *constructivist* with emphasis on establishing dialogues designed to support constructive learning (theories of learning and teaching are discussed in more detail later in this chapter).

The concept of the supportive dialogue as being a vital element in RBL has been enshrined in the literature as a 'tutorial in print' (Rowntree, 1990) or the 'learning conversation' (Harri-Augstein and Thomas, 1991). The conversations may be between student and tutor, as part of support systems using telephone, computer mediated communication (CMC) or face-to-face contact. They may take the form of commentaries in study guides or elsewhere on 'how to learn'. They may be built into learning materials as activities with formative feedback.

2. The extent to which the materials are prescribed and structured

Here we have in mind a particular dimension, which ranges from, at one extreme, little or no structure to, at the other extreme, very detailed specification and structure.

As an example of the former, consider project-based learning, where students are set a learning task and required to identify and locate their own resources, using libraries and the Internet.

As an example of the latter, consider a distance learning course, where all the materials are contained in course units and where the content is structured to form a very specific exposition of subject matter content.

3. The extent to which learning experiences are prescribed and structured

Later in this chapter, when discussing course design, we refer to the concept of a *tutorial strategy*. This offers another range of possibilities, ranging from students taking responsibility for their approaches to learning, to students being taken through very prescribed and structured experiences designed to ensure that learning is effective.

4. The ways in which different kinds of media are deployed

As discussed in Chapters 3, 5, 6 and 7, media and forms of delivery may be classified in a variety of different ways. We can classify different kinds of information such as verbal, visual and auditory and we can also classify the ways in which the different kinds of information are made available as text, audio, video, or multimedia. The Internet is in many respects breaking down these distinctions. The Web enables the delivery on one 'page' of all these media types in a coordinated and synchronized manner (see the discussion of SMIL in the next chapter). Moreover, students can control and interact with these Web pages and receive feedback on their interaction. The student can converse directly (synchronous communication) or via messages (asynchronous communication) with teachers and other students. The importance of this for education will become clearer after a brief excursion into learning theory.

An excursion into learning theory

Introduction

> Fundamentally, a university is a community holding conversations about knowledge. (Daniel, 1998)

In this section we introduce some theoretical frameworks designed to make clear what takes place when effective learning and teaching occur. The emphasis is on the usefulness of the models, rather than on detailed appraisal of the theories. The models were developed prior to the impact of the Internet on RBL, but this does not affect their relevance. The contexts in which learning and teaching take place may change, but not the underlying principles that inform good practice.

What is learning?

When considering what learning is and how it occurs, it is useful to recall that humans, like all other biological organisms, are dynamic, self-organizing systems, surviving and evolving in a hostile world. Such systems survive by adapting to their worlds and by actively becoming 'informed' of how their worlds work. 'Learning' as biological adaptation happens incidentally in the context of the pursuit of current 'need–satisfying' goals.

These processes of adaptation are going on all the time. In this sense one cannot *not* learn. In humans, learning finds its highest expression. Our 'need to learn' is so strong that often we experience boredom and actively seek out novel environments. We readily acquire new habits and actively construct mental models of problem situations. In addition to the processes of adaptation, we humans learn *intentionally*. We consciously set ourselves goals. We practise new skills. We reflect, conceptualize and converse. We come together to learn and to teach. We engage in tutorial dialogues and peer-peer discussions.

What do we learn?

When we learn, we are said to acquire 'knowledge'. In this section we look more closely at what knowledge is.

Often, different sub-types of 'knowledge' are distinguished. Bloom (1956), for example, distinguishes between 'knowledge', 'skills' and 'values'. Gagné *et al* (1992) distinguish motor skills, discriminations, intellectual skills, defined concepts, concrete concepts, cognitive strategies, attitudes, problem solving, verbal information (names or labels, facts, knowledge), rules and higher-order rules. Romiszowski's (1984) classification is even more complex. He distinguishes four main kinds of 'knowledge' (facts, procedures, concepts, principles) and four main kinds of 'skill' (cognitive, psychomotor, reactive, interactive) with further subdivisions.

We do not use these more elaborate schemes for describing 'what is learnt', chiefly to avoid unnecessary complication but also because (in our experience) the distinctions made are not always easy to apply. We do, however, make considerable use of one particular distinction: between 'knowing why' (theoretical, conceptual knowledge) and 'knowing how' (practical, performance knowledge). In the discussion of course design below, we introduce the concept of 'learning outcomes' and distinguish between cognitive outcomes that emphasize 'knowing why' and performance outcomes that emphasize 'knowing how'.

Learning as a process of cognitive construction

As noted above, 'learning' implies that new cognitive structures are acquired, if only as a consequence of adaptation. *Constructivist* theories of learning emphasize that some cognitive structures and processes actively guide these constructive activities. Learners have intentions, they form plans and adopt particular strategies. Learners can learn to learn; cognition can pull itself up by its own boot straps.

Kolb (1984), using ideas from Lewin and Piaget, provides a simple but useful (and frequently cited) model of the processes involved in constructivist learning (see Figure 2.1). Kolb proposes that learning is a cyclic activity with four stages. These are: *concrete experience*, followed by *reflection* on that experience, followed by *abstract conceptualization* (the derivation of general rules or theory construction, the construction of models and methods) and, finally, *active experimentation* (testing out rules and theories, models and methods). The important point to appreciate in terms of RBL is that the learner is not conceived as a passive recipient of 'knowledge' but rather as an active participant in the process of learning.

Rescher (1973; 1977), also building on Piaget's ideas, has constructed a more detailed model than that of Kolb. Two cycles of activity are distinguished: one corresponding to the acquisition and justification of 'why' knowledge, the other corresponding to the acquisition and consolidation of 'how' knowledge (see Figure 2.2).

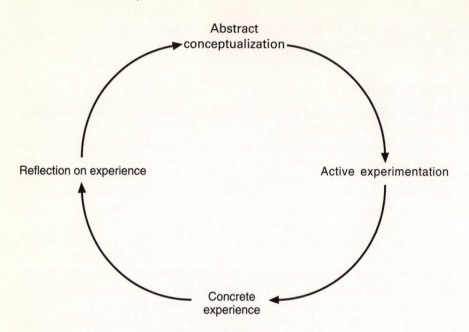

Figure 2.1 *Learning as a cyclic activity (after Kolb)*

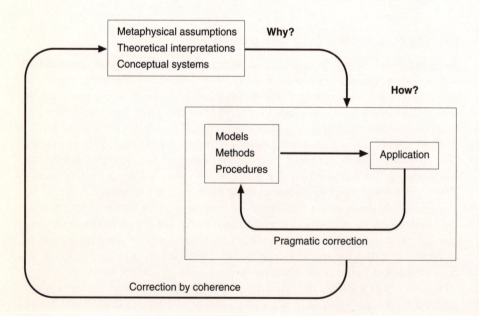

Figure 2.2 *Rescher's 'two-cycle' model of learning*

In the 'why' cycle, new conceptual knowledge is integrated with existing conceptual knowledge to form a coherent whole. Achieving coherence may necessitate revision or modification of existing knowledge (Piaget's classic terms for these processes are 'assimilation' and 'accommodation'). In the 'how' cycle, new 'methods' (procedures, operations) are constructed and tried out and are subject to pragmatic correction: do the models work, are problems solved, are predictions shown to be correct?

Learning as conversation

Here we describe theories of learning that include the role of the teacher, where the key idea is that learning takes place through learner and teacher being in conversation with one another.

The late Gordon Pask is the thinker who has most thoroughly developed a theory of conversations. Throughout several decades, he actively applied his ideas in education and in the development of man-machine teaching systems (Pask, 1975; 1976). Pask refers to his basic model, shown in Figure 2.3, as the 'skeleton of a conversation'. It shows a 'snapshot' view of two participants (learner and teacher) in conversation about a topic. Notice that the model distinguishes verbal interaction (questions and answers) from behavioural interaction via a shared modelling facility or 'micro-world'.

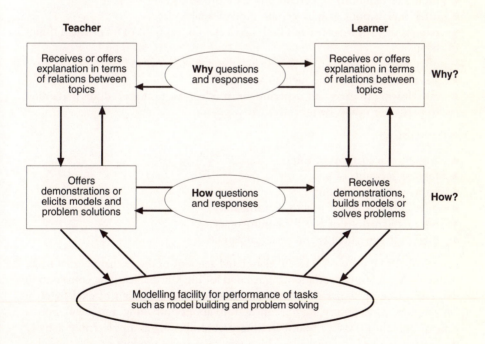

Figure 2.3 *The 'skeleton' of a conversation*

The horizontal connections represent the verbal exchanges. Pask argues that all verbal exchanges have at least two logical levels. In the figure these are shown as the two levels 'how' and 'why'. As in Rescher's model, the lower 'how' level is concerned with descriptions of how to 'do' a topic: how to recognize examples, construct models, achieve and maintain states of affairs and so on. The higher 'why' level is concerned with cognitive, conceptual understanding: defining, explaining or justifying what a topic means in terms of other topics. Critically one asks, 'Are explanations coherent?' If a student asserts that he or she understands a particular topic, does the student also understand other topics that are logically entailed? As a simple example, if a student says cake making requires that ingredients are mixed, does he or she have a clear understanding of what it means 'to mix' things and what is meant by the term 'ingredients'?

The modelling facility allows the teacher to instantiate or exemplify the topic by giving non-verbal demonstrations. Typically, such demonstrations are accompanied by verbal commentary about 'how' and 'why'. In turn learners may use the modelling facility to solve problems and carry out tasks set. They may also provide verbal commentary about 'how' and 'why'. Note that the form of what constitutes a canonical 'world' for construction and demonstration is itself subject to negotiation and agreement. Here, a brief example will have to suffice.

Consider topics in chemistry, which as noted by Marcel some 200 years ago (Marcel, 1805) is very suited to conversational learning. A teacher may:

- model or demonstrate certain processes or events;
- offer explanations of why certain processes take place;
- request that a learner teaches back his or her conceptions of *why* certain things happen;
- offer verbal accounts of *how* to bring about certain events;
- ask a learner to provide such an account;
- ask a learner to carry out experiments or other practical procedures pertaining to particular events or processes.

A learner may:

- request explanations of *why;*
- request accounts of *how;*
- request demonstrations;
- offer explanations of *why* for commentary;
- offer explanations of *how* for commentary;
- carry out experiments and practical activities.

Laurillard (1993) provides a useful elaborated account of the exchanges that make up the skeleton of a conversation, interpreted for the kinds of learning conversation that take place in higher education. She distinguishes a domain of exchanges of descriptions, conceptions and misconceptions about both 'how' and 'why', from a general domain of 'tasks'. 'Tasks' are interpreted liberally as any learning activity the learner is asked to engage in which generates some product or outcome that can then be the subject for further discussion.

Pask refers to learning about 'why' as *comprehension learning* and learning about 'how' as *operation learning*. He conceives them as being complementary aspects of effective learning. These distinctions allow Pask to give a formal definition of what it means to *understand* a topic, ie the learner can 'teach back' the topic by providing both non-verbal demonstrations and verbal explanations of 'how' and 'why'.

The components of a 'learning conversation'

In order to round out our discussion of 'learning as conversation', following Harri-Augstein and Thomas (1991), we will elaborate the Pask model in a different way.

Pask notes that conversations may have many logical levels above a basic 'why' level: levels at which conceptual justifications are themselves justified and where there is 'commentary about commentary'. Indeed, reflexively, the conversation itself may be the topic of conversation.

Harri-Augstein and Thomas make this notion central in their work on 'self-organized learning', where the emphasis is on helping students 'learn-how-to-learn'. In brief, they propose that a 'learning conversation' has three main components:

1. conversation about the *how* and *why* of a topic, as in the basic Pask model;
2. conversation about the *how* of learning (for example, discussing study skills and reflecting on experiences as a learner);
3. conversation about purposes, the *why* of learning, where the emphasis is on encouraging personal autonomy and accepting responsibility for one's own learning.

The model in Figure 2.4 shows the relationships between the components. Laurillard makes many similar points about the importance of these higher levels in the conversations that take place in universities.

Given the importance of conversational interaction as a component of effective learning, the challenge for designers and developers of RBL materials is to ensure that learning conversations do occur. We noted above Rowntree's concept of the 'tutorial in print'. In distance learning materials, activities such as self-assessment questions are used to promote constructive learning and reflection. Learners are encouraged to imagine themselves in conversation with the author of the learning materials. Minimally they are in conversation with themselves in carrying out reflection. Other ways of promoting learning conversations are through student support systems such as telephone tutorials or the occasional face-to-face session where students may engage with their peers as well as with their tutor. We pay particular attention to the use of computer mediated communications to support student learning in Chapter 7.

Individual differences – styles and strategies of learning

Our discussion of RBL and theories of learning and teaching would not be complete without some reference to individual differences: learning styles, learning

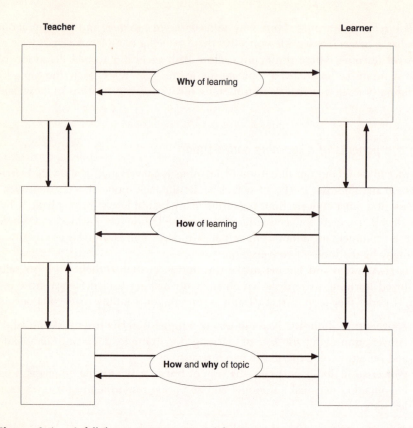

Figure 2.4   *A full 'learning conversation' (after Harri-Augstein and Thomas, 1991)*

strategies and approaches to learning. The reason for this is that, as an ideal, good RBL will accommodate a variety of learning styles but will also ensure that effective learning strategies and approaches are followed.

There is a very large literature on individual differences covering many aspects of emotional, motivational and cognitive mental life and behaviour, all of which may have some effect on the quality of learning. Here, our chief concern is with the cognitive aspects of the learning process. We present a very brief summary of some generally accepted research findings and models; if you would like to read more on this topic, the standard sources are Biggs (1987), Jonassen and Grabowski (1993), Marton *et al* (1984), Morgan (1993) and Schmeck (1988).

By learning *style*, we mean a fairly enduring characteristic of a learner that biases him or herself to adopt a particular strategy or approach. By learning *strategy* or *approach*, we mean descriptions or models of what learners may do.

Holists, serialists, comprehension learning and operation learning
Pask and associates (Pask, 1975, 1976; Pask and Scott, 1972, 1973) are responsible for a pair of distinctions: *holist* and *serialist,* and *operation learning* and *comprehension learning.* A learner with a *holist* bias prefers to work globally, in parallel, on many

topics at once; conversely, a learner with a *serialist* bias prefers to work locally, serially, on one topic at once.

A *holist strategy* is then a 'many-at-once' approach and a *serialist strategy* is a 'one-step-at-once' approach. A learner who can adopt either approach to fit task demands is said to be *versatile*.

A learner with a bias towards *comprehension learning* tends to focus more on *why* than *how*, whereas a learner with a bias towards *operation learning* tends to focus more on *how* rather than *why*.

As noted above, comprehension learning and operation learning are necessary and complementary aspects of any effective learning strategy. A learner who does both well is said to be an *effective learner*.

Pask and associates carried out empirical studies of learning style over a 10-year period, using different student populations and different subject matters. They commonly found associations between type of strategy adopted and type of learning engaged in (see Pask, 1988, for a summary of the research findings). Pask argues the observed associations reflect competence requirements, as follows:

- *operation learning* often calls for the adoption of a *serialist* strategy;
- *comprehension learning* often calls for the adoption of a *holist* strategy;
- *effective learning* often calls for versatility with respect to learning strategy.

Bias in learning style leads to what Pask refers to as *pathologies of learning*.

Operation learning without *comprehension learning* may lead to *improvidence* – essentially, failing to see similarities, so learning the 'same' things over and over again. *Comprehension learning* without *operation learning* may lead to *globe-trotting*, possibly *vacuous globe-trotting* – essentially, citing similarities and differences but failing to operationalize one's concepts and running the risk of engaging in mere 'talk'. Table 2.1 summarizes these ideas about learning style.

Table 2.1   *How biases contribute to learning style*

	Serialist bias	Holist bias	Versatile
Bias to operation learning	Improvident		
Bias to comprehension learning		Globetrotting	
Effective learner			Versatile and effective

Approaches to learning: deep, surface and achieving

Marton *et al* (1984) and Morgan (1993) distinguish two main approaches to learning: *deep* and *surface*. In his summary of work on deep and surface learning, Biggs (1987) proposes that learning may be surface or deep and more or less *achieving* depending upon a learner's 'cognitive competencies and biases' and 'motivation and purposes'.

A learner adopting a *deep approach* has the intention to understand and will:

- focus on an author's intent;
- relate new to old knowledge (elaborate);
- relate knowledge to personal experience;
- actively organize and structure knowledge content.

A learner adopting a *surface approach* has the intention of completing the task set and will:

- focus on content items;
- memorize facts and procedures for requirements of assessment.

A learner adopting a *strategic approach* has the intention to maximize attainments and will:

- analyse course requirements in the light of resources and commitments;
- use a mix of deep and surface approaches.

Learning, RBL and the Internet

The Internet can provide 'non-linear' learning environments that are rich in different media forms and interactive in a variety of ways. Such environments may be an exciting and worthwhile challenge for the versatile learner who has 'learnt how to learn'. However, for many learners they may also be sources of confusion and anxiety.

Clearly, as educators, we need to follow a dual strategy: providing some environments that are carefully designed to support a variety of styles, strategies and approaches, while ensuring effective learning takes place; and supporting students in becoming reflexively aware, skilled learners, who can cope with less structured and supportive environments.

Pask and Scott's (1973) CASTE (Course Assembly System and Tutorial Environment) is a prototype for the former that supports holist and serialist approaches in a hypermedia domain, while ensuring learning to 'mastery' (see also Scott, in press a).

With respect to the latter, we know from the work of Perry and others (Perry, 1970) that for many learners there appears to be a maturation process, during which period they do indeed need to be nurtured and 'educated' (Latin, *educare,* to lead out). They need to have good quality learning experiences in order to reflect on how to learn effectively. In the next section, we look at course design and principled ways in which good quality learning can be facilitated.

A framework for course design

As noted above, the use of RBL implies that the learner is being given access to learning materials and experiences in a chiefly teacher-independent manner. The resources in question may take a variety of forms: they may or may not be structured or organized in some way; they may or may not have supporting study guides and assessment procedures.

Resources having some or all of these features may have to be integrated and used alongside other resources that also lack some or all of these features. It may be the case that a particular programme of studies may have non-RBL components, such as traditional didactic lectures or small group seminars, tutorials and supervised project work. It is against this backdrop of a variety of possible teaching and learning scenarios that we shall address the question of how to effectively develop RBL, embed it into the curriculum and evaluate outcomes.

In keeping with the Coopers and Lybrand (1996) findings, cited at the beginning of this chapter, the solution as to how to cope with this variety is to 'take account of pedagogic issues in a systematic way'. The framework for course design that we propose has four major components:

1. a description of desired learning outcomes (these are commonly expressed as course aims and objectives);
2. a specification of course content (describing knowledge and skills and desired learning experiences);
3. a specification of the tutorial strategies to be employed (issues covered here include sequencing of learning experiences, choice of media for delivering learning experiences and the role of dialogic interactive activities designed to encourage and reinforce effective learning);
4. the assessment strategy to be used (encompassing both formative and summative assessment aims).

We believe that these four components are essential for effective learning and teaching. They are closely interrelated and, indeed, a major aim of course design is to ensure their interrelations are meaningful in justifiable ways.

The essential principles of good quality course design can be summarized as follows:

*   there should be a clear mapping between the statements of learning outcomes and the specification of course content;
*   an analysis of course content should be carried out in order to specify appropriate tutorial strategies;
*   there should be a clear mapping between course content and assessment activities which preserves the mapping between learning outcomes and course content.

These ideas are summarized in Figure 2.5.

The whole process of course design is overviewed in Figure 2.6. The diagram shows the several stages involved and indicates how they may interact, as decisions made at later stages may necessitate revision of decisions made earlier. Later stages include evaluation studies. Ideally, these should be part and parcel of an HEI's quality assurance procedures. Guided by the above principles, we will now examine the components of effective course design in a little more detail.

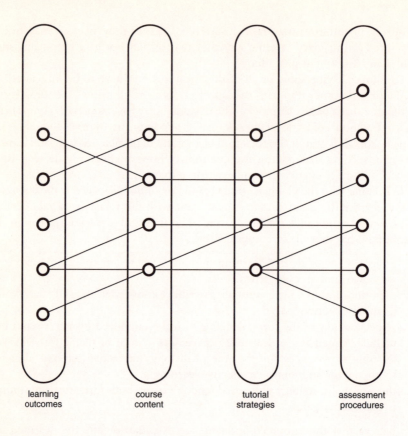

learning
outcomes

course
content

tutorial
strategies

assessment
procedures

Figure 2.5 *A framework for course design – all items of any of the four components should map on to corresponding items of other components*

Learning outcomes, aims and objectives

There is a variety of terminology for specifying what it is the course is intended to achieve. Our favourite term is 'learning outcomes', rather than the widely used 'aims and objectives'. 'Aims' and 'objectives' are often used in association, implying a distinction is implied. Aims are usually broad-brush statements of intent used as a way of framing the activities of a course team. Objectives are more specific statements of desired learning outcome. We prefer the term 'learning outcome' since it lacks the narrow behaviourist connotations that some people give to the term 'objective'. The term also reminds us that the outcomes belong to the learner.

Following our earlier distinction of 'why' and 'how' knowledge, we shall generally distinguish two main categories of learning outcome: cognitive (or conceptual) and performance. As an example, here are some learning outcomes for the topic 'cake baking':

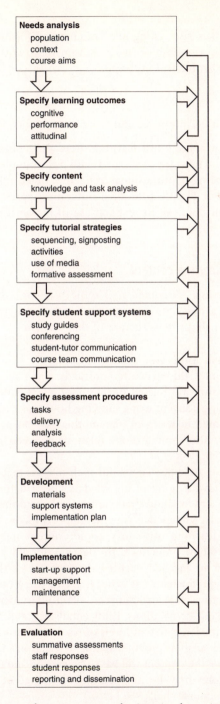

Figure 2.6　*The course design process – the iterative loops indicate the possibility of parallel activities and revisions in the light of experience*

Cognitive outcomes:
- explain why cakes 'rise', citing relevant chemical formulae and equations;
- explain why it was foolish of Marie-Antoinette to say, 'Let them eat cake', when told the people had no bread.

Performance outcomes:
- bake a cake;
- recall what Marie-Antoinette said when told the people had no bread.

In the literature on teaching and learning, it is also common to distinguish 'attitudinal outcomes'. These are concerned with, for example, having the appropriate attitudes for being a professional, reflective practitioner. Although very important, we shall not discuss attitudinal outcomes separately, except to note that their achievement does call for explicit use of higher level conversations, as shown in Figure 2.4.

The specification of course content

A description of learning outcomes goes some way towards specifying course content; however, as a description of course content it is incomplete. What is lacking is information about the structure of that content.

Knowledge and task analysis

For conceptual outcomes, this structure consists of some account of how topics within the subject matter are related one to another. Relations between topics can be represented using concept maps, showing how topics may be derived from one another or explained in terms of one another. As well as relations of logical entailment, maps may also show analogy relations between topics or subsets of topics (Pask, 1975, 1976; Pask *et al*, 1975).

The important thing to appreciate about such maps is that they show possible ways of coming to know a body of knowledge. The structures show the forms that possible teaching and learning strategies may take and the range of 'narrative structures' that particular knowledge content supports (Scott, 1999).

For performance learning outcomes, topic content needs to be specified operationally, as the set of procedures the learner should be able to perform satisfactorily. In order to provide detailed descriptions of the procedures that constitute satisfactory performance, it is necessary to carry out a task analysis. As with conceptual structures, task structures are often conveniently displayed using graphical techniques and conventions. Both entailment and task structures may be mapped and described at different levels of resolution or granularity.

Knowledge and task analysis provides a clear description of the overall content of the course. However, the content still has to be created and compiled as tutorial materials. The structures may be mapped and described at different levels of resolution within the 'course shell' (see below).

See Rowntree (1990) for examples of different kinds of concept map and task structure representation. In Chapter 4 we describe 'Webmapper', a concept mapping tool to aid the design of courses delivered via the Web.

The 'course shell'

It may be helpful at an early stage of course design to agree upon the form of a 'course shell', in which it is clear how particular 'learning chunks' may fit into the overall learning programme that is the course. Figure 2.7 is an example of a typical course shell that distinguishes the smaller chunks: module, unit, lesson. A common alternative in the world of CAL is 'book, chapter, lesson'.

A 'lesson' may be specified as being equivalent to a certain amount of study time, for example, 'one hour' or '20 minutes'. Clearly, such specifications impose constraints on the amount of material that can be included in particular chunks. As shown in Figure 2.7, an even more fine-grained analysis may specify key terms and topics that are contained in each lesson and make explicit links to particular learning resources. Distance learning materials are typically compiled according to a course shell, at least down to 'lesson' level. Many text-based examples can be found (UK Open University, UK Open Learning Foundation, UK National Extension College).

CAL authoring tools such as Toolbook and Authorware readily accommodate the creation of course shells. In Chapter 8 we describe Web-based 'virtual learning environments' (VLEs), such as WebCT, in which working to a course shell is a standard feature of course design.

Tutorial strategies

By 'tutorial strategies' we mean decisions about teaching sequences and tactics. Given that knowledge and task analysis has clearly revealed the course structure, there may be many different orders in which topics can be presented while still conforming to the course shell. The essential requirement is to come up with sequences or 'narrative structures' that are psychologically appealing while respecting the logic of the course structure (Pask *et al,* 1975; Scott, 1999).

By 'tactics' we mean the deployment of a number of tutorial aids, devices and procedures. These are well documented in the course design literature; see, for example, Rowntree (1990). We have in mind aids such as 'advance organizers' (Ausubel, 1968) that help learners anticipate what is to come. These may take the form of a listing of learning outcomes, textual introductions, or maps of course content. Icons or other devices may be used to clearly signpost to students where they are within course materials. Different media may be used to enhance the effectiveness of the learning materials. Expository text may be accompanied by activities and self-assessment questions, designed to reinforce understanding and mastery and provide formative feedback. These latter devices and procedures may overlap with the course's assessment strategy, as discussed below.

Other aids to support effective learning include glossaries, indices, note taking, copying and printing facilities. With learning and distance materials it is also

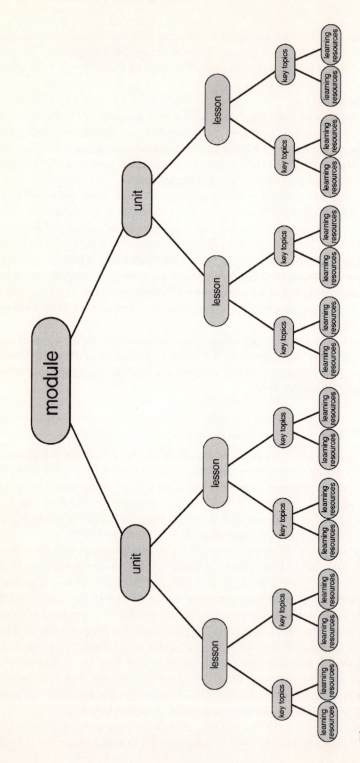

Figure 2.7 *A generic 'course shell'*

common practice to include a study guide that provides overall information about the course, possibly with advice on study skills and learning strategies.

When writing for the Web, specific structuring and organizational considerations come into play. Gahran (online) makes some useful points about the quality of the information presented, and the contextual structures that surround it such as summaries, headlines and topic sentences. This article also demonstrates a medium-sensitive feature that is largely ignored by academic sites: the 'print-friendly' page. There are two versions of the Gahran article, one being graphics and link rich, divided into several Web pages and meant for viewing onscreen and linking away from. The other version is the one printed for reading offline away from the computer – free of graphics, divided into sections by typical paper-based devices, without the side-bars of the Web version, and in one fast-loading page.

A particularly useful article for Web authors is 'Concise, SCANNABLE, and Objective: How to Write for the Web' (Morkes and Nielsen, online). One of the most interesting conclusions of the paper, and the reason for the uppercase 'SCANNABLE' in the title, is that Web page users usually do not read pages on the Web but scan for the information they want. The implications for authors of educational Web sites are enormous, suggesting that we must relearn how we write. They argue that writing for the Web is much closer to the inverted pyramid style of newspapers, where conclusions and summaries are presented first, followed by detail and background later. The authors conclude that, 'scannable, concise, and objective writing styles each make a positive difference in Web users' performance and subjective satisfaction'.

In his Alertbox of 24 January 1999, 'Differences between print design and web design', Nielsen (online d) summarizes the differences between the high-resolution environment of the modern newspaper and the low resolution but multimedia, hyperlinked environment of the Web, identifying strengths and weaknesses on both sides.

Assessment strategies

It is common practice in education and course design to make a distinction between formative and summative assessment. We have already made use of the terms but it may help to review the distinction.

Summative assessment refers to carrying out assessment in order to be able to award a mark or grade that indicates how a particular student's performance compares with that of his or her peers or set criteria.

Formative assessment refers to assessment carried out in order to obtain information about a particular student's progress, in order to provide feedback to that student and his or her teachers. This feedback may provide motivational reinforcement. It will also provide knowledge of results so that learning and teaching strategies may be adapted or modified to be more effective, including implementing remediation programmes. It may also provide information about other strengths and weaknesses that the student may have such as preferred learning style, or the effectiveness of his or her study skills.

Effective assessment

Effective assessment procedures should address both the 'how' and 'why' aspects of understanding, although in the context of a particular course, given its aims and desired learning outcomes, there may be more or less emphasis on one aspect or the other. Sometimes, the emphasis is on mastery of performance skills (can you really bake that cake?); sometimes the emphasis is on theoretical, conceptual knowledge (why was it foolish of Marie-Antoinette to suggest giving the people cake instead of bread?).

It is, of course, absolutely essential that the assessment tasks set do indeed reflect the course content – that, as in Figure 2.5, there is a fair mapping between what is studied and what is assessed. Typically, many assessment procedures only sample the subject matter content. Assessment to a high level of mastery may require that all aspects of the subject content are assessed (Block, 1971).

Thus far, we have assumed that assessment takes the form of questions posed and tasks set. As noted above, Pask's model (Figure 2.3) suggests a more general framework in which the process of assessment can be placed. He argues that what is being asked for in assessment is that students should 'teach back' what it is they have learnt. For performance outcomes, this may mean carrying out tasks and demonstrating competence and skill but, for conceptual outcomes, it also entails giving a narrative account about what is being done and why.

Pask is very clear, though, that such teach back should not be mere repetition or regurgitation. As evidence of insightful understanding and the ability to generalize, novel tasks may be set and performed. Expository narratives may be assessed for conceptual coherence and accuracy rather than for rote ability to recall. Credit may be given for originality, and the integration of material from distinct but relevant related topics. In the absence of full, narrative-style teach back, overall coherence and understanding can be assessed by setting more complex questions whose parts are interrelated and which lend themselves to objective, mechanical scoring.

In recent years there have been a number of interesting attempts to construct question forms and assessment activities that approximate to eliciting a full conceptual teach back (roughly equivalent to eliciting an essay). Some of these assessment activities are presented interactively using a computer.

Formative assessment activities, in order to play their full role in tutorial strategies, require the delivery of appropriate kinds of feedback and knowledge of results. Again, there are a number of computer-based delivery systems designed to do this, either as part of a specific tutorial package or as more generic computer aided assessment (CAA) tools. We review a number of these in Chapter 8.

Conclusion: the question of quality

We began this chapter by noting that good quality RBL can enhance and improve learning. We also noted that such good quality is not arrived at by accident, nor is it readily achieved even by the most enthusiastic 'amateurs'. What is needed is the competent application of relevant theories of learning and teaching and principles of course design, augmented as necessary by other competencies, such as programming and media design. Thankfully, there appears to be an emerging consensus about the importance and form of these several competencies (see, for example, Schultz *et al,* online) and of the importance of evaluation and quality assurance procedures (Calder, 1994).

We have provided an overview of some well-tried models and approaches to learning, teaching and course design. In later chapters we also discuss the course development process, noting the need for 'course teams' who have the right mix of skills. As well as subject specialists, programmers and media designers, there is a need to have input from educational technologists who can advise on pedagogy and course design. In Chapter 9 we discuss the changing role of the teacher, noting that many may become increasingly involved in the production of RBL materials and become effective instructional designers in their own right.

Chapter 3

Technologies of delivery and interaction on the Internet

Introduction

In the previous chapter we examined resource-based learning and provided a brief overview of some key learning theories. We saw that our models of learning require interaction and a 'learning conversation' to take place. This learning conversation may occur directly between the teacher and the student or be mediated through a variety of RBL materials. We also saw that, as an ideal, good RBL will not only accommodate a variety of learning styles but will also ensure that effective learning strategies and approaches are followed. We suggested that the Web, with its ability to include a range of powerful media forms and its interactive capability, enables us to support a sophisticated range of interaction and provide a rich environment for teaching. How can the Internet support such interaction?

This chapter examines the nature of the Internet in more detail and focuses on a number of interlinked issues relating to the use of the Internet for teaching and learning:

- What is the Internet, and what is its relationship with the World Wide Web?
- What resources – sources of stimulation – may be delivered to users via the Internet?
- What is the nature of the interaction that is enabled, or impeded, between users and the Internet?

Some of the content may appear quite technical, but we strongly believe that if teaching staff are to fully exploit the possibilities offered by the Web and engage in constructive dialogue with developers and technical specialists, it is necessary to have a broad overview of the possibilities and limitations of the Web. At the end of this book is a glossary that deals with the technical terms you're likely to meet in this chapter, such as HTML, URL, XML and Java, and you can refer to it as necessary.

We will first take a broad look at the nature of the Internet, then at the software (the browser) that acts as a window onto the information space that comprises the Internet. We will then look at the types of information that can come and go through that window.

The Internet and the World Wide Web

The Internet is an interlinked network of networks that allows any computer in the world connected to it to exchange data with any other computer in the world. This is possible as all computers linked to the Internet have a unique address that enables data to be sent to and from it. The Internet's origins have been well documented elsewhere (for example, Gilster, 1994), but to understand the current focus on the Web and the browser (such as Netscape Navigator or Microsoft Internet Explorer) we need to look for a moment at its technology.

Let's start with a metaphor: on our road system the rules that govern the way in which drivers behave are embodied in the Highway Code. Similarly, the Internet is a network of electronic roads, and the information that traverses it is broken down into small pieces called 'packets' which are routed according to a set of rules laid down in a specification called TCP/IP (Transmission Control Protocol/Internet Protocol). Each of these packets has its destination written in a language that all of the attached computers can understand.

What's in a packet?

Just as we can classify traffic on the basis of a vehicle's nature or contents, so we can group Internet packets by the structure of their contents, which is defined by several sets of rules or protocols. There are six major types: HTTP, e-mail, News, Gopher, FTP and Telnet. In the past (relatively speaking, of course) each different packet could only be understood by a different type of software application. For example, packets of HTTP (HyperText Transfer Protocol) could only be read by a Web browser, while packets of News (as found in bulletin boards and newsgroups) could only be interpreted by applications that understood NNTP (Network News Transfer Protocol).

Today, browsers are very different to what they were even four years ago. Now, Web browsers can deal almost seamlessly with HTTP, FTP, e-mail, Gopher and News protocols. For this reason we'll focus on the browser as the main software application for the delivery of information over the Internet. More information on the technical aspects of the Web and the Internet can be found in many places on the Web, particularly WDVL (The Web Developer's Virtual Library – http://WDVL.Internet.com/Internet/web/About.html).

There are other metaphors for the Web. Jakob Nielsen's Alertbox (Nielsen, online b) suggests that the telephone may be the best one. His approach is rather different to the one taken here initially, in that it does not consider the electronic nature of the Web, but rather the nature of the interaction between people and the Web. Both the Web and the telephone support one-to-one communication; the Web of course supports one-to-many communication. An obvious similarity between the Web and the phone is that 'calls' are initiated by the user, at their convenience. The telephone and the Web are interactive in the way that a TV show is not: direction and content are determined by both partners in the conversation. Finally, everyone is a publisher on the telephone, as are the millions of Web users who have their own pages.

Using the Web – interacting with a range of resources

The Web is a non-linear hypertextual environment that works with a multiplicity of media types such as:

- text, plain or formatted;
- hybrid documents containing high resolution text and graphics, such as Acrobat documents;
- images, colour, still and animated, and video;
- sound;
- 3-D environments;
- scripted interaction (through JavaScript, VBScript, Java, ActiveX).

It also supports real-time chatting via text and real-time audio/video communication through, for example, InternetPhone and CU-SeeMe videoconferencing. (These terms are described in more detail below.)

The essential characteristic of the Web has nothing to do with the media it delivers, but the movement between different media environments that it supports: the Web is a hypertext environment, where non-linear movement is the defining process that users engage in.

Hypertext consists of pages (or nodes) that contain anchors (or hotspots), that link to destination pages. Usually, the anchors in a Web page are the coloured and underlined words. Clicking on one of these loads in the destination page. This linking is the key property of the Web that makes it so attractive to educationalists. Unlike courses delivered in, say, printed form that have to be self-contained, a course on the Web can contain links to materials and resources located anywhere. This may be anything from resources on the same server that provide additional help, or support that can be accessed as required by the student, or links to the latest reports from a research organization located on the other side of the globe.

Interaction on the Web

What is the nature of the interaction that is enabled, or impeded, between users and the Internet?

There are two dimensions by which the technologies of the Web can be defined and described. The first is concerned with the *nature* of the different media types; the second with the *type and quality of interaction* that may occur. These two are closely bound together.

For example, let's consider the medium of text. In its most passive mode it is the one-way transmission of information, fixed in form (on the screen) and content. At the other extreme we have chatting, through IRC (Internet Relay Chat). Through the browser, and the medium of text, one person can interact in real time with one or many other people, from anywhere in the world, on any subject. While the medium, the mode and the software are the same, the degree of control and intellectual investment is quite different, and it is in these terms that we'll be discussing the multimedia of the Web.

Media and interaction

This section deals with some of the media that a Web author can use to support learning. The ideal design process in any medium amplifies its strengths and diminishes its weaknesses, and we will try to demonstrate the characteristics of the different media you may meet on the Web by describing a potential teaching resource.

We will start with what Tufte (1983) describes as 'what may well be the best statistical graphic ever drawn'. This is Charles Joseph Minard's graphical description of the fate of Napoleon's army in Russia, redrawn for the Web by Saglamer (online), shown in Figure 3.1. The graphic combines data, map and time series in which Tufte identifies six variables: the size, direction and location of the army, and the temperature at various locations and dates. What can the Web add, or detract, from this graphic, and how might we use this medium to interest and stimulate learners?

Text and graphics

We need little text to describe the data of the graphic, yet we could have information on the Web page about Napoleon's campaign. This text could be structured by the use of headlines, subheadings, tables and lists, and so far there's not much that's different from the printed page. As you can see, the graphic itself is horizontal, and to see the detail it needs to be fairly large on the screen. However, by using frames we can add to the information in the graphic without detracting from its impact.

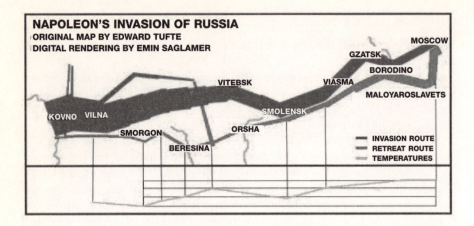

Figure 3.1 *A version of Minard's map, reproduced in Tufte (1983) and digitally rendered by Saglamer (online)*

Frames

Frames are a way of dividing the browser window into several independent parts. The example in Figure 3.2 illustrates one use for frames (we'll return to Napoleon shortly).

This site is about an area of Leicester, UK, called Highfields. The site describes the place from a variety of standpoints, using text, images and sound from people who lived in the area in the past and some who have recently moved into it. To help visitors to the site get a feel for the different viewpoints, a list of the most popular items of interest and concern was created; and it can be seen on the left-hand side of the browser window: this is a frame. When the user clicks on one of the headings the text appears in the right-hand window. In this example, the heading 'Entertainment' has been chosen. Note that the top frame of the window contains navigational links, and they are always there whatever selection is made in the left-hand frame.

Framing Napoleon

If we put Minard's map in the top frame of a browser we could divide it into four or more active areas so that, with a click on each, an enlarged and annotated image could appear in the lower window. Similarly, using a list of headings in a frame to the left-hand side (like the Highfields site) we could put contextual information into the central frame that supports and embellishes the richness of the map.

Animation and video

By animating the graphic we could see the flow of Napoleon's army first to the east and then to the west. This could add a time dimension, indicating the speed

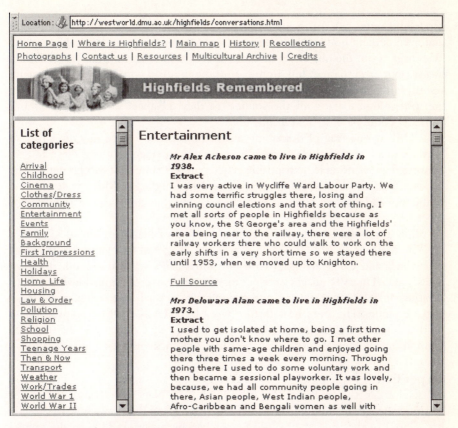

Location: http://westworld.dmu.ac.uk/highfields/conversations.html

Home Page | Where is Highfields? | Main map | History | Recollections
Photographs | Contact us | Resources | Multicultural Archive | Credits

Highfields Remembered

List of categories

Arrival
Childhood
Cinema
Clothes/Dress
Community
Entertainment
Events
Family
Background
First Impressions
Health
Holidays
Home Life
Housing
Law & Order
Pollution
Religion
School
Shopping
Teenage Years
Then & Now
Transport
Weather
Work/Trades
World War 1
World War II

Entertainment

Mr Alex Acheson came to live in Highfields in 1938.
Extract
I was very active in Wycliffe Ward Labour Party. We had some terrific struggles there, losing and winning council elections and that sort of thing. I met all sorts of people in Highfields because as you know, the St George's area and the Highfields' area being near to the railway, there were a lot of railway workers there who could walk to work on the early shifts in a very short time so we stayed there until 1953, when we moved up to Knighton.

Full Source

Mrs Delowara Alam came to live in Highfields in 1973.
Extract
I used to get isolated at home, being a first time mother you don't know where to go. I met other people with same-age children and enjoyed going there three times a week every morning. Through going there I used to do some voluntary work and then became a sessional playworker. It was lovely, because, we had all community people going in there, Asian people, West Indian people, Afro-Caribbean and Bengali women as well with

Figure 3.2   *A screenshot of a Web page showing frames*

of advance and retreat of the army. The commonest form of animated graphics on the Web uses the animated GIF format, but the speed of animation is not under viewer control. An alternative is the compressed digital video formats that can be used on the Web, QuickTime (Apple Computer) being a common one. It's not necessary to use video to take advantage of QuickTime. A series of graphics could be made into a moving sequence whose advance may be controlled by the mouse, so users can either let the sequence play at the speed intended or step through it a frame at a time.

QuickTime can also be used to produce compressed digital sound files, so links to annotated descriptions and samples of contemporary French, English and Russian music would be possible. Using a QuickTime video with a soundtrack, your students could hear the music and see the highlighted place in the music score at the same time.

Virtual reality
Another way of enlivening the display might be to build interactive three-dimensional models of the soldiers using QuickTime VR or VRML (virtual reality

modelling language). An image of a soldier might be rotated, viewed in close up and even contain hotspots. For example, a click on a weapon could take you to a Web page about the object, an animated description of its workings, its evolution as a weapon, and so on. A link from part of the uniform could move to a museum resource on textiles. Even complex information about the change in the nutritional and physiological status of the soldiers as they advanced in the cold towards Moscow could be described in this way.

VRML is one way of describing a 3-D object. The source files are small, so they are quick to download (especially compared to video or sound files), and are converted into movable, expandable objects by software that works within the browser. This resource might be used to model a building in Moscow at the time of the war, and students could examine it from many angles, measure and describe it.

While there may not be any VR sites for any of Napoleon's battles, there is one site that does have 360 degree panoramic images of two famous battles – of Gettysburg and Chickamauga, two of the American Civil War's bloodiest battle-fields. QuickTime VR images were put together from over 975 individual snapshots, creating 46 panoramic images and a spectacular visual representation of these historic scenes. The site's host (http://www.JATRUCK.COM/stonewall/) tells us that his great, great grandfather was a private in Company D of the 79th Pennsylvania Volunteer Infantry at the battle of Chickamauga.

HyperText
What else can the text add? An introduction to Napoleon's campaign might mention the nationalities of the soldiers, their dress and their own histories. While not central to the issue, they could be reached by hypertext links in the text to other pages either on the same Web site or on others.

Sound

Among the 813 pages of one Web development book, the topic of sound gets just two pages. The author's reason is that sound encoding and manipulation systems aren't as available or as easy to use as the graphics equivalent, and we'll agree with that. However, we suspect the main reasons are more complex, and to perceive them we need to look at the way in which we interact with the Web page.

Links are visible, stationary and activated by an eye-brain-hand process. Sound, in contrast, has no such accessibility: it can't be seen, can't be 'clicked' on, and it changes with time in a way that we can't control as we would an animation (say by slowing it down or playing it frame by frame). As any listener to a radio play will attest, sound is a powerful and stimulating medium, yet it is used to very little effect on the Web and in resource-based learning in general. And, unlike vision, which focuses on one image at a time, we can 'focus' our hearing on several things simultaneously – it is possible to hold a conversation while listening to music, and even follow several conversations going on at once.

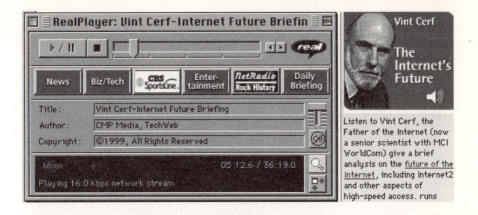

Figure 3.3   *A RealPlayer window sitting on top of a Web page, showing a streaming audio version of a talk by Vinton Cerf (http://byte.com)*

Increasing bandwidth, rapidly developing software, faster computers and pressure from those wishing to place commercials are now bringing audio onto the Web in a big way. For example, the 'Real' stable of products started out with 'RealAudio', best know for the streaming audio technology that allows you to listen to a radio broadcast or a music track without having to download the whole file.

Figure 3.3 shows an audio broadcast over the Web by Vinton Cerf, known as the 'father of the Web' because he defined the TCP/IP protocol. Once the broadcast has reached the computer it can be replayed and saved as you wish.

Many radio stations now broadcast live to the Web, as the image in Figure 3.4, taken from the 'RealGuide' site at http://www.real.com, shows clearly. As the image suggests, there are literally thousands of sites delivering audio content. As a resource it can be used in at least two ways: first, as a place for your students to do some research on issues of the day, directly from live news feeds. Alternatively, you can save sound files and even edit them, creating your own resources for students to use on demand.

Sound has other functions than to relay news. At the New York Public Library, Schomburg Center for Research in Black culture, Louis Armstrong Jazz Oral History Project (http://www.nypl.org/research/sc/scl/MULTIMED/JAZZHIST/jazzhist.html), you can listen and see jazz musicians talking about their favourite subject. The sound and images bring the names on the record sleeve alive, and inhabit the subject area with real human beings.

While loudspeakers attached to a computer in a public space represent an annoyance, a pair of headphones can bring immediacy to a topic that's hard to achieve in any other way, especially if the sound resource uses stereo. In this way the movement of an object across a space can be represented in two media channels: sound and vision. In the introduction to this chapter we questioned how educational designers might represent aspects of real objects such as touch and texture – here is a way.

Figure 3.4 *A screenshot of part of a Web page from the RealGuide site showing the range of audio channels available (http://www.real.com)*

MP3

One of the newest developments in audio on the Web is MP3 (MPEG 1 layer 3). This is a compression format that allows a digitized sound, such as found on a music CD, to be compressed to a size that makes it possible to stream it over the Web – so you can hear high-quality renderings of your favourite music CD as you sit at your machine. What's more, you can download the file and put it back onto a CD, hence making your own compilations and saving yourself some money. This means that educational developers can now represent audio interviews on the Web in relatively small files and with high quality, so adding another medium for stimulation to their existing technologies. We could, for example, add interviews with experts on the Napoleonic era to our Web page.

Adding interactivity

So far the only form of interaction with the material has been the mouse click. This may enable navigation and provide the ability to start and stop video, animation or audio files, but if we want to enable more advanced forms of interactivity, it requires Web authors to use the scripting languages that are now available, such as Javascript, Java and ActiveX.

At the simplest level we could ask multiple choice questions and mark answers directly on the same Web page as our Napoleonic map. For this we'd use JavaScript because it's fairly easy to manage and is embedded within the Web page. If we wanted to collate student answers or to collect group information then we'd have to use an application designed for this purpose such as QuestionMark or WebCT. We discuss these in Chapters 7 and 8.

Java is a programming language developed by Sun Microsystems that enables complex interaction at Web level. Perhaps you want your students to develop experience in graphing information, so you might use a Java applet (a Java programme loaded when the Web page loads) to take data about the size of Napoleon's army plotted against distance travelled. A Java applet would present a table to hold the data and a space for the graph to be created. Directing the graph to a separate page, together with some student-generated text, allows a printout to be made, saved and submitted to you. Alternatively, the whole page, with the graph as an image, might be e-mailed to you.

Example 1: FlyLab

An excellent example of meaningful interaction through the Web browser that uses a Java applet is the fly laboratory. FlyLab (http://www.cdl.edu/FlyLab/) is an educational application for learning the principles of genetic inheritance. Typically, the way to use small fruit flies to learn about genetics is to breed them in small bottles, knock them out with chloroform or ether (killing most in the process), pick the types you want (short or long, hairy or bald, black or yellow) using a microscope and a pair of tweezers, mate these, wait a week, and count the variations that result.

The alternative is to use a computer program to build the flies you want, mate them in large numbers (100, 1000 or 10,000) and get the results immediately. The advantages are that the flies don't die, you can create mating types that might not survive naturally, and the images are larger on the computer.

In Figure 3.5 the student is about to choose the type of hair found on the body. You might just be able to see that this is a female (you repeat the process for the male). Along the left-hand side are the different characteristics that can be chosen for the mating – one is body colour; see Figure 3.6. The chosen body types are shown prior to mating (Figure 3.7) and the results in Figure 3.8.

Since this is a carefully written simulation, you'll see that not everything seems to work out fine. For example, there are more female than male offspring. Note what the students can do now: they can enter the results in a summary form, do a statistical test, add to their laboratory notes or do another mating with a fresh set of flies or, better still, with one of the two types that resulted from the first mating.

This experiment was written in Java and was running within a Web browser, Netscape Navigator, on a Macintosh. We could just as easily have run this under Windows in Internet Explorer and not noticed the difference. Indeed, this is one of the strengths of Java: the programmer would only have to create the code once for it to run under several different operating systems.

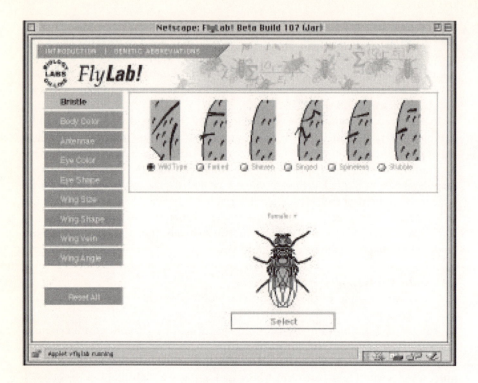

Figure 3.5 *A Flylab window where the user can choose the hair type for the mating*

Figure 3.6 *Another Flylab window where the user can choose the body colour type for the mating*

What is also interesting is that this experiment resides on a server at California State University, and we ran it in Leicester, UK at 10 am local time, very early morning US time. The Web gives us time and place independence and, as in this case, can provide very high quality stimulus and interaction.

Figure 3.7   *The Flylab window showing the chosen body types prior to mating*

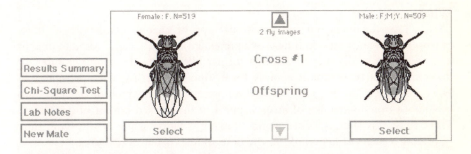

Figure 3.8   *The Flylab window showing the offspring of the mating*

Example 2: Facilitating interaction between individuals and groups

We saw in Chapter 2 the importance of the conversational, dialogic process for teaching and learning. This can be supported directly through the Web. In 'Creating an interactive student medium for learning about the Holocaust', Klevan and Kramer (online) describe their rationale and methods for a project that linked the US Holocaust Memorial Museum and the students of public high schools of the District of Columbia. One of their creative leaps was to enable the spontaneous and/or prompted transfer of ideas among students, teachers and museum personnel by scattering throughout the Web site special input boxes that allowed individual students to send a message to individuals (a teacher, say, or another pupil, or a member of museum staff) or to groups. All messages are stored in a database and can be reviewed by museum staff and teachers.

Responses to questions act as adjuncts to the main resource and may be as illuminating for the person who answers as the person who asked originally. Eventually, the database of questions, answers and comments becomes a resource in itself for teachers and students to mine. We explore these ideas in more detail in Chapter 6.

SMIL(e), it's getting better

Part of the process of creating any educational resource is the identification of structure and sequencing: where does object X go in relation to concept Y? In a lecture, the placement of any demonstration is determined by the content and occurs at a specific time within the lecture. On the Web the usage of time-based media such as video and sound is still developing. We see the browser window most often as a page in a book, with all the implications for linearity that that suggests, but with the development of a new Web standard things are changing.

SMIL allows a developer to 'describe the temporal behaviour of a presentation, describe the layout of the presentation on a screen, and associate hyperlinks with media objects'. Because SMIL is a relatively simple language that can be created with a basic text editor, it has the potential for widespread adoption and to have as revolutionary an impact on computer-delivered content creation as HTML.

What can it do?

SMIL allows for the layout and synchronization of various media types – audio, video, graphics and text – in time-based presentations. SMIL can be used to present a sequence of media files in a timed format like a slide show, or a number of different media types simultaneously for a sophisticated 'TV-style' presentation. For example, a SMIL file might describe a presentation in which, after 10 seconds of audio, a timed sequence of images appear in the top left corner of the screen. Fifteen seconds later, it could begin showing a video while at the same time displaying a series of hyperlinks in the bottom left corner of the screen.

One of the most important features of SMIL is that, like HTML, it is possible for each of the files referenced by a SMIL document to reside on a different server, so an author can integrate information from many different sources to create something unique.

What will it do?

SMIL is an important step forward for computer-based multimedia because it is based on open standards, which means that content can be delivered across a broad range of devices and in a wide range of circumstances and conditions, and that the content will not become unavailable due to technological obsolescence.

One of SMIL's strengths is the ability to reuse media sources. Because SMIL has the ability to display a selected segment of a larger file, multiple presentations can use the same source file. For example, users may be given the option to view an entire video sequence or just edited highlights using the same video file. The same source file could be used along with simultaneous text or audio translations in a variety of different languages. In education this means we can reuse educational video material in new ways. We will be examining the reuse of educational objects in Chapter 8.

Back to Napoleon

Earlier in this chapter we looked at Napoleon's advance and retreat from Moscow as a means of introducing some of the media types available through the Web. Using SMIL we could create a rich presentation that, say, showed an animated version of the map in the picture window, video of an expert talking about Napoleon's motives and the progress of the march in the adjacent window, and a scrolling text window below that included links to other material. All of the resources would be under the learner's control.

Conclusion

At the start of this chapter we posed three questions:

- What is the Internet, and what is its relationship with the World Wide Web?
- What resources – sources of stimulation – may be delivered to users via the Internet?
- What is the nature of the interaction that is enabled, or impeded, between users and the Internet?

As a conclusion to this chapter we should stand back from the Web and be slightly cautious about the claims made about its potential as an educational environment. Developments on the Web are driven by a mixture of commercial, information and technology forces, so its educational functionality derives from a forced union of these groups: in other words, don't be surprised if you can't do all that you would want. This rich and complex medium is like a racing car: it needs to be handled carefully, have lots of time and money spent on it, is glorious when in action, but has a propensity to go out of date rapidly and fail at the most inopportune moments.

Chapter 4

Using the Internet: course development and delivery

Introduction

In Chapter 2 we looked at general principles of course design and the stages in course development. This chapter provides an overview of some of the key issues that need to be worked through when developing a Web-based course. It describes tools that may assist in this process of course development and delivery. We will address issues such as:

- When should faculty staff be developing RBL for their students?
- What resources will be required?
- What are the major constraints staff face?
- How should staff go about developing Web-based RBL materials?
- What delivery issues need to be considered?

These issues will also apply to some extent if you are planning to make materials available on the Web to support conventional face-to-face teaching.

Identifying potential students

An essential point to consider when developing any educational materials is to clarify who these materials are intended for. Without this clear focus, the materials may not sufficiently address the needs of the target group and may fall between a number of stools. This is particularly important when developing RBL where, as direct contact with the students is likely to be limited, a number of assumptions based on the best information available will need to be made about them and their needs.

Rowntree (1990, p.40) identifies four types of information about prospective learners that will help the development process of any course using RBL. We will apply this framework to online delivery.

First of all, he identifies demographic information. This will include considerations such as the number of students likely to be on the course as well as their geographic distribution. These demographic factors may influence the way you plan to deliver your course in a number of ways. For example, the number of students will clearly have an important influence. In terms of the 'bottom line', if the initial projections of student numbers are small, the institution may not consider the course viable if considerable course preparation and technical development are required. Options using existing Web-based resources with relatively little new development may still be appropriate. The Instructional Management Systems project and the reuse of educational objects discussed in Chapter 8 may be particularly relevant here.

If the numbers are large enough, then very substantial development costs can be justified. This can be seen clearly in the case of the UK Open University where development costs can run into hundreds of thousands of pounds, and as we saw in Chapter 1, this figure may be dwarfed if speculation about future mega-courses becomes a reality.

There are excellent examples of Web-based courses running with small numbers of students dispersed worldwide (Birkbeck College, online) and of prestige courses charging premium fees to students for studying online:

> At Duke University's Fuqua School of Business, almost half the students at its brand-new online Global Executive MBA program live outside the US, 'commuting' by e-mail from as far away as Switzerland and Hong Kong. These students are willing to pay a premium for the convenience of the remote access and the prestige of a Duke degree: $82,500 (frequently picked up by students' employers), compared with $50,000 for the regular on-campus MBA. (Gubernick and Ebeling, 1997)

Student numbers will heavily influence the choice of support and assessment strategies. If your student numbers are relatively small, it is quite easy to develop a computer conferencing system that you will be able to manage and support (although very low numbers can lead to problems in developing and sustaining interaction). As numbers increase, ways of subdividing the students into different groups and having additional tutor input will need to be considered.

Another important consideration relates to assessment strategies. If you are dealing with large numbers of students, you will not be able to provide detailed personal comments on all their work single-handed. You will either have support from colleagues also acting as tutors, or some other form of assessment strategy will need to be considered. We examine computer-aided assessment in Chapter 7.

Motivation

Rowntree invites us to consider the likely motivations of potential students and how that might influence the construction of the course. Why, for example, are the students studying this course online? Did they have any choice? Was it a positive decision on their part to study using the Internet rather than conventional means? Or was it forced upon them? Are they taking the course to update their skills, or for advancement at work? Or does it form part of a degree programme? With RBL we are asking students to take a major responsibility for their own learning and progress, and their motivation for taking this particular course may well influence their approach. Students who prefer flexible study, for example, may well be more motivated than others.

The need for students in full-time education to take paid employment while studying in order to finance their studies has long been a feature of student life in the USA but is relatively new in the UK. This has led to the rise of the 'part-time full-time student'. Students may not, because of work commitments, be able to attend all their timetabled lectures or practical classes. This increases the need for RBL with the potential for greater flexibility of delivery. Students can access materials at any time online, making the combination of paid employment and study more manageable.

Learning factors

Here Rowntree clusters together a whole range of different issues including:

- prior experience with RBL;
- time, support and facilities;
- subject background;
- mode of delivery.

We will use his headings but apply them specifically to Web-based delivery.

Prior experience with RBL

This is a key issue. Will this be the first time that your students have undertaken an online course, or are they already familiar with such approaches? If the former, what information is available about their level of readiness in terms of study skills, IT literacy, time management and other core skills that are very relevant to their progress? If there is reason to believe that students may not have adequate prior core skills, what strategies can be offered to deal with this situation? Is it appropriate to suggest that students undertake additional work in, for example, IT skills at the same time as studying the course? Will this lead to overloading and the likelihood of placing unrealistic demands on students who have to complete a course within a restricted time period? Rather than recommending that students improve their study skills outside the course, should you be incorporating the development of these skills within the materials? If so, how are you going to make room for them? Will this lead to unnecessary duplication between your course and the courses of others who may also be attempting to cover these skills?

Clearly there are no easy answers to the above questions, but they are ones that must be worked through at the planning stage. The advice and input from your colleagues can be of great help here. It is likely that over time, as institutions develop more and more online courses, policies and strategies will be in place relating to study skills issues and RBL. It will then be possible to design courses with a clearer understanding of the likely level of student preparedness.

Time, support and facilities

It is essential that students have the facilities necessary to complete the course and also sufficient time to work through the materials. The question of access to facilities applies to online courses delivered on campus as well as remotely. If the course is being delivered on campus, where will students access it? Will it be from a library or resource centre and if so will there be sufficient PCs available at the right time for the numbers of students studying the course? This issue may be particularly acute for institutions in the early stages of online course development.

If students are studying the course from home, they may be liable for connection charges while on the Internet. Bear in mind also that not all Internet links are the same. What works satisfactorily on a fast link within an institution (and many links within institutions are not fast), may prove to be a disaster on a slow modem link at home. Adequate technical support must also be provided for these remote students.

An example

A student is studying a course from home, delivered by a remote institution, which requires him to access material online. He buys a new computer and subscribes to an internet service provider (ISP).

This works fine at first, but then he has a technical problem. The problem may be due to:

- faulty hardware – the manufacturer's responsibility;
- a problem with the connection – the student's or the ISP's responsibility;
- a problem with the institution's server or network – the institution's Network and Communications team's responsibility;
- a technical problem with the online materials – the course team's/ developer's responsibility;
- a combination of the above!

The student will want a solution to the problem and fast. Who should he contact and where should he start?

The lesson from this example is that institutions offering online courses need to put in place help desks or other student-support devices. When students have technical difficulties they need to have one point of contact. This contact may not be able to solve all the technical problems, but is at least in a position to advise on where the student should go for help and what kind of questions should be asked.

Subject background

Rowntree poses the question, 'What knowledge, skills and attitudes do they (the students) already have regarding the subject of your course?' (Rowntree, 1990, p.40). Here he is distinguishing between more general issues relating to study skills and specific preparedness for studying within a particular discipline. At the planning and development stage, the key issues to consider are related to the level at which to pitch your material. This will depend in part on your students' existing knowledge and expertise. If you feel it is likely that your students will have a wide range of knowledge and skills relating to your subject area, what strategies can you develop to assist those who are less knowledgeable at the same time as satisfying the more advanced student?

It is here that opportunities offered by the Web can be particularly helpful. Individual topics can be pursued at a general level and, where appropriate, students can 'drill down' and explore specific areas in more detail. Individual students can also call up background or supporting material as necessary without interrupting the 'flow' of the treatment for those students who do not require that information. This is shown diagrammatically in Figure 4.1.

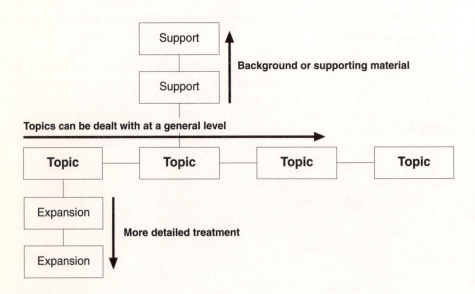

Figure 4.1 *Dealing with topics at different levels*

Mode of delivery

Based on your knowledge of potential students, you may decide that online delivery is not appropriate in this context or that an approach that mixes face-to-face delivery with the use of the Internet will work best. At De Montfort University there are examples of students studying online materials within the classroom with a lecturer present; see Chapter 9 for more details. The lecturer can provide help and advice while individual students are working at different rates.

Developing an online course

Web-based materials by their very nature are public, or at least semi-public. What happens in a conventional lecture is usually only known by the lecturer and the students and, in the case of the latter, possibly only for a short time. Web-based materials may be viewed not only by the students for whom they are developed but also by colleagues, specialists in other institutions and, in some cases, the general public and potential students.

Clearly then, it is important for the credibility of the institution that Web-based materials are of a high standard. One way of achieving this is to work with others in their development, thus ensuring that a range of insights and perspectives are brought to the course.

The course team

It is for these reasons that we recommend that a course team be set up when developing RBL materials. The course team need not be as formal as the name sounds; it may be a loose collection of a few individuals who contribute varying amounts of time to the development of the course. Of course the situation is different if a teacher decides to put up supporting materials such as handouts or lecture notes on the Web. This can be done quickly and easily and may be of considerable value. However, in the example shown in Table 4.1 we are thinking of the development of a complete Web-based course.

Often the same person will perform a number of these roles. Nor is it likely that many, if any, of the people will be working on the course full-time unless it is a large funded project. This flexibility of role raises important staff development issues; in particular there has been considerable debate about the extent to which academic staff should be involved in the direct production of Web pages.

It will also be of value if you connect into the wider online academic community where, via discussion groups, information, ideas and opinions are shared and debated. You will find details of where to find out about such groups in Chapters 5 and 6.

Table 4.1 *Typical roles for a course team*

A Course Team Chair. This person will have overall responsibility for the development and delivery of the course. He or she will usually be an academic actively writing and producing the materials.

Contributing authors. Specialists who will write and contribute to different parts of the course.

Readers and commentators. These will be colleagues who will be invited to make appropriate inputs by reading and commenting on the materials so that they can be refined and further developed.

Educational Technologist. The person who will advise on planning development and structuring the materials, choice of media, assessment and evaluation.

The Production Team. This may include people with responsibility for Web design, video, graphics, administration and support.

Development timescale

One thing that must be very clear by now is that developing a good Web-based course takes considerable time and resources – more than is the case with conventional teaching materials. The potential 'pay-back' is that once such materials have been developed, because they can be used flexibly and can overcome constraints of time and location, they could be used by a more diverse range of students. This widens student opportunities, increases the number of potential students for an institution and may offer some cost savings. Empirical evidence on this last point is scarce but support is provided by the SCALE reports (Arvan *et al,* 1998).

Estimating development time

When planning RBL, it is vital to obtain realistic estimates of how long it is likely to take to produce the materials. You will find that estimates published in the literature vary widely. The Report of the Committee of Enquiry into Higher Education (Dearing, online) provides some estimates of how long it takes to produce RBL materials. For the development of materials with low production costs (and here the writers were thinking of paper-based materials), they use an estimate of 20 hours to develop one student study hour. For developing IT-based materials, the figure used is one to two hundred hours per student study hour. The appendix concludes by saying:

But for the high quality of materials needed for the majority of university study, development will have to be of a high order, and therefore not in-house, in general. IT methods must achieve their promise of greater efficiency both by improving the quality of student learning and by amortising the cost of development over large student numbers. (Dearing, online, Appendix 2)

The above arguments reinforce the point that, before committing time and resources to developing new materials from scratch, time should be spent seriously investigating whether resources already exist on the Web that could form at least part of the new materials.

However, some of the points made above require closer examination. The development of the Web has started to break down the distinction made in Dearing between low production RBL and the more expensive IT-based methods. The Web, with its facility to link diverse resources together wherever they are located, means that the distinction made in the report between internal and external resources may not be as clear cut as first appears. Indeed, in some contexts, it is cheaper to produce materials for use on the Web than for print. The rapid growth of electronic journals, electronic versions of conference proceedings and similar, is indicative of the savings that can be made using the new technology compared with conventional print. This linking ability also facilitates reuse, so that relatively expensive software elements can be customized and reused, potentially offering savings over the cost of development from scratch (Twining *et al,* 1998).

We will return to issues of using existing resources later in Chapters 5 and 8, but for the moment we would emphasize that, in whatever medium you are developing RBL, there needs to be careful planning, structuring and organization, linked to the development of activities and assessment systems. This by its nature will be time-consuming.

Scheduling your development

It is very easy to underestimate how long it will take to produce a good Web-based course. Developing RBL is not something that can be done 'in your spare time'. Rather, it is a major commitment that needs to be planned in and scheduled as part of your work activities. What is as important is the distribution of time. In other words, it is no use trying to pack a hundred hours into the last few weeks when what is needed is a clear development schedule. This schedule, if followed, will allow for the development of ideas and approaches, as well as the writing, structuring and commenting on the materials.

It is difficult to provide firm guidelines as to how long it will take to develop a course, but based on our experience a typical schedule might be something like the one shown in Table 4.2. This schedule is for the development of a module that typically would involve 13 weeks teaching if delivered conventionally and assumes a student study time of approximately 120 hours. Clearly this is not a blueprint or formula, but it does indicate the way in which a typical module might be developed and the kind of time periods that may be required.

Table 4.2 *A schedule for development*

September to December	Initial planning of module. Identification of content, analysis of student characteristics, agreement of release of staff time and assembly of course team. Provisional consideration of media selection and student support systems. Formulation and agreement of learning outcomes.
January, February	Development of short two-page summaries of content of the units forming a module with cross-referencing to learning outcomes to ensure all are covered. Identification of existing resources on the Web. Specification of any interactive elements for development.
February to April	Production of initial drafts of work units. Development of interactive elements.
April, May	Commentary and discussion of first drafts. Development of interactive elements.
May to July	Development of assessment and student support systems. Graphic design, Web site development.
July, August	Graphic design, Web site development and other production activities that might be required.
September	First delivery of module.
The next year	Ongoing modification and updating.

Lockwood (1998) examines this issue in more detail. He provides examples of RBL materials being produced in much shorter timescales, in some cases in a matter of weeks. But what is certainly the case is that, with the development of good tools for producing Web pages and the advent of online assessment systems and virtual learning environments (see Chapters 7 and 8), courses can be assembled and produced in a technical sense for the Web relatively quickly. Where considerable time may still be required is in the planning, development and structuring of the course content and associated learning activities.

One common problem we have encountered is that, because the work may be scheduled over a relatively long time, other more immediate activities such as teaching a class next week are given priority. The time allocated for development gets squeezed and then disappears. In some cases this can lead to the cancellation of the project; in others, course team members have worked desperately hard to try and complete a project while still undertaking a heavy teaching load. Producing a schedule will not in itself overcome this problem, but an agreed schedule does provide a clear reference point in any disagreement about workload.

Scheduling technical development

It is important to pay particular attention to the scheduling of the development of any media-based elements, especially in relation to technical input from staff and the availability of resources.

A key consideration is getting the involvement of technical staff at as early a stage as possible. An educational technologist will advise on an appropriate 'mix' of media, then technical specialists can assist in planning its development. What you should avoid doing is trying to do too much yourself, or making technical decisions without sufficient knowledge. At De Montfort University, video production staff tell stories about lecturers who come to them with masses of videotape that they want editing into teaching material. Often it is better to start again from scratch. Equally, when developing multimedia or Web sites, some things may sound complicated but are in fact relatively easy to do, while others are the opposite. Getting specialist advice can save a lot of difficulty later.

Understanding costs

The cost of different media elements has changed considerably over the last few years. New high-quality copying and colour printing techniques have changed the traditional view that it is necessary to have long print-runs to produce high-quality material economically. A new generation of software tools has made the development of Web sites much quicker and Web-based 'virtual learning environments' such as WebCT mean that a variety of interactivity can be supported at a technical level relatively easily. The costs of producing video sequences are also being reduced by the use of digital cameras and digital editing facilities.

It is important that you obtain up-to-date information on the costs of different elements at the planning stage rather than assume a particular element will be too expensive. However, Rowntree's advice is worth bearing in mind:

> As with most things in life, you get what you pay for. Quality learning materials need thoughtful planning, writing, testing and rewriting until *they work*. This takes time. Inferior materials (the 'quick and dirty') can be produced more cheaply – by skimping on or omitting some of those stages. This is what happened with programmed learning in the 1960s, when bad (but cheap) material drove out the good (but expensive) – leading to the discrediting and collapse of programmed learning. I hope we can ensure that history does not repeat itself with open or distance learning in the 1990s. (Rowntree, 1990, p.86)

Tools for planning, structuring and development

Two of us have been involved in a project to develop tools to assist with this process. We have argued that courseware is best developed in a team context, whereby individuals with a range of skills (subject experts, instructional designers, programmers) work together to agreed aims and objectives.

The development of powerful Web authoring tools, and tools for the conversion of word-processed documents into HTML format can tend to encourage the collapse of these various roles into one person – the universal courseware expert. When using such tools there is a tendency not to map out the courseware first, but in the act of marking up, to try to structure it at the same time. In effect, what happens is that the producer is attempting to structure and plan the courseware and produce it simultaneously, and in the process of so doing may lose sight of the main pedagogic structures and navigational routes.

Courseware on the Web may have a number of additional features not normally found in stand-alone computer-based packages. As well as the core sequence and structure of the material, whereby the user will proceed via a menu, 'next' or 'previous' buttons, clicking on an image map or some other navigational device, typically it will contain hypertext links to other pages or to information held on other Web sites. Examples are definitions of terms, references, additional material or links. The student may explore these before returning to the main sequence of the courseware.

These additional features mean that overall planning and structuring of the educational project are critical in order to reduce the possibilities of the student becoming 'lost in cyberspace' at worst, or at best wasting time and effort following secondary links of little or marginal relevance. It is therefore important to spend time conceptualizing the total project and considering what links (if any) have primacy.

Webmapper (Freeman and Ryan, 1997) is a tool of two parts. The first is an icon-based concept mapping tool developed from previous tools we have used for the development of stand-alone multimedia projects (Freeman and Ryan, 1995). It allows a subject expert working alone or, where appropriate, an instructional designer, to map out and plan the entire courseware project before that courseware is created. An initial concept map is shown in Figure 4.2. Using the system the developer may, via the manipulation of icons, try out the different links and routes, add and delete proposed sections and run through various sequences without being concerned about the actual delivery. This encourages top-level planning of the entire courseware prior to any attempt to construct it. The act of planning and structuring is therefore separated from the production. The second part of the tool is the Editor, which converts the map into HTML ready for use on the Web; see Figure 4.3.

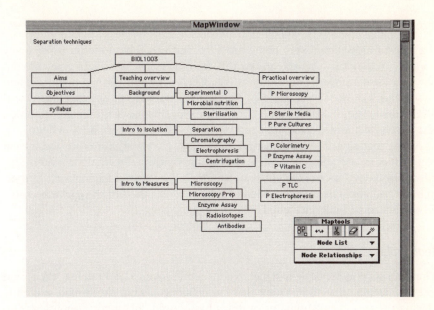

Figure 4.2 *An initial concept map*

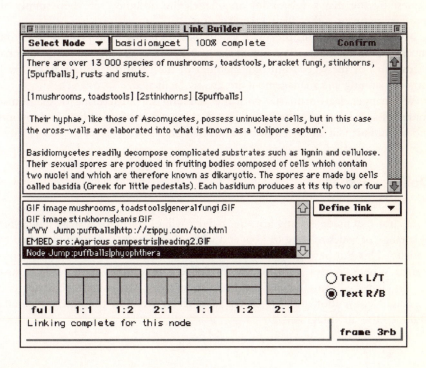

Figure 4.3 *Developing the Web page*

Integrating planning and development

If a map of ideas alone were being provided, this could be done on paper or by using a commercially available package. Part of the planning process is to consider how the ideas mapped out will be realized and delivered via various media and how features of the media can best be used for teaching purposes. Therefore, as part of the conceptualization, it is necessary to specify how, for example, graphics, text, video or sound will be used and incorporated into the delivery system.

At the mapping stage, Webmapper provides a means of indicating the way in which media and content will be integrated within the final structure. This information developed at the concept mapping stage serves as a template for others to build and implement in the delivery system. Other parts of the package enable prototypes to be built and tested.

Team roles

These tools provide ways in which team members can clearly define their own role and at the same time locate that contribution within the overall structure. Having the concept mapping software and associated documentation available to all course team members greatly facilitates project management. For example, the graphic designer may examine the concept map to understand the context of a request by the map's author for an image. The designer can then supply an appropriate image rather than a generic one.

Most importantly this process is documented. At any time print-outs can be obtained showing the latest version of the map, details of all links plus any additional instructions or messages from one member of the team to another. In this way project planning and management are greatly facilitated.

Webmapper deals primarily with the planning and structuring of the course content. Issues relating to the use of conferencing systems for teaching and support and assessment will also need to be scheduled in.

Delivery issues

Your choice of media for any learning activity will of course be heavily influenced by a range of issues relating to how and when that activity will be undertaken by students. This can be a grey area, particularly where Web-based delivery is concerned. Where courses are primarily for delivery on campus, parts of the course may be delivered using the Web and conferencing systems, while other elements are taught 'conventionally'. Care needs to be taken over how the various elements of the course are integrated.

A framework for considering delivery issues

Canole and Oliver (1998) offer a framework for working through considerations relating to delivery of courses using media. They identify a number of factors, including:

- time dependency;
- location dependency;
- requirement of a co-present group;
- facility requirements.

Lectures, for example, are time dependent: they only 'happen' when scheduled. The same is also true for synchronous conferencing using either audio or video links. Lectures are also location dependent, as is video conferencing when large room-based systems are used. Asynchronous conferencing, such as the FirstClass system, is neither time nor location dependent, although these factors still play a part in the sense that access to suitable computers and networks will only be available at certain times and places.

The requirement for a co-present group will only apply to activities programmed to occur at certain fixed times and that require interaction from peer students.

Sometimes the use of multimedia or simulation software will only be practicable in group sessions. This may be so that lab sessions can be timetabled for groups of students and support staff to be on hand.

Table 4.3 indicates the facility requirements for different media types.

This approach shows that the delivery of courses is more complex than a simple division between campus-based and Internet-based courses. Some Web-based courses may be time and location dependent if, for example, they require a co-present group. There need be no hard and fast distinction between campus and off-campus courses. The increasing use of Web-based delivery on campus can provide advantages of flexibility while still retaining a large measure of direct contact and interaction between students.

Conclusion

This chapter has emphasized the importance of commitment in terms of time and resources to the development of Web-based courses. We do not believe it is advisable for lecturers to attempt to produce courses for the Web single-handed; it is unlikely to produce satisfactory results. We have for this reason emphasized the course team approach.

A good starting point for development is a careful analysis of who your potential students are and their likely characteristics. This analysis will help inform your delivery strategy and hence the process of development.

Table 4.3 *Delivery constraints comparison chart (adapted from Canole and Oliver, 1998)*

Media type	Time dependent		Location dependent		Usually involves a co-present group	Usually involves group work	Requirements	Location of students
	Tutor	Student	Tutor	Student				
Lecture	✓	✓	✓	✓	✓	✗	Presentation equipment	Lecture room
Hypertext	✗	✗	✗	✗	✗	✗	Web, PC	Campus/off campus
Multimedia	✗	✗	✗	✗	✗	✗	PC	Campus/off campus
CAL	✗	✗	✗	✗	✗	✗	PC	Campus/off campus
Chat system	✓	✓	✗	✗	✗	✓	Web	Campus/off campus
Asynchronous conferencing system	✗	✗	✗	✗	✗	✓	Web	Campus/off campus
Sync. video conference	✓	✓	✗ (to some extent)	✗ (to some extent)	✓	Sometimes	Web, video link	Campus/off campus
Whiteboard	✓	✗	✗	✗	✗	✓	Web	Campus/off campus
SAQs	✗	✗	✗	✗	✗	✗	Web or PC	Campus/off campus

Where your course is primarily campus-based, your analysis also needs to consider how best the various elements of the course, delivered both traditionally and via the Web, can be integrated so that the most appropriate balance can be reached for you and your students. In the following chapters we will consider how these elements, including other people's resources, conferencing and assessment systems, can be used.

Chapter 5

Resources on the World Wide Web

Introduction

In the previous chapter we discussed some of the major development issues to be considered when producing Web-based teaching materials. An important consideration is whether suitable materials exist already and, if so, can you use or adapt them? We have seen that one of the major strengths of the Web is the ability to use existing resources and materials by linking to them. Equally you will find on the Web a vast array of materials that you may not wish your students to access directly but are of great use to you in researching and developing your teaching materials. Either way, in order to make use of these resources you need first of all to locate them and, given the wealth of resources available, have some means of evaluating them.

This chapter examines the range and variety of Web-based resources relevant to educators, and considers how we assess the appropriateness of what has been located. The final section is about the future of searching, storage and management of information on the Web.

What is a Web-based resource?

In Chapter 3 we looked at the different media types that comprise a page in a browser. Now it's time to look at the range of information carried by those media, whether it's an article from a journal such as *Scientific American,* an electronic pop 'fanzine', a virtual reality walk through the corridors of the London Natural History Museum, or an online course from a leading university.

Types of Web-based resources

Digital/online libraries

In any discussion of electronic or digital libraries it has become almost *de rigeur* to mention Jorge Luis Borges' short story, *The Library of Babel*. The library, infinite in extent, contains all human knowledge but has no order, a catalogue that can't be found and many false catalogues. Knowledge and wisdom abound but are just out of reach, and the library comes to stand for chaos and ignorance.

Borges died in 1986 but his imaginary library is being brought to life, at least in part and in a systematic and ordered fashion, through a $25 million dollar research programme called the Digital Library Initiative. One aspect of the research is the development of multimedia search and retrieval tools that will enable semantic federation – the ability to search diverse repositories as if they were a single collection. In part this goal has already been achieved, for example by the OCLC – Online Computer Library Center (http://oclc.org), a non-profit computer service and research organization whose network and services link more than 24,000 libraries in the United States and 63 other countries. WorldCat (part of OCLC) is a merged electronic catalogue with 36 million records in eight bibliographic formats, and growing by 2 million records per year.

A search for the whole phrase 'online library' returned 40,451 results from a Web search engine. The first few references are to the Library of Congress, the National Institutes of Health sites and ERIC, the world's largest source of education information. The question, then, is what do we mean by the term *digital* or *online library*? The results from the searches include everything from the expected catalogues and collections of digitized books to personal home pages, collections of e-mail, images and others. In fact the only common feature is that they are digital in form, so it is reasonable to include digitized movies and sounds as well as texts.

Harter (online) refines the question elegantly by asking instead about the *library* half of the term. Clearly the traditional library system works; how can its best features be adapted to the digital domain? One characteristic of the physical library is its place. On the Web the collection owned by a digital library may be stored anywhere.

The traditional library contains information sources that are catalogued and described. The objects in the library are selected on the basis of need (expressed by institution and users) and quality, and are then organized within a known framework by librarians expert in the field. Who will perform these functions in the digital library? To whom will the researcher turn in the digital library – where is the equivalent of the help desk? This debate is ongoing, and collections of digital objects will increase in number nevertheless.

In the ideal digital library the resources will be multimedia objects, classified, archived and accessible by search engines' software agents that understand our needs, where works exist in initial form and in subsequent variations, and where authors have their rights respected and protected.

In this section we'll consider a sample of the best-known and highest quality 'online libraries' and describe their limitations and advantages.

The Library of Congress

Perhaps one of the best places to start is the world's largest repository of knowledge. A visit to the site's statistics section (http://lcweb.loc.gov/stats/) provides some indication of the interest and usage of this site (see Figure 5.1). On a normal weekday during February 2000 the number of hits on the site was over 2,695,000. The number of hits at the weekend was still over 1 million per day.

Shortcuts to Sections on This Page:

The Library of Congress Home Page
Using the Library: Catalogs, Collections & Research Services
THOMAS: Congress at Work
Copyright Office: Forms & Information
American Memory: America's Story in Words, Sounds & Pictures
Exhibitions: An On-Line Gallery
The Library Today: News, Events & More
Bicentennial: The Library of Congress, 1800-2000
Help & FAQs: General Information About the Library

Figure 5.1 *The site map of the Library of Congress (http://lcWeb.loc.gov/help/sitemap.html)*

One of the major projects hosted by the Library is the American Memory Project, consisting of documents, photographs, movies and sound recordings that tell America's story. For those more interested in the present, there is full text access to current bills under consideration in the US House of Representatives and Senate. These and other subjects contribute to the Library's stated aim of getting 5 million items from its archive digitized and online by the year 2000. Unfortunately, even this seemingly large number only represents less than half a per cent of the total 110 million item collection.

US National Library of Medicine

The National Institute of Health gives free access to the US National Library of Medicine's MEDLINE bibliographic database, which covers the fields of medicine, nursing, dentistry, veterinary medicine, the health care system and the pre-clinical sciences. The database covers more than 9 million references to articles published in 3800 biomedical journals published in 71 countries. To access full articles, one must use either traditional methods or register to join a service and pay a fee. An alternative access path to 11 free databases hosted by the NLM is via the (charmingly named) Internet Grateful Med site (http://www.igm.nlm.nih.gov/).

The Internet Public Library

This isn't a library in the traditional sense, but a meta-library; a library that refers *to* and stores information *about* publications and other institutions rather than the original sources themselves. You can't take a book out or read a newspaper in the reading room, but in a sense you can go one better and read it wherever you can go online. This library refers to online books, magazines and serials in every subject category. Every entry is written by a trained librarian and provides an abstract, Web address (URL), publisher, language, frequency, type (eg, magazine, journal, e-zine) and the subjects covered.

The mission statement establishes its credentials in no uncertain way: 'The Internet Public Library is the first public library of the Internet... Our mission directs us to serve the public by finding, evaluating, selecting, describing and creating quality information resources'. For those using or directing others to use the Web as a source of information this might be an excellent place to start (http://ipl.org/about/newmission.html).

One of the sections at this site is called 'Great Libraries on the Web', and a link or two away is the Rare Book, Manuscript and Special Collections Library of Duke University, USA (http://www.scriptorium.lib.duke.edu/). This resource is special in that you get as close, digitally, as you can to the real object. For example, the Duke Papyrus Archive provides electronic access to texts and images of 1373 papyri from ancient Egypt, with the content searchable by keyword or subject; images of the papyri are available at several magnifications. Indeed, this resource is better than the real thing for many schoolchildren, who would never be allowed to get so close to these resources.

The WDVL: The Virtual Library of WWW Development

The Virtual Library of WWW Development is one of the best sites on the Web for finding Web-focused materials. It's worth visiting the home page for this 'library', at (http://www.wdvl.internet.com/Vlib/) to see the structure. However, the site illustrates the successes and failings of the Web. First, it's a great resource for any issue to do with the Web, but it's another meta-resource because the full information isn't here but somewhere else. However, each resource has an abstract and evaluation.

The Electric Library

This particular library demonstrates some very good features of libraries on the Web, as well as pointing the way for future developments. For example, it is very large, with real resources, ie the actual articles rather than references to them. In its own words, 'the Electric Library currently contains 9,463,735 newspaper articles,

711,632 magazine articles, over 446,016 book chapters, 1523 maps, 129,727 television and radio transcripts, and 98,859 photos and images'. However, while the search engine is powerful, and lists finds in terms of relevance, date, size and reading difficulty, a click on a link only takes you to a page asking you to subscribe to a paying service. The results of a search at Electric Library are shown in Figure 5.2.

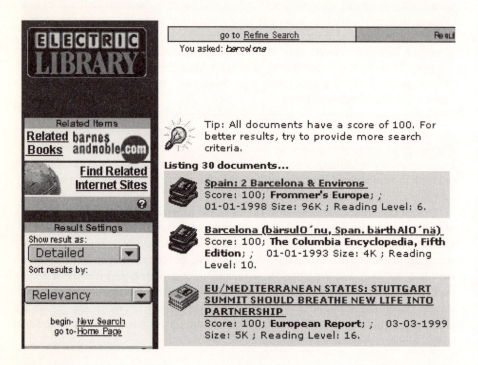

Figure 5.2 *The results of a search at Electric Library (http://www.elibrary.com)*

Electronic publishing

There is a tendency in academic circles to equate *electronic publishing* with the electronic publication of scholarly journals. Let's take a broader view for the moment and expand the interpretation to include any subject or opinion-focused Web document. This now means that the term includes the electronic versions of:

- scientific journals such as *Nature, Science and Scientific American;*
- magazines such as *MacWorld, Internet Design Magazine* and the Conde Nast stable;
- newspapers such as the *New York Times, The Guardian* and *The Sunday Times.*

Some Web-based publications don't have a physical equivalent but they are included in our definition:

- the contents of e-mail discussion lists (lists or listserves), such as the women professors of adult education list (http://www.womynwit@listserv.tamu.edu) or the distance education list (http://www.utksisde@utkvm1.utk.edu);
- the 'zines' with interesting titles such as 'Abnormalia', and 'O Shenandoah! Country Rag';
- perhaps your version of the history of the local football team, the activities of the philatelic society or your hobbyhorse views on films and books.

An optimist might cite the explosive growth in published material as an increase in the level of free speech and freedom of expression, and the pessimist might raise issues of plagiarism, racism, sexism, veracity, cataloguing, archiving and access. Either way, relatively unimpeded access and right to publish on the Web is a phenomenon as radical and challenging as the introduction of the printing press.

Scholarly journals

Some scholarly electronic journals on the Web are exact copies of their paper relatives; others don't have a physical equivalent at all but both have one thing in common – the role of taking academic conversations and discussions, via a panel of respected peer referees, to a wider domain (Hatvany, online). But journal contributors and publishers have several goals, some conflicting. Traditional journals communicate the latest research, act as an archive of information and data, define and record scientific/academic endeavour, claim precedence to an idea/concept and support career development (Pullinger, online).

The electronic publishing of journals is unpacking these goals, separating them to the advantage/disadvantage of authors, researchers, publishers and librarians. Let's consider the arguments. Edwards (online) briefly lists the advantages of electronic journals as being 'speedy delivery, availability unlimited by time or geography and searching facilities', but then goes on to discuss their problems for academic librarians, focusing on administrative issues rather than the opportunities of added value, rapid publication and forward referencing. In contrast, Holoviak and Seitter (1997) describe the originations of a new, totally online journal, 'Earth Interactions'.

There are several advantages of Web publication. Some are obvious in that they supersede the possibilities of the printed word, and some are functions of the medium itself and so are completely novel to the field. Edwards' stated advantages of delivery as fast as your connection to the Web, 'unlimited by time or geography and searching facilities' are the least exciting opportunities of this new format. At the very least readers can build their own archives and search for specific terms across many hundreds of articles from different publications. But the real changes will be in the areas of a release from paper limitations, added value and an enhanced review process.

Every author has faced the tyranny of an enforced page limit: on the Web this is unlikely to be a problem. It is likely that the number and nature of illustrations in an article will change dramatically in e-journals. Where black and white, static images are the norm in the print world, on the Web we can look forward to animations and virtual reality, 3-D images that can be rotated and viewed from any angle. Musicians can illustrate their articles with sound bites by attaching sound files; meteorologists can include animations of weather systems and whole data sets can be included or linked by hypertext. The e-journal 'Earth Interaction' currently supports the inclusion of Mathematica notebooks (a highly regarded mathematical software package) so readers can examine the mathematical treatment of data sets presented in the paper.

The subject of electronic peer review has formed the core of most of the discussion about the pros and cons of electronic publication on the Web. Harnad (in Peters, online) suggests that the Web offers the possibility of implementing peer review more efficiently, particularly through interactive publication in the form of open peer commentary on published work. Since that article, many e-journals have adopted a form of open peer review, typified by this statement from the 'Journal of Interactive Media in Education' (http://www-jime.open.ac.uk/):

> All JIME articles are integrated with a structured Web discussion space. Reviewers and authors debate a submission, after which open peer review is invited. An edited version of this discussion is preserved with the final publication, providing a forum for subsequent commentary and links to related material.

This approach seems to take the best practice from established procedures and adds value in a form that is unique to the medium. Commentary is likely to be broad-based, considered and informed, perhaps providing authors with ideas for new avenues to examine.

Magazines and e-zines

Newspapers and magazines on the Web represent an enormous source of novel and up-to-date information. The following list is a typical example of what can be found:

Ladies Home Journal
MacWeek
Nuke
Science Magazine
Sports Illustrated
Tennis Online
Time Magazine
Wired

Some have their own search engines and archives; they are the electronic versions of their larger, print-based cousins, and most of them are free. Typically, they include references to other Web-based information sources, and in keeping with their electronic nature, possess characteristics that the paper versions cannot. For example, the computer magazines enable the downloading of shareware and demonstration software, such as *MacWorld* and *PCWorld;* others will lead you into tutorials about Web-based issues which are interactive and have animations, sound and video with them.

There is a very big difference between an electronic magazine and an e-zine (or zine). The traditional e-zine is unique and idiosyncratic, as befits an object that is run, researched and written by one person. That's not to say they are peripheral or unimportant or uninformed: one link from 'The Zine and E-Zine Resource Guide' site (http://zinebook.com/) takes you to 'Elissa's Essay About Zines' (http://www.members.aol.com/erickalyn/elissa.html). The author raises issues about the theory behind e-zines, their history, the different genres, the place of e-zines that exist to review e-zines and personal reflections on the implementation and history of her own zines.

Newspapers on the Web

The number of newspapers with electronic, Web-based versions is growing all the time. Ecola Newsstand (http://ecola.com) lists access to over 6100 Web-based newspapers and magazines worldwide, and claims to be the 'Gateway to English-language media online'. The characteristics of these online newspapers are similar to their paper-based versions, maintaining a close style and content relationship to the parent.

News brokers

One interesting development within the domain of electronic newspapers can be found at NewsHub (http://newshub.com/). This site integrates and reports headlines from the world's premiere news sources every 15 minutes. NewsHub also provides customized versions to corporate customers who distribute specialized information to employees, stockholders or customers. Corporate policy manuals and news releases are among the categories that adapt well to NewsHub's format. The site is broken down into categories such as technical, financial, world, science, health, entertainment, and so on. Selecting a category leads to a page where news releases are sorted by time of appearance, ranging from the last two hours to 22 to 24 hours old, in increments of two hours. The aim of these companies is to provide paid services to large, information-rich organizations, and they use a news-based Web presence to advertise their wares and attract potential clients. Having said that, as a by-product they provide a potentially useful service to researchers and students.

Another similar site is Reuters' (http://reuters.com/). It doesn't just advertise its commercial arm (http://online.reuters.com/), but provides news reports complete with audio and movies, so it's a true multimedia resource.

E-mail discussion lists, newsgroups and 'chat'

Discussion lists

If the best resource is another human being, then discussion groups and usenet newsgroups are the places to find the answers to your questions. Liszt (http://liszt.com), one of the most comprehensive of the discussion site directories, numbers its lists as 90,095, the most popular groupings being in humanities (254 lists), computers (250) and music (216). The least popular include science, education and religion (97, 112 and 111 respectively). Internet discussion lists are communities of people discussing their favourite or work-based topics by e-mail. For example, 38 discussion lists were returned on a search for 'multimedia'. An example of a search listing is shown in Figure 5.3.

Subcategories:

Academia (11)
Administration (10)
Adult (6)
Alumni (4)
Distance Education (7)
Early Childhood (3)
Elementary (4)
English (6)
Exchange Students (1)
Financial Aid (1)
Gifted (2)
Health (1)
History (2)
Home Schooling (36)
Internet (12)
K-12 (12)
Languages (19)
Law (2)
Math (2)
Mathematics (1)
Medicine (3)
Methods (6)
Minorities (2)
Multicultural (2)
Music (7)
Philosophy of (1)
Physical (3)
Religion (4)
Research and Theory (6)
Science (5)
Special Needs (5)
Statistics (1)
Technology (14)

Figure 5.3   *Liszt – the subcategory listing for educational lists, with numbers of lists per category in brackets (http://www.Liszt.com)*

Internet discussion lists have been around for a number of years. The way they work is simple: having found a list of interest, you make a request to the list manager for a subscription to be opened. If you satisfy their requirements for membership you will be sent, by e-mail, copies of all mail that other subscribers send in to the list. Many lists are open to all, but some require you to present some proof of occupation in order to join, particularly medical and religious lists.

Another common type of Internet discussion list is the newsletter or announcement format, where a single writer (the list owner or moderator) broadcasts a periodical e-mail to a willing audience (and where the audience doesn't participate directly). SCOUT, EDUCOM and TidBits fall into this group.

Newsgroups

Newsgroups differ from discussion lists in that you don't have to make a request to any 'owner' in order to participate. You just look up the list that reflects your interest, read the latest postings and reply to the group. The other difference is that postings don't land in your e-mail: they are read online, at the newsgroup's home, so to speak. Also, with the correct software it's possible to read the submissions to the newsgroup as 'threads', that is a listing of postings organized by topic. Any message sent to a newsgroup is distributed all over the world by thousands of different 'news servers', the equivalent of the corner newspaper shop. However, these news servers keep old posts, sometimes for days, often for weeks or months, so it's possible to reach back into the archives for material of relevance. The largest newsgroups are international, have hundreds of regular participants ('posters'), and tens of thousands of regular readers. They can also be hostile environments, where naive questions or ignorant posts can stimulate a barrage of less than polite responses.

'Chat'

Discussion groups and newsgroups are asynchronous – conversations between posters doesn't take place in real time, but in chat groups they do. One advantage of the format is its immediacy of communication; a disadvantage is that it lacks the opportunity for consideration between replies. There are no archives to the chat system, unless you choose to save everything to your own computer, so searching of archives is not an option. One of the Web's best directories for chat sites is, again, Liszt (http://www.Liszt.com).

Museum resources and the Web

In this section we'll look briefly at the relationship between museum resources and the Web, and the way in which some museums have put their collections 'on' the Web.

What do we mean by 'museum'?

Definitions from the International Council of Museums, UK Museums Association and the American Association of Museums, quoted in Ambrose and Paine (1993) focus on the features of permanence, service to society, availability to the public, acquisition, conservation, research, education and publication. Within the scope of these definitions we'll include botanical gardens, zoological parks, aquaria, planetaria, art galleries and historic houses and sites. This rather bland summary seems to cover all bases, yet doesn't indicate any of the effects that the Web is having on the nature of museology and increased access to museum collections for learners.

Teather (online) states that 'the museum experience is about meaning and knowledge building that is based on the visitor's experience of the museum'. The electronic visitor has quite a different experience to the physical one: on the Web the museum is a two-dimensional place where objects are often separated from one another either because of screen constraints or the temporal constraints of connection time and computer speed. In the physical world the visitor is immersed in objects that form an interrelated world, where a simple step in any direction, and on the basis of many types and styles of stimulus, can reform a perspective and sharpen an interest. The experience of getting the physical object cannot be replaced by electronic means, except in the 'ideal' world where money, time and network constraints are not issues. An example of an interactive museum site is shown in Figure 5.4.

Figure 5.4 *Exploratorium – one of the most interactive museum sites on the Web (http://www.exploratorium.edu)*

The virtual and the real: virtual laboratories

The notion of a laboratory on the Web is a peculiar one: laboratories are not very high in the public's mind as places to explore, tending to be littered with complex and arcane equipment. As with all things to do with the Web, the notion and nature of virtual laboratories has changed a lot over the last few years. Initially, a search for 'virtual laboratory' would have returned a list of sites of the 'this is my room in the lab' type, with a few photographs of the lab leading to or from a list of publications or information about the parent institution. In their own way these guided tours described the differences and similarities to be found in 'the lab' as work environment.

Doing the same search now would yield similar results, but several new types of resource would also appear, each quite different from the other. Some, for example, would be about virtual reality, and some would focus on visualization issues, particularly of information spaces (such as the Web). Another site would be a place to find information, so under this heading would be recipe sites for chemical and biological processes, such as dealing with the staining of tissues or the growth and identification of microorganisms.

The collaborative laboratory

We've already discussed the idea of a virtual library that encompasses more than one physical location. The same idea can be applied to the virtual laboratory, a space in which real experiments can be performed in real but physically separate places, and such sites are becoming more common. One example of such cooperation is described in documentation at the Sandia National Laboratories site (http://www.cs.sandia.gov/SEL/projects/GII.TESTBED/SC95.presentation). The physical laboratories that constitute the parts of the virtual laboratory include the microscopy laboratory at the National Jewish Center for Immunology and Respiratory Medicine and the Paragon supercomputer, Synthetic Environment Lab and MPCRL Visualization Lab. The different facilities were used to obtain, modify and visualize from computer-generated data different views of cells and tissues obtained microscopically at the medical site.

A slightly different approach was used at the NASA Research and Education site (http://www.nren.nasa.gov/vlab.html). The Virtual Simulation Laboratory (VLAB) project allowed engineers from Boeing, Rockwell and Lockheed Martin based at the Johnson Space Center to remotely participate in the astronaut training programme using the Vertical Motion Simulator. They could remotely and interactively participate in live experiments, simulation models and control and display developments.

The thinking behind both of these examples is that scientists and researchers require remote access to national simulation and computing resources, and that collaboration between specialist facilities should be encouraged. Unfortunately there are barriers to such useful collaboration, mainly based on finance: both examples used very high speed networking technologies that are costly to install and maintain. Also, where different laboratories or research programmes are funded by different sources there may be difficulties over payment and ownership of work done.

An ambitious project for the use of a virtual laboratory has been proposed by Cardiff University, UK (http://www.info.cf.ac.uk/uwcc/psych/stevensonwc/vp-lab/proposal/overview.html). The lab, called VP-Lab (Virtual Psychology Laboratory) will provide teachers, students and researchers with a tool that supports the analysis, modification and re-execution of archived experiments. The archive will include experimental data, methods and computer-based procedures, meaning that users can gain practical experience of a much wider range of experiments than that normally found in a single department and, at the same time, be able to re-research previous experiments and the data they generated. The VP-Lab is as much an archive of data from pre-run experiments as a place to generate and analyse new data.

The simulation laboratory

The final type of virtual laboratory to be found on the Web is the simulation laboratory, where students experiment with interesting physical artifacts such as power plants and jet engines that are too expensive and/or dangerous to employ in normal teaching environments. There are many examples to be found on the Web, and we'll only provide pointers to a few.

Let's revisit for a moment the advantages of simulation. While nothing can replace the real, hands-on experience of lab work, the rise in class sizes and the reduction in per capita resources has meant that students either have access to fewer lab facilities or carry out fewer experiments, or have to work in larger groups. Virtual labs can enable all students to do all the experiments, alone or in a group, in their own time; experiments can be done to generate experimental data or to sensitize/contextualize students before they enter the real lab. Experiments such as breeding programmes in genetics that might take days or weeks can be telescoped into minutes, and repeated several times, without the need for living organisms.

The real question concerns the upsurge in availability of simulation experiments on the Web. What has changed since, say, 1996 that has enabled the appearance of all of these sites? The answer is not that educators have realized the potential of simulation to reduce costs and, in a challenging and motivating way, reach students and entice them into an interactive learning situation. It is the appearance of Java, a platform-independent programming language, created by Sun Computers, that can create programs (applets) that will run within the major Web browsers on any platform.

One example of a Java-rich site is the thermodynamics lab at the University of Oregon (http://jersey.uoregon.edu/vlab/Thermodynamics/index.html), shown in Figure 5.5. This is an ideal example, as it uses a straightforward model that is easy to code to describe visually a subject that instils fear and loathing in many students. Another good example that possesses all the characteristics of simulation

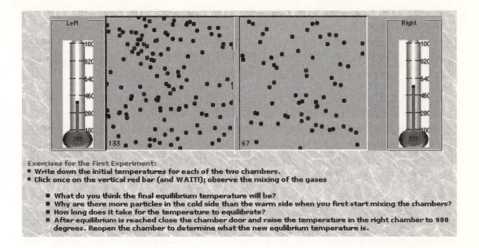

Figure 5.5 *An experiment in thermodynamics at the Oregon University virtual thermo-dynamics laboratory (http://jersey.uoregon.edu/vlab/Thermodynamics/index.html)*

mentioned above, is the lab techniques site at the Howard Hughes Medical Institute (http://www.hhmi.org/gui/dir1/dir1sub3topic5.html).

It would be unfair to close any discussion of virtual labs without mentioning one of the earliest on the Web, the Virtual Microscope demonstration of the UK Open University (http://www.met/open.ac.uk/vms/swave/vm1.html). This isn't a demonstration of the way in which a microscope works, but an illustration of the effect of using polarizing filters in the examination of thin sections of rock.

Evaluating Web-based resources

Think of the last few Web pages that you've visited. On what grounds did you believe the information within them? As an example, consider a search on Charles Dickens. You might find sites ranging from student theses located on university servers, to personal views of the novelist's life and writings, hosted on a Japanese site. Which one contains information that you, as a student perhaps, would include in an essay?

As we've already seen in our discussion of e-journals, peer review underpins the perceived value and status of a document, but on the Web as a whole there is no equivalent. Any opinion or datum has the same weight and value as any other. Sometimes the normal signals about quality and value may be overturned: we'd probably believe something written in sober terms on a rather 'bookish' Web page and dispute information on a gaudy, psychedelic page. Unfortunately neither dullness nor exuberance are good indicators of veracity or reliability. To find some guidelines on the issue let's turn (where else) to the Web.

The World Wide Web Virtual Library is as good a place as any to start when looking for information about the evaluation of information sources. Clearly this issue doesn't only refer to Web-based information, but the Web has some special characteristics that mean we should be more circumspect about information than that obtained from traditional sources. The World-Wide Web Virtual Library site concerned with the evaluation of information sources can be found at http://www.vuw.ac.nz/~agsmith/evaln/evaln.htm. Most of the URLs on this page point to pages written by information specialists, librarians or researchers in the field, and therefore we consider them to be reliable, of good coverage, objective and current. In fact most of these authors use effectively the same main headings to discuss the subject, and there are several subsidiary headings that cover most other issues. We'll use the checklist suggested by Harris (online) in CARS: Credibility, Accuracy, Reasonableness and Support.

Harris, in one of the best articles in the list, suggests a common sense approach that users take before they do any 'surfing' – ask, 'What is my research goal, what is the context of my search, is it facts, opinions, resources, statistics or descriptions?' Once contextualized, the researcher has a much better chance of remaining focused and sensitive to the issues we're going to discuss.

Credibility

Also referred to as 'authority' in many of the articles, this issue is about trust. There are several tests to apply in determining the value of this source to your work, and several indicators to look for. For example, who is the author and what evidence is there that the information is reliable, timely and truthful? Does the author give biographical information, a job title, a contact e-mail address, and can you glean anything from the URL? If the site has a 'good' location then there's more chance of the information being credible than if it were a user's own page, for instance. Evidence for peer or editorial control should be obvious if, for example, the site is that of an online journal or a chapter from a book.

The presence of abstracts, summaries, tables of content and indexes are summary information sources that enable rapid scanning of a site, while evidence of evaluative information such as recommendations, ratings or commentaries add to the weight of the site. On the other hand, there are indicators for lack of credibility: the site may be anonymous, opinionated and show poor quality control in terms of spelling, grammar and syntax.

Accuracy

This test also covers what some evaluators call 'timeliness', and is meant to assure us of the currency, comprehensiveness and purpose of the information. If a site claims to be absolutely comprehensive about a subject then you should be suspicious, though you'll never be able to gauge the value of that claim unless you've done some other reading in the area. What's important is that salient features, facts and issues haven't been missed out on purpose.

Accuracy can only be measured within context, so look at the intended audience for the site: if it's for children or a general audience you might be better looking elsewhere for accurate reports on the latest research findings in the field. Indicators suggesting a lack of accuracy are harder to identify: lack of a date might be one, the presence of sweeping generalizations another, but the best test is your own knowledge of the field.

Reasonableness

This ugly word covers objectivity, bias (and fairness) and consistency. A site discussing the health issues of smoking should offer a balanced argument representing documented evidence and opinion from all sides. In such an area there may be conflicts of interest, but being alert to them means they can be accommodated. Another way to value the site is to do 'a reality check'. For example, ask how close the claims are to your experience. Does it make sense? If the site claims that 50 per cent of Americans have suffered abduction by aliens, does this pass your reality check? One indicator of reasonableness might be to speak the text aloud: does it sound like someone on a soapbox or on a brains trust? Is the tone angry or exaggerated? Are claims outrageous (50 per cent of Americans...)? Is there clear evidence of a conflict of interest?

Support

This is concerned with the source and corroboration of the information, and in some ways overlaps with issues of credibility. Summary or review articles depend on other sources. If these are cited then the credibility of the information is strengthened, so look for bibliographies, properly referenced citations, meaningful information about statistical methods used on raw data and honest uses of graphics for the representation of numerical data (see Tufte, 1983, on this issue). The only way to measure the credibility of this information is to assess it in the light of your own experience of other information sources. The same is true of consistency – does this article agree or describe information in the same way as other, established articles? Tests for lack of support are almost as before, such as unattributed statistics or source information, or a stance that is away from the norm for the subject.

Web resources management

Metadata and the Web browsers

The Web is a chaotic mixture of unclassified information; it's the marketing medium for the new millennium; it's a democratizing and educational source for the world. Take your pick. It's also growing and changing at an almost undefinable rate, both in terms of the number of Web pages and in terms of the user profile.

For it to be a useful resource for education, management and marketing, it's essential that some globally acceptable means of classifying, describing and maintaining Web pages and sites be developed and used by Web authors. In an educational context there is a lack of support for the collaborative and dynamic nature of learning and a lack of incentives and structure for developing and sharing content.

Several interlinked projects are underway with these objectives, and this section will introduce some of them. All of the projects, however, use additions to the HTML language collected under the heading of 'metadata', meaning data about data. This metadata sits in a part of an HTML document that's never seen onscreen by end users – the 'HEAD' section. If you use Web-page authoring packages such as Claris HomePage or Microsoft FrontPage, and examine the HTML code they produce, you'll find information in the 'HEAD' area that names the package used to create the code. This space is used by Webmasters to store information about the type of content in the page, and it's used by some search engines as a first stop in indexing your pages. The Dublin Core project and the Instructional Management Systems (IMS) project both use metadata tags in this space to describe documents. We examine IMS in more detail in Chapter 8.

XML

The language of the Web, HTML, is simple to write: schoolchildren are using Web-authoring tools to produce HTML. Unfortunately it also suffers from some drawbacks, such as lack of flexibility in formatting, control over items on the Web page, fonts and so on. Also, managing a site of 10,000 pages can be a time-consuming activity, and open to degeneration at every change. If the material in the pages has to be transferred to paper or CD ROM then a lot of reformatting is required. As we write, new tools and standards are beginning to come onto the scene to redress the limitations of HTML. We've already discussed some of the changes that will make HTML documents easier to search and use across local and international boundaries in the educational world (see Dublin Core and IMS, above). The new technologies and standards have acronyms such as XML (extended mark-up language), CSS (cascading style sheets) and DHTML (dynamic html). Each works on a slightly different set of issues: XML helps to organize and find data; CSS determines Web page inheritance and presentation; and DHTML controls dynamic aspects of Web page presentation. An excellent source of information on all three is in Mace *et al* (1998, p.58).

XML is becoming 'the syntax of choice for the exchange of structured data' (Marchal, online). Because of that it appeals to organizations that publish large numbers of documents, such as a big company working on an intranet, or an educational establishment hosting documents containing teaching and learning materials and seeking to use materials from other institutions.

Conclusion

The Web is a very large information space, and we make no apologies for not attempting the impossible task of classifying all objects within it. Change is a feature of the Web, where experienced Web authors constantly introduce new technologies to their sites, thus driving the need for users to have the latest browsers and plug-in technologies. These sites sometimes offer all that is good and useful about the Web. At the same time new authors and their sites commit all the same sins of slow access, variable quality content and impermanence.

The future will bring easier and more specific access to educational resources, through the use of XML and IMS. It will bring greater and better interactivity as the Java language improves, as computers become faster, as network bandwidth gets wider and educational users become more critical of extant provision and clearer about the role of the Web in traditional and electronic educational systems.

Chapter 6

Computer mediated communications for collaborative learning

Introduction

In this chapter we try to answer some questions related to:

- what we mean by computer mediated communications (CMC);
- what opportunities are offered by CMC for human-to-human interaction;
- how it can be used in the learning process and how it affects the nature of learning;
- how the roles of the teacher and students change;
- learning collaboratively: what works and what doesn't.

We have already seen that the Internet's greatest potential for education is its capacity to bring people separated by space and time together online and to give them access to learning resources from around the world. This form of communication mediated by the computer offers great opportunities for interaction that is essential to the learning process. Bates (1995, p.52) makes the distinction between individual interaction and social interaction:

> There are two rather different contexts for interaction: the first is an individual isolated activity, which is the interaction of the learner with the learning material, be it text, television, or computer programme; the second is a social activity, which is the interaction between two or more people about the learning material. Both kinds of interaction are important in learning.

Interaction with a myriad of resources on the Internet is described elsewhere in this book and in particular in Chapter 5. We will focus here on human-to-human interaction.

The learning process

Learning is essentially a social process, which needs to take place in an environment where learners can share resources, communicate with each other and their tutors, and provide mutual support.

The university campus is designed to provide a protected environment where students come to get access to teachers, scholars, books and equipment to develop their knowledge about their subject of interest through debate, discussion and by obtaining guidance from the 'experts'.

The reality in most campus universities today is that, due to the growth in student numbers, courses are structured around large impersonal lectures, where the teacher dispenses the 'knowledge', and small tutorial groups where some level of interaction takes place about the subject matter. Individual interaction between student and tutor is limited and often rare. Campus-based students are an important part of the pedagogical structure of the course, both as *teachers* and as *learners* (Rowntree, 1981). They learn a great deal from each other about what it means to be a student as well as about course-specific information. This informal support network is as crucial a part of the learning process as regular contact with tutors through formal classes.

In distance learning the majority of learning takes place in the student's home or workplace, with little face-to-face tuition or contact with fellow students. Learning materials are designed to be 'interactive'. The emphasis is much more on the individual student to achieve set goals, such as understanding subject matter or mastering a set of skills. The role of the tutor is one of learning facilitator or coach.

In Chapter 2 we described how resource-based learning encourages the 'constructivist' model of learning and explored the ideas developed by Pask and Laurillard on learning as conversation. Supportive dialogue is recognized as a vital part in both distance and campus-based education. CMC gives us the capability to 'talk' to one another through text, audio and video communication over the Internet. Utilized effectively, this ability to 'interact' using CMC can offer new methodologies for supporting these pedagogical paradigms and enhance good practice in current educational practice (Chickering and Ehrmann, online) especially in important aspects such as:

- frequent contact between students and tutors in and out of class to encourage student motivation and involvement;
- cooperation and collaboration to enhance learning – sharing and discussing ideas deepens understanding and team working can increase involvement in learning;

- talking, reflecting and applying their learning facilitates students' active engagement in learning, which enables them to make what they learn a part of them;
- continuous feedback to enable students to reflect on what they have learnt and what they still need to know;
- diverse learning experiences – different students bring different talents and learning styles to learning, which add to the richness of the learning process.

Computer mediated communications (called telematics in Europe) offers opportunities to deliver more flexible learning programmes, where all the participants can work interactively whether they are located on campus or studying at a distance, without the constraints of time and place.

In this chapter we explore the different aspects of CMC for human-to-human communication and the role they can play in developing supportive virtual learning environments and the strategies which need to be put in place to make these new learning environments effective.

What is CMC?

As used in this book, CMC defines the ways in which telecommunications technologies have converged with computers and digital networks to create a new set of tools to support human communication. In our model the computer network is primarily a mediator of communication, which facilitates both synchronous (real-time) and asynchronous (time-delayed) modes of communication. In this chapter we discuss three different mediums of communication:

- text-based computer conferencing;
- audio-conferencing; and
- video-conferencing.

Let your fingers do the 'talking' – text-based conferencing systems

Text-based conferencing enables synchronous as well as asynchronous communication and includes interactive messaging systems, electronic mail, and group conferencing support systems. In this section we look at some of the technologies that are available for both real-time and time-delayed interaction and their use in the learning process.

Real-time interactive 'chat'

Many computer systems enable users to 'chat' to people who are online at the same time as themselves by sending text messages interactively. These forms of interactive messaging systems (chat) on the Internet follow a similar model to that of citizen's band radio, in that they are multi-user chat systems in which people get together on 'channels' and participate in an interactive textual dialogue on topics of interest. Many Internet Service Providers (ISPs) and Web sites have chat rooms for users. There are thousands of chat rooms on all sorts of topics and you get the software to access them when you sign up. Users often have to pay extra for access to these chat rooms.

A free and popular form of chat programme is Internet Relay Chat (IRC). It was developed in 1988 by Jarkko Oikarinen and came to international prominence during the Gulf War when it was used to send out live and uncensored reports of the conflict. To use IRC you have to run a local IRC client program, which connects you to one of many IRC servers on the Internet. You have to select a 'nickname' for yourself and a 'channel' for communication. The channels are chat spaces each devoted to a particular topic. If a channel does not exist, IRC will create one and you will be the 'owner' of that channel.

In these chat sessions participants have to accept an invitation to join before they are hooked into a 'conversation'. This avoids unsolicited messages. The lines of 'text chat' appear as a rolling script of sequential entries visible to all participants. The sequence of entries is dependent on when an individual presses the return key; this often makes the conversations difficult to follow. Although this type of communication is good for informal chat and for creating affinity between users, it is currently not widely used in formal education apart from building rapport between learners and for socializing.

Real time chat features are also sometimes built into asynchronous conferencing systems such as the FirstClass system (see below). In FirstClass, users can call up information to see who is currently online at the same time as them and then invite one or more participants to 'chat' with them. This invitation can be accepted or declined by the invitee. We have found that on courses using FirstClass at De Montfort University this feature is little used by students. This is in part because prior arrangements need to be made between the individuals who wish to chat to ensure they are online at the same time. Another disadvantage identified was that chat messages were not saved by the system. This is not a problem if the chat is purely social, but if it is being used to discuss course related matters, the lack of a record of what has been said that can be referred back to is a disadvantage.

MUDs and MOOs

Multi-User Dimensions or Dungeons (MUDs) are text-based virtual reality environments on the Internet. They are virtual meeting places where participants can meet people from all over the world. Users can take on particular identities and the environment can be set up for interactive role-playing games where users can try out ideas, theories and fantasies. MUDs were originally created to play a multi-user version of a role-playing game called Dungeons and Dragons (Multi-User Dungeons – MUD) on the Internet, and are still popular for playing other interactive multi-user games.

Users can explore the virtual environment, and extend it, creating new objects and places. The MUD is organized into 'virtual rooms' in which users can chat with other people in the same room and move in and out of different 'rooms' through specific exits. They interact with objects or create new objects, which will stay after they leave and which other users can interact with in their absence, allowing the virtual world to be built progressively and collectively.

A MOO is a MUD built on object-oriented principles. To log into a MUD you either need a MUD/MOO client or you can *telnet* to the server on which the MUD or MOO program resides.

MOOs have immense potential for use in educational environments where there is a need for virtual 'face-to-face' communication. An example is the BioMOO, used as a part of an online course in Principles of Protein Structure offered by Birkbeck College, University of London (http://www.cryst.bbk.ac.uk/PPS/). The BioMOO is a virtual meeting place for biologists to meet other biologists and colleagues from related fields to brainstorm, to hold seminars and conferences; see Figure 6.1 for an extract from a discussion. More information about the BioMOO can be found at http://www.ls.huji.ac.il/~idoerg/mooguide.html.

```
Gustava says, "If I understand it properly, there are
currently 13 entries in HotMolecBase?"
Rebhan says, "yes"
Rebhan says, "The information is collected manually, and
focusses on selected proteins that are of interest for a
large group of researchers."
Gustava wonders how big such a personally-curated database
can get.
EitanR likes the detailed, human readable presentation, but
can you efficiently run searches to find things expressed
"mainly in brain?"
Morna says,"who selects the researchers?"
Rebhan says, "That's a good question. Those researchers who
have interesting homepages and who have publications in good
journals."
```

Figure 6.1 *An extract of the discussion in the BioMoo (http://bioinformatics.weizmann. ac.il/~lvrebhan/rebmoo.html)*

An evolution of the MOO/MUD concept is 2-D and 3-D virtual reality worlds created using the Virtual Reality Modelling Language (VRML). These are still new and developing but they have immense potential for collaborative learning in the future (Tiffin and Rajasingham, 1995).

Interesting Web sites for information and links to educational MUDs/MOOs covering a range of topics and several languages can be located at http://tecfa. unige.ch/edu-comp/WWW-VL/eduVR-page.html, and http://www.cms.dmu. ac.uk/~cph/moos.html.

Time-delayed 'chat'

Time-delayed 'chat' or asynchronous communication does not require all participants to be present and active at the same time. They are not required to respond
immediately to questions or other participants' interventions. Contributions and
responses can be read and replied to at a time that is convenient to the individual.
E-mail, discussion lists, newsgroups and group conferencing systems facilitate this
type of asynchronous communication.

E-mail

Electronic mail has long been used as a mode of communication on the Internet
and is now ubiquitous in some parts of the higher education community; it is still
not universally accessible.

In general most e-mail systems enable the user to compose and send outgoing
messages to one or more people. Messages are routed by the system to the
addressee's mailbox and wait there until the next time the addressee logs on. The
addressee can respond to incoming messages in various ways – read the message,
reply to it, edit and forward it, delete it or leave it for later attention. Users can
also attach files to a message. With the latest generation of e-mail systems one can
attach any type of file, eg, text, spreadsheet, graphic or audio and, provided the
person receiving the mail has compatible software, the file can be opened and
used immediately or downloaded for later use.

Discussion lists

Discussion lists are essentially an extension of electronic mail that have particular
relevance to tele-learning for group conferencing. With an e-mail system you can
send a message to a group of people as easily as to one person, provided all the e-
mail addresses are known. A group conferencing distribution list enables you to
send messages to lists of persons through a single address. These lists can be small
and closed: a group of people working on a project or specific to a course. They
can also be very large and open: a discussion list on a particular topic, eg, scuba
diving, that anyone who is interested in the topic can subscribe to.

One discussion site directory (http://www.liszt.com/) currently has 90,095
mailing lists (see Chapter 5). Many of these discussion groups are maintained via
special software programs such as Listserve, Major domo and Listproc. Discussion
lists can be moderated or unmoderated. If the list is moderated, all the messages
are initially sent to the moderator or list owner, who will check the messages
against some criteria that govern what is of interest to the list's readership and
either sends the message on to the list, edits it and sends it on to the list, or
returns it to the sender.

Some interesting information about education-focused discussion lists can be
found at http://edweb.gsn.org/list and at http://www.mailbase.ac.uk/.

Newsgroups

Newsgroups differ from discussion lists in that you don't have to make a request to any 'owner' in order to participate. You just find the list that reflects your interest, read the latest postings, and reply to the group. The messages are not sent to individual mailboxes: they are read online, ie the reader has to go to the server, where the newsgroups are stored. With the correct software it's possible to read the submissions to the newsgroup as 'threads' – a listing of postings organized by topic. Any message sent to a newsgroup is distributed all over the world by thousands of different 'news servers', the equivalent of the corner newspaper shop. However, these news servers keep old posts, sometimes for days, often for weeks or months, so it's possible to reach back into the archives for material of relevance. The largest newsgroups are international, have hundreds of regular participants and tens of thousands of regular readers.

Group conferencing management systems

Group conferencing management systems encompass the concepts and technology of e-mail, distribution lists and newsgroups; however they have additional features and impose a structure on conferences that enhance group communication and support the participants. The systems all make one-to one, one-to-many and many-to-many communication easy to handle. They are closed systems with each participant needing a User Identification and password to access the conferences. This gives a level of control over who can participate and the size of the group.

Conferencing management systems use database management features to give users access to common databases of shared messages. These can be organized in sub-conferences or branches for special topics or groups. A range of different discussions can run simultaneously. Users can 'thread' through a particular line of discussion. This enables the user to isolate the messages related to a particular line of discussion and track the evolution of the ideas in the debate.

Most conferencing systems offer a range of facilities to aid group communication and information retrieval. These include directories of users and conferences; a 'history' function, which allows a user to see who has read or responded to a particular message; a 'résumé' feature that allows participants to put a few biographical details and a photograph onto the system; search facilities to find messages on particular topics; conference management and customization tools.

Examples of computer conferencing systems used in higher education include FirstClass, Lotus Notes, CoSy, Participate and VaxNotes. Modern systems such as FirstClass have a graphical user interface and a Web interface which make them easy to learn and use and to integrate with other Internet-based resources.

Figure 6.2 shows some screens from a FirstClass conference on a module on resource-based learning that formed part of a Master's level course on learning and teaching at De Montfort University. We discussed this course in Chapter 4.

The middle screen, entitled 'RBL MALT', shows the structure of the conferences associated with the course. The folder 'Pen pictures' contains biographical details and photos submitted by all staff and students associated with the course.

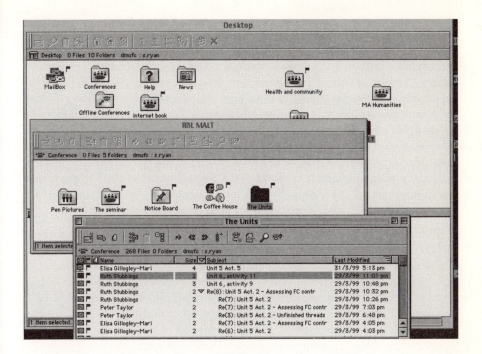

Figure 6.2 *Screens from a FirstClass conference*

This is to help participants find out a little more about each other. It formed the first posting students were asked to make and provided them with a gentle way of getting used to the system. The second folder, 'The seminar' was an area reserved for a virtual seminar on the future of higher education. Students were given background reading and an initial input from the tutors. They were required to make a substantial contribution during the first week of the seminar and then respond to each other's contributions.

In the final week of the seminar students were required to make a further contribution summarizing their views. The seminar was spread out over a number of weeks so that students had an opportunity to undertake background research and collect evidence before responding. The discussion was 'threaded' so that a number of different discussions were happening within the conference. This is illustrated in the third window of Figure 6.2. It shows part of the discussion from 'The Units' conference. This conference focused around discussion of the course materials (the units) and the activities they contained. The window shows a discussion thread around Unit 5 Act(ivity) 2.

Notice also 'The Coffee House' conference. This is a discussion area for any topic not specifically part of the course. It serves as a virtual social area and an area to air views on any topic, without mixing it in with more directly course-related discussion.

Computer conferencing and the learning process

We use computer conferencing as a generic shorthand to describe the different systems for text-based chat. Asynchronous computer conferencing represents a unique domain of educational interaction (Harasim, 1989) especially suited for supporting learners. The freedom from time and space constraints allows learners to work with each other, asynchronously and at a distance, enabling them to gain the benefits of collaborating and interacting with their peers and tutors. This, combined with the simple equipment (computer, modem, and telephone) and relatively inexpensive software required by the learner to access the system, potentially makes computer conferencing a powerful teaching and learning tool for creating 'virtual classrooms'. Even when computer conferencing software was relatively unsophisticated, its potential for education was recognized:

> Computer conferencing will ultimately emerge as a new educational paradigm, taking its place alongside both face-to-face and distance education; at the same time it will change the nature of 'traditional' multimedia distance education... CMC has the potential to provide a means for the weaving together of ideas and information from many people's minds, regardless of when and from where they contribute. The educational potential of such computer mediated interactivity, and the openness of multiple discourse and perspectives that it permits is enormous. (Kaye, 1989, p.3)

More than ten years on, it is widely used in both campus-based and distance learning to enable interaction between students and tutors who cannot meet face-to-face. The UK Open University has nearly 40,000 FirstClass users who use computer conferencing to discuss course materials, have queries answered and to provide mutual support to each other. The UK OU uses FirstClass for over 80 of its courses, with over 5000 conferences in operation. On average, every day 15,000 connections are made, 20,000 mail messages are sent and more than 150,000 conference messages are read (http://www.higher-ed.softarc.com/use/openu.shtml).

Communication via computer conferencing has uniquely been described as 'preserved conversation' or 'say writing' (Mason, 1992). As written communication it can be more thoughtful and coherent and it can be stored (for later reference). However, the nature of interaction tends to be 'conversational', similar to spoken dialogue, with the potential for expansive and unmediated feedback.

Contributions to the discussions can be searched, printed and perused at the learners' convenience. Learners can review earlier messages, make a thoughtful analysis and phrase their contribution more carefully, than in a conventional classroom.

Computer conferencing is particularly conducive to collaborative learning through conversation, argument, debate and discussion that facilitates deep level understanding. Learning occurs through a process of social interaction, planned and unplanned, between learners, peers, tutors and experts. Having to make explicit one's own knowledge and understanding to others through writing enhances one's own understanding. The 'little and often' nature of the medium encourages a regular engagement with the subject and 'combined with the collaborative work' engenders deep learning.

The power structure of the learning process changes in a conferencing environment. The time delay inherent in computer conferencing ensures that discussions are more democratic then in a conventional classroom, as turn-taking is not an issue. Opportunities to contribute are not missed because the conversation has moved on; the 'loudest voice' is not the only one heard. The more introverted students can reflect on other contributions, contribute in their own time and increase their level of input. Everyone can contribute more equally. This is particularly important in international courses where students are studying in a second language.

Using computer conferencing in the campus environment, students can make contributions to discussion topics whenever and from wherever it is convenient for them, rather then during scheduled class times. For example, at De Montfort University FirstClass is used to support student interaction on several full- and part-time courses outside of the scheduled class times. This is particularly important to part-time students who have limited time for interaction with their tutors and peers in face-to-face meetings.

Mutual support among learners and tutors enables learners to participate more fully. Participation in group conferences and regular contact with the tutors has a beneficial effect on student motivation (Soby, 1992). They have a sense of commitment to their peers, and they develop into true learning communities, which enhances the tutor's role (Prendagast, 1996). CMC enables more personalized education. Teachers can interact with the group or with the individual on a one-to-one basis, whichever is most appropriate.

The textual nature of the contribution means that race, gender, physical appearance or age is not apparent and participants do not form preconceived prejudices about what is written before they read it (Rhiengold, 1992).

As in spoken dialogue, where a chance remark or a conversation in a corridor can develop new ideas and trains of thinking, computer conferencing facilitates serendipity (Kaye, 1989). Students can follow up comments and ideas made in group conferences with any other students, develop tangential strands of discussions, discover common areas of interest – in effect develop an electronic version of the corridor or coffee room.

CMC breaks down geographical boundaries, so 'virtual online classrooms' can draw on global expertise and bring a multicultural perspective to any subject. Small groups with specialist interests can draw on expertise from further afield. This is especially true for professional development where employees work in global environments and where the flexibility of distance learning is required. One example is the use of Lotus Notes by Ford of Europe and its partner universities to deliver postgraduate training to its employees wherever they are geographically located (Johnson and Chatterton, 1996).

Engaging in face-to-face conversation involves complex forms of behaviour (Feenberg, 1989). Facial expressions, the tone of the voice and body language all give us cues to the reaction of the listener to the conversation. These can convey irony, sarcasm, compassion and other subtle nuances, which are all missing in computer conferencing. This limitation of the communication bandwidth can lead to misunderstandings and frustration. This can cause passionate verbal 'warfare', a phenomenon commonly known as 'flaming'.

The one-to-many and many-to-many communication adds uncertainty as to whether the audience will get the message and who will get the message. Unlike face-to-face conversation, a person does not get immediate feedback. The unpredictability of responses can be irritating if participants read the message but don't reply ('lurkers') or they miss the point (Rhiengold, 1992). Learners often learn just by 'listening to the discussion' without contributing to the conversation. This can be problematic for the active participants.

Computer conferencing can facilitate many different types of learning methods that involve group interaction such as debate, simulation, role-play, transcript-based assignments, brainstorming, Delphi technique and project work (Paulsen, 1995). All these methods take advantage of the group communication, which is the real power of computer conferencing as a teaching and learning tool.

The moderator's role

The role of the online tutor or conference moderator is crucial to the success of a computer conferencing application for collaborative learning. Experience reinforces the view that success or failure of a computer conferencing application is often due to social rather than technical factors (Kaye, 1992).

Several authors (Brochet, 1989; Feenburg, 1989; Mason, 1991; Paulsen, 1995) have written comprehensively about the roles and responsibilities that computer conferencing moderators must fulfil. These fall broadly into four categories: pedagogical, social, managerial and technical (Berge and Collins, online).

The main role of the online tutor is that of educational facilitator: to contribute specialist knowledge and insight, focus the discussion on the critical points, to ask questions and respond to students' contributions, weave together disparate comments, and synthesize the points made to foster emerging themes.

They also need key social skills for nurturing online collaboration, similar to those of a tutor, facilitator or chairperson in a traditional peer learning situation. They must be able to create an atmosphere of openness, assuring all participants that their contributions are valued and welcome, building rapport within the group to help group members to explore ideas and different perspectives and to take ownership of their learning.

It is important that the moderator sets the context, agenda and timetable for the conferences, defines and clarifies the ground rules for interaction, the objectives of the discussions and manages the interaction and flow of the conference with strong leadership.

The moderator/administrator of the conference must be comfortable with the technology. They must ensure that the participants are familiar with the software and hardware. In addition, they have to handle the permission rights (eg, who has access to which conferences, whether they have read only or read-write access), design the organization of the conference and set up sub-conferences for smaller groups for group project work or special discussion topics, and move or delete messages from conferences.

The role of the moderator will change as the conference develops and students gain confidence and experience in using computer conferencing. Salmon (1998) offers a five-stage model for developing effective online moderation (see Figure 6.3). She highlights the following five stages:

1. access to the system and motivation – give instruction on how to use the system and build user confidence, encouraging them to log on regularly;
2. socialization – develop group cohesion and culture, develop systematic ways of working online, raise awareness of style, eg how messages may come across;
3. sharing of information – encourage all participants to contribute to the discussion, acknowledge and cater for different learning style and summarize and weave together the information and ideas being exchanged;
4. construction of knowledge – encourage interaction, make links to learning issues, handle conflict and give feedback, reduce moderator intervention to allow students to interact with their peers and generate their own knowledge;
5. development of students as moderators.

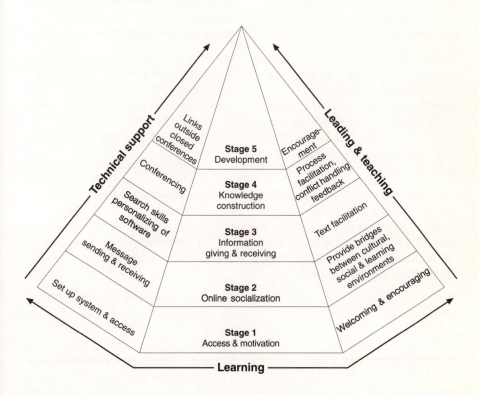

Figure 6.3   *Salmon's model for teaching and learning online*

This is further developed in Salmon's recent book, *E-Moderating – Teaching and Learning Online* (Salmon, 2000).

Changing roles of tutors and students

Computer conferencing offers a unique educational paradigm that encourages learners to take greater control over their own knowledge construction and understanding of the subject, and changes the role of the teacher from 'knowledge expert' to learning facilitator. Table 6.1 provides a summary of these changing roles (see also Chapter 9).

Table 6.1 *Changing teacher and student roles (adapted from Berge and Collins, 1996)*

Changing Teacher Roles	Changing Student Roles
From oracle and lecturer who provides the answers to an expert questioner who is a facilitator, guide and resource provider	From passive receptacles for hand-me-down knowledge who memorize facts to complex problem solvers who construct their own knowledge
Teachers become designers of student learning experiences, providing the initial structure to student work, encouraging increasing self-direction and presenting multiple perspectives on topics, emphasizing the salient points rather than just being providers of content	Students refine their own questions and search for their own answers and see topics from multiple perspectives as they work, in groups, on more collaborative/cooperative assignments. Group interaction is significantly increased
The teacher-learner power structure changes. From a solitary teacher in total control of the teaching environment to a member of a learning team, sharing a learning environment with the students as fellow learners	More emphasis on students as autonomous, independent, self-motivated managers of their own time and learning process. Access to resources is significantly expanded
More emphasis on sensitivity to student learning styles	Emphasis on acquiring learning strategies (both individually and collaboratively). Emphasis on the use of knowledge rather than the observation of the teacher's expert performance or just learning to 'pass a test'. Discussion of students' own work in the classroom

These changing roles have raised questions about the security of academic jobs and there has been much talk of the cost savings that may be possible with the introduction of technology. This as yet is unproven. The SCALE study in the United States (Arvan *et al,* 1998) is one of few which have conducted large trials using computer conferencing to identify the efficiency savings. They found that although most tutors reported increased time involved in greater contact with students, some productivity gains where made through the successful substitution of graduate students for tutors to moderate conferences on courses with a large number of students. Additional gains emerged from student interaction with peer tutors.

Moderating conferences can be an arduous, time-consuming task, but the rewards for both students and tutors in enhancing the learning experience through greater interaction makes computer conferencing a 'killer application' (Daniel, 1996) for education.

See me, hear me! Video and audio conferencing

Advances in digital compression technologies, the increases in bandwidth and the power of computers is making it possible to send audio and video in relatively small amounts across the Internet. Software products such as RealAudio and RealVideo are making the handling of audio and video easier on the Web in terms of the capacity of computer power, storage and network required. However, they are still mainly used as one-way broadcast technologies rather than as communications technologies for human-to-human interaction. Internet radio stations are a popular implementation of this technology, as are music sites. Video-broadcasting is used to Web-cast conferences and music concerts, although the quality is fairly poor.

Audio conferencing over the Internet

Internet phones allow you to have live audio conversations over the Internet. Internet telephony works by digitizing audio data, compressing it and transmitting it over the Internet.

Internet phones allow you to talk to other people on the Internet all over the world without the expense of an international phone call. Using Internet phones is far from simple: the person you want to talk to must be online when you are and they must have compatible Internet phone software. Most conversations are only possible one-to-one. The emerging developments (the collaboration of Nokia, Ericsson with Psion in Europe) in mobile telephony, combined with palmtop computers for Internet access, could revolutionize this type of conferencing.

Audio conferencing is also now becoming common in products such as Net-Meetings, which facilitate two-way chat. This is often used in conjunction with a 'white board' to create a multimedia conferencing environment that can be used for genuinely interactive one-to-one teaching and learning (see Multimedia conferencing below).

Live audio streaming on the Web is still primarily one-way, but it can be effectively used in conjunction with other Web-based technologies such as text-based chat rooms. The UK Open University Knowledge Media Institute has successfully used Internet-based audio delivery for several large-scale applications, including a series of expert lectures and seminars based on the concept of talk radio, and a Pub Quiz (Scott and Eisenstadt, 1998). Archives of some of these applications can be found at http://www.open.ac.uk/kmi/.

Videoconferencing

Videoconferencing is becoming more widely available in higher education institutions. It offers two-way audio and video communication in real time, allowing individuals or groups of people in different locations to hold interactive conversations. Videoconferencing covers a wide range of applications using a variety of hardware, software and network facilities, including the person-to-person videophone, desktop videoconferencing systems and sophisticated studio-based systems.

All the systems allow you to send and receive audio and video information to and from a remote site. The audio and video are compressed for transmission and decompressed on arrival at the remote site. Compressing the information causes a very small time lag and reduction in the quality of the video and to a lesser extent the sound, although the main factor affecting the quality is the bandwidth of the network. The compression and decompression causes a loss of 'redundant' information that often translates to some loss of 'body language' and facial expressions. This can cause misunderstandings. Later in this section we look at how to compensate for this loss in a learning situation.

The equipment

All videoconferencing systems have five basic components – cameras that capture images; microphones to capture sound; a device known as a 'codec' (COmpressor/ DECompressor) which compresses and decompresses the audio and video signals for transmission over the network; a monitor for viewing participants, and loudspeakers to hear the participants.

The networks

An important element in the quality of audio and video in videoconferencing is the bandwidth of the network used for transmission of the signal.

The most commonly used network for videoconferencing is ISDN (Integrated Services Digital Network). ISDN technology is a global standard that allows the simultaneous use of several digital telephone lines to make connections to most parts of the world. The more lines you use the better the quality of the sound and video, but it is obviously more expensive. The main disadvantage of ISDN is the recurrent call charges.

ATM (Asynchronous Transfer Mode) networks which give high speed data transfer are starting to emerge as a high-quality vehicle for videoconferencing applications in education. In the UK the development of high bandwidth ATM Metropolitan Area Networks (MANs) which link educational and other relevant organizations in a particular Metropolitan area are paving the way for testing ATM videoconferencing. For example, the Scottish Higher Education Funding Council (SHEFC) has supported the use of the Scottish MANs by providing funding for ATM videoconferencing studios to be installed in most Scottish HEIs (http://www.use-of-mans.ac.uk/Video.html).

Room or studio-based systems

Roll about systems or room-based systems are better suited to traditional classroom applications. All the equipment can be fitted on a trolley for ease of movement.

There are usually at least two cameras. The main camera, which is normally pointed at the participants, can pan, tilt and zoom. The document camera can function as an overhead slide projector. There are normally two monitors, one showing the image you are sending and the other the image from the other site. One omni-directional microphone, echo cancelling unit and one set of speakers usually serve for a small room. The controls are usually on a remote control keypad or an LED menu display.

To make a connection with the remote site you just dial the correct telephone number of the site and with luck you make contact. Currently it is important that your equipment is compliant with the generally approved H320 standard to which most systems comply, although new standards are being developed as the hardware and software improve.

Most room-based systems have facilities to use support materials such as videotapes, computer applications, charts and photographs.

In addition to the equipment, issues such as acoustics, room layout and lighting have to be considered when setting up a dedicated room-based system. A very good source of practical information on all aspects of designing a distance learning classroom using videoconferencing is *Classrooms for Distance Teaching & Learning: A blueprint* (Hegarty *et al*, 1998).

Desktop systems

For desktop videoconferencing you can use a personal computer, with the appropriate videoconferencing card and software. The bandwidth (only two lines for ISDN applications) and the standard of the cameras and microphones reduce the quality of the picture and sound and limit the number of participants at each site. However, this form of videoconferencing has the advantage of enabling you to share and exchange files and to collaborate using shared software applications via a 'white board'(see below). Some popular desktop videoconferencing systems which support this type of videoconferencing and applications sharing include Intel's Proshare, PictureTel's Liveshare and Apple's QuickTime Global Phone.

Internet-based systems

These systems are in their infancy and are still developing. White Pine's CU-SeeME, which was developed at Cornell University, was the first Internet video-conferencing system. It allows people to communicate with each other in real time using both video and audio over the Internet via a modem connection to an analogue telephone line. There are now other competitors in the market such as RealVideo by Progressive Networks and Microsoft's NetMeetings.

One-way video streaming on the Web is now being used in institutions such as Stanford (DiPaolo, 1999) to broadcast lectures directly to distance learning students on their computer desktop. An example of this can be accessed at http://stanford-online.stanford.edu/demo/index.html.

Internet-based videoconferencing has great potential as some systems can offer the facilities for real multimedia conferencing with applications sharing (see below). However, the current bandwidth limitations of the Internet make this type of videoconferencing very low quality for teaching and learning.

Point-to-point or multi-point

The simplest type of videoconferencing is point-to-point, which establishes a connection between two sites. In this mode each site receives a live picture of the other location. Using room-based system where most locations have two monitors, it is usually possible to see both the incoming and outgoing images simultaneously.

Using a multi-point bridge, it is possible to make a connection to many sites simultaneously. Each site makes a connection with the bridge and the bridge manages the interaction between the sites. Multi-point bridges can be voice activated, that is they react to sound so the speaker is always seen and heard by all the other sites as soon as he or she starts to speak. This is the most common form of protocol used in higher education in Europe; however, it requires discipline from all the sites not to make any noise when they are not addressing the other sites or to make appropriate use of the 'mute' function.

Another option is to have chairperson control, where the control over who is seen and heard is with a chairperson at one of the sites. A good example of this type of system is used in some French universities, particularly for distance teaching. The presenter sits in a separate room with a computer and small TV screens which show the current image seen by students at all the sites. The students press a button if they want to make an intervention. This is displayed on the tutor's computer screen and he or she can see who wants to make the intervention and can decide whether to allow the intervention or not. Each button is linked to a pre-set on a remote controlled camera. This type of system offers all the sites equal attention from the tutor and gives the tutor greater control.

Using videoconferencing for teaching and learning

Videoconferencing is widely used in higher education to support many different activities that require real-time visual and audio communication between participants in different locations. Some examples of the use of videoconferencing in higher education are:

- to give remote learners the opportunity to participate in a 'traditional class-room', without having to travel between campuses, and to show them overhead slides, videotapes, computer applications charts, etc;
- to enable staff to teach students across the world remotely;
- to enable students and staff to interact with experts from related fields from all over the world;
- to enable students to work with their peers, across the world;
- to enable students to participate in courses not offered at a particular campus;
- to enable students to participate in courses at different European partner institutions;
- to support students on international exchange programmes by enabling staff to have regular meetings with the students;
- to train students working in business;
- team teaching with remote teachers;
- holding meetings between several sites and with partners in other parts of the world;
- interviewing candidates for jobs or carrying out assessment at a distance;
- to demonstrate surgical procedures to medical students, using broadband networks.

Factors to consider when using videoconferencing

Interactivity is the key to using videoconferencing effectively for teaching and learning. Although videoconferencing enables 'face-to-face' visual and audio communication similar to a traditional classroom, the videoconferencing tech-nology changes the classroom environment and can cause concern for the tutors and students alike. Participants at different sites have to make adjustments for the use of the technology and communication mediated 'through a television monitor' with limited picture quality. Preparing tutors to use the technology is an important issue, but more important are the skills involved in personalizing the teaching and incorporating student interaction strategies into the teaching and learning experience.

Videoconferencing is not broadcast television, where participants passively watch a slick presentation. The picture quality is not yet good enough. The use of cameras can restrict movement. Too much movement can appear as a blur at the remote site.

In face-to-face communication we constantly use body language to augment our understanding of what is being said. A tutor can identify whether students are interested and understand the subject through visual cues and the students' body language. Videoconferencing loses some of this information in the com-pression and decompression of the image and viewing the image on a TV monitor. The loss of some facial expression and body language can lead to a loss of interest and miscommunication. Therefore the tutor needs to compensate for this through clear instruction to the students, constant vigilance of the remote site and regular verbal interaction with the students.

Role of the tutor

Videoconferencing happens in real time, which means pre-planning is essential. Some factors to consider are:

- The logistics of organizing connections with the remote sites and making sure the technology works. Videoconferencing is a fairly stable technology; however, it is advisable to plan what to do in case of a technological failure, particularly with learners at the remote site.
- Ensuring all the participants have access to course materials. Make sure students have course material in advance and that they know what is expected of them.
- Compensate for the tutor and students viewing each other through a monitor. Start the session with an informal roll call and use student names frequently. Look at the camera and maintain good eye-contact with participants at the remote site, otherwise they can lose interest. Don't make fast, abrupt movements. Speak clearly, slowly and continuously. If feasible make a seat chart and use it for the first few sessions so students get to know the names of students at the remote site.
- Make things clear, tell the students exactly how the session will be organized and what is expected of them, explain assignments, etc. Plan for interaction early on, to set the rhythm for the rest of the session. Inform students interaction is expected and how they should take part. Make sure your visuals and the commentary match.
- Provoke interaction, ask questions and wait for responses, facilitate local and cross-site group activities, encourage students to participate.
- Not every aspect of the teaching and learning should happen on screen: group work conducted locally or asking students to turn to a workbook to complete an exercise helps to add interest to the session. Use silence while students are doing self-study, or reading or writing.
- Listening to someone talking on a TV monitor with a poor picture for any length of time is tiring. Use variety, plan for short segments. Variety keeps interest levels high and this leads to more active listening. Instead of delivering a 30-minute lecture on a complex topic, provide short segments of concentrated listening (10 minutes), then alternate with other activities, using a different teaching method for a couple of the segments.
- Get familiar with the technology (eg, selecting which images are sent to the remote site, controlling the camera image and the other audio-visual aids). Be in control of what is on screen, use pre-sets, avoid meaningless camera movements, and operate the camera at the far end if necessary.
- Give enough time for students to take notes – sometimes students feel that everything on a screen needs to be copied. Provide printed back-ups to reinforce the message.

● Use repetition and summary to help students remember the important points. Repeat new words, concepts or phrases at least three times.

One widely used technique to ensure all these factors are planned for is to develop a lesson plan using a matrix or script, with detailed timings and stage directions (Fraeters *et al*, 1997) – see Figure 6.4. It describes in columns what all those involved in the session need to know about the lesson. The advantage is that at a single glance it is clear what content is going to be communicated at what time, in what manner and with what support material. Condense it as much as possible.

Teaching using videoconferencing requires a much greater degree of advanced planning than conventional face-to-face teaching. Maintaining the interest of students at the remote sites is particularly difficult. Teachers therefore need to redesign courses with carefully planned activities to promote interaction. Practical guidelines for teaching using videoconferencing have been produced at De Montfort University (Burns *et al,* online) and are available at http://www.jtap. ac.uk/reports/htm/jtap-037.html.

Multimedia conferencing systems

Although the quality of video and audio are still very limited on the Internet, software is available that enables you to use not only videoconferencing and audio-conferencing but software applications between computers. Desktop video-conferencing systems and products such as NetMeetings allow users to share applications remotely via a 'white board', similar to a desktop videoconferencing system. Two people can 'talk' to each other using text or voice (with a microphone), they can videoconference using a small camera attachment, and they can work on the same file, be it a word-processed document, a spreadsheet or some other software, in real time.

One person always has control at any one time and although audio and video is only possible point-to-point, several people can be connected at the same time and they can see the 'controlling' screen. Despite its current limitations, this type of multimedia applications-sharing has great potential for one-to-one as well as one-to-many teaching at a distance. It is already being used in educational and training environments to create virtual workspaces.

One example of the successful use of this type of system is at De Montfort University where applications sharing (NetMeetings) is being used to teach Java and C++ programming to Computing Science students in the face-to-face laboratory sessions. NetMeetings enables a group of students and the tutor to 'see' the same computer screen, the tutor uses the 'white board' facility to show students the screen with the relevant programme, or to discuss a particular question or problem a student may have by displaying the screen to the class. Students can work in groups on the same programming problem. When the class is over, students can contact the tutor remotely via NetMeetings to discuss any programming problems. Using the NetMeetings audio conferencing facility, the tutor can view the programme, identify the problem and point the student in the right direction.

timing	activity	content/goal	support	remarks
10'	• introduction	to be completed		
10'	• show video excerpt • invite reactions • have learner read part of article *The Economist*	• icebreaker • give essentials of 'Belgian problem' • test previous knowledge	• video excerpt 1 • article 1 • provide slides?	• do learners understand English? • video player?
10'	• form groups of four • brainstorming • have 1 spokesperson report • invite others' reactions	• State structure of Spain? centralist? federal? draw up chart • basis for comparison	• assignment brainstorming on slide • result = chart. transmit by doc.cam.	• doc.cam. available? • does seating plan allow group formation?
10'	• ask questions • lecture • questions & answers	• State structure of Belgium?	• slides • photograph Prime Minister?	• adapt slides • look for photograph
10'	• lecture • invite reactions • have learners talk about Spain during same period	• 1800–1831: advent of Belgium. End Napoleonic era. Rule by Holland. Belgian revolution. • anecdote about opera at start of revolution!! • what was happening in Spain at that time?	• slides • audio excerpt opera?	• look for audio excerpt (or score of the opera?) • CD? Tape?
10'	• lecture • invite questions	• relevant aspects 1831–1945 • anecdotes language situation!	• slides • tables (language situation, etc.)	
10'	**BREAK**			
15'	• lecture • invite questions	• 1945–1970; changes after WWII	• slides • tables (demography)	
20'	• lecture • show excerpt tv news • interview politician 5' • invite questions	• from 1970 on: consecutive State reforms	• slides • video excerpt 2 • phone	• phone available? • agree on subject!! (does politician speak Spanish??)
10'	• have learners read provocative points of view • brainstorming • group discussion		• slides	• involve Spanish colleague!
5'	• end			

Figure 6.4 *Example of a lesson plan (Fraeters et al, 1997)*

This is now being extended to be a regular service within the student resource centre, where a research student will be available to deal with queries from students over NetMeetings (Smith, 1999).

Collaborative course development

NetMeetings has been successfully used to support academic staff in universities in four different European countries to develop a joint course. The applications-sharing software was used to train staff in the use of software applications (available at one site) which were being considered for integration into the course. The applications–sharing has also been used to demonstrate multimedia being used at one site to the other sites so that they can use it and evaluate it. The software also enabled participants to jointly visit several Web sites that had relevant resources for the course, to discuss the usefulness or otherwise of the resources.

Academics are just beginning to explore the potential of collaborative work tools. The possibility of groups of students collaborating and working together although separated by considerable distance is a real and exciting one. It is far removed from the notion of the isolated student passively reading large volumes of text from the computer screen.

Creating the virtual learning environment using CMC

Virtual learning environments have long been written about, but it is only with the recent advances in communications technologies that they are becoming a reality. CMC offers the interactivity of campus-based courses with the flexibility of distance learning courses.

Bringing various aspects of CMC together can 'virtually' provide all the elements of an educational system based on the traditional campus model. Telecommunications are used to deliver education to the learner as opposed to using transport to deliver the learner to the campus (Tiffin and Rajasingham, 1995).

The advances in satellite and cellular telecommunications and the availability of more portable computers make it possible for students to work from anywhere, at any time. The student can download the learning materials and assignments, and access online services such as databases or information on the Web. More importantly, with CMC students can interact with the tutors and fellow students, discuss topics and complete their assignments and send them to be marked. It is irrelevant whether the student is at work or at home, on campus or off campus.

The combination of synchronous and asynchronous technologies has been used in another model that is emerging for creating a 'virtual classroom'. Groups of learners physically get together and meet in local centres with facilities such as videoconferencing to interact in real time with a wider 'virtual' learning community. This community could be national or international. The human interaction at the centre provides additional support. This is supplemented by interaction using computer conferencing for asynchronous communication. This model has been tried and tested in various European initiatives we have been involved in, as illustrated in the case study below.

Case study: European Open University Network/WIRE

Members of the European Association of Distance Teaching Universities (EADTU) have set up a network of EuroStudyCentres (ESC), which are based in traditional and distance learning universities in 15 countries across Europe. They offer students access to distance learning opportunities using all forms of asynchronous and synchronous technologies.

The European Open University Network project and the WIRE project have used CMCs including point-to-point and multi-point videoconferencing to create a 'European Virtual University'.

Some examples of courses delivered

Students in ESCs in England, Belgium and France were able to participate in a multinational course which consisted of expert seminars on international business delivered in Helsinki, by CEOs of prominent Finnish businesses and political leaders (including the Prime Minister), via videoconferencing. Students were able to listen to and question people they would not normally have access to. They then discussed the content of the seminars with their peers across Europe using computer conferencing and finally completed group projects for which they were accredited by the Helsinki University of Technology.

In another instance, multi-point videoconferencing was used to bring together students and professional workers, including social workers, the police, and voluntary organizations from across Europe, dealing with the sensitive issue of physical and domestic violence. The videoconferencing enabled students to share their perspectives with the professionals and to debate issues raised with other students from different countries where the law and how the professionals dealt with the issues differed. These discussions were augmented by a very active computer conference where each fortnight students from a different institution posted a topic for discussion.

Videoconferencing in conjunction with satellite television was also successfully used to provide two-way interaction for interactive television broadcasting to create international 'virtual classrooms', to deliver courses ranging from medicine to chaos theory. These courses also used computer conferencing to develop the discussions between television transmissions.

Similar technologies were again used to deliver a course on sustainable development in Europe. It included expertise and satellite pictures and simulations from the European Space Agency, academics, other experts and students from several countries. This enabled students to gain a European perspective on environmental issues, which was particularly useful in relation to cross-border pollution. For example, Swedish students had a totally different perspective to their British counterparts on acid rain and the burning of fossil fuel in the UK.

These are a few examples of a series of courses on different subjects that have been delivered jointly between ESCs based in different universities and different countries. These courses offered students opportunities to work with their peers in Europe and to gain perspectives on the subjects from experts and peers, which would not have been available to them in a conventional course.

All these examples show the potential to entirely reshape the 'place' of education – what constitutes a course, where and who delivers it, the groups in which students learn. Learners will no longer be restricted to a choice between distance learning and campus-based courses. They can participate in courses on the other side of the world and still 'talk' with their tutors and peers on a regular basis. We discuss virtual learning environments further in Chapter 8.

Conclusion

Computer conferencing is a unique form of communication which promotes interaction that is often lacking in traditional classrooms. It enables learners who are geographically and temporally separated to exchange ideas and information, to work collaboratively, explore alternative pathways and develop their own learning styles. Learning depends on the active involvement of students in constructing knowledge on their own, which leads to better understanding of the subject.

The role of the teacher changes from a teacher controlling the content and process, to that of a facilitator whose primary role is to guide and support the learning process. The students must also accept responsibility for their own knowledge creation (Gunawardena, 1992).

Video and audio conferencing over the Internet are still inhibited by the limited bandwidth of the network. The use of studio-based videoconferencing over ISDN for remote classroom teaching is now integrated within most universities. It has enabled learners to gain access to expertise not previously available to them, as well as giving universities access to new learners in geographically remote locations.

Multimedia conferencing systems with applications-sharing capabilities are still developing as a technology, but with the increase in bandwidth and improvements in digital compression, they offer the greatest potential for collaborative working in the future.

All these technologies are tools for creating interaction, but they do not foster interactivity in themselves. The role of the tutor, although changing, is still central to the success or failure of the learning process. Technology does not substitute for the key roles of mediation, inspiration, annotation and provocation (Heppell and Ramondt, 1998) that teachers would recognize from conventional pedagogical paradigms.

CMC supports RBL through offering learners the interactivity of campus-based education with the flexibility of distance education.

Chapter 7

Using the Internet: Computer Aided Assessment

Introduction

The assessment of students' work in higher education is one of the most important aspects of teaching and learning but it can also be one of the most resource-intensive. If CIT is to produce real savings in staff time and resources then Computer Aided (or Assisted) Assessment (CAA) systems will play a key role. The Internet has given a new lease of life to some forms of CAA as well as stimulating the development of others.

This chapter examines the following:

- CAA and the Web;
- the purposes of assessment;
- the range and types of tests now available;
- some future developments.

Web-based assessment

The adoption of CAA, in the UK at least, has been slow, certainly compared to the United States, but this may be changing. Kleeman (online) has argued that:

To achieve the full benefits of computerized assessment, you need the computers to be connected to each other. This allows instant publishing of new questions and instant marking and retrieval of the results. A local area network is an excellent means of connecting computers, and much existing computerized assessment runs on a local area network. But with testing at a distance, until recently electronic connection has been more troublesome, with either no connection at all or no standard means of connection. A lot of organizations distribute questions and return answers by floppy disk, but a reliable electronic connection would be so much easier. Even the most unobservant reader will probably realize what is coming next... the Internet/intranet is the key enabling technology for computerized assessment.

Kleeman has in mind forms of assessment such as multiple choice questions where student scores from tests can be collated together over the Internet very easily, unlike systems that rely on floppy disks being sent back with the students' answers on them. While the technological changes identified by Kleeman will certainly help, they are only part of the picture. There has been, and to some extent there still is, caution in the UK towards the adoption of CAA. Questions such as the following are often asked. Does CAA offer a sufficient range of assessment strategies or does it encourage the testing of superficial learning and knowledge acquisition? Are the procedures secure? Can meaningful feedback be provided?

An indication of this increased interest is the establishment of a Web site on CAA aimed at HE in the UK as part of a nationally funded initiative:

By identifying existing good practice in the use of CAA, the project aims to demonstrate how to overcome the organizational, pedagogic and technical difficulties of using CAA in higher education. (CAA Centre, online)

The CAA Centre is undertaking research and development, providing information and resources and is serving as a focus for CAA development in UK HE.

Advantages and disadvantages of CAA

McCormack and Jones (1998) have provided a useful summary of the main advantages of CAA when used online; see Table 7.1.

However, CAA also has important limitations. Below are some common ones:

- Implementation of a CAA system can be costly and time-consuming.
- Construction of good objective tests requires skill and practice and so is initially time-consuming.
- Because of the above, testing of higher order skills is difficult.
- Hardware and software must be carefully monitored to avoid failure during examinations.
- Students require adequate IT skills and experience of the assessment type.
- Assessors and invigilators need training in assessment design, IT skills and examinations management.

- a high level of organization is required across all parties involved in assessment (academics, support staff, computer services, administrators). (CAA Centre, online)

Table 7.1   *Advantages of online assessment (based on McCormack and Jones, 1998, pp.236–7)*

Saving time. Assessments can be created using software tools and adapted and reused as needed. They can be distributed and collected using a Web-based system. This saves development and distribution time.

Reducing turnaround time. Using a system whereby assignments are corrected by computer or the computer is used to reduce the correction time means the results (and appropriate feedback) can be returned to students as quickly as possible. This will enable students to use the knowledge obtained from their corrected assessments to address their deficiencies as soon as possible.

Reducing resources needed. Human resources can be reduced because simple assessments can be electronically corrected and software can reduce the processing and correction time for essay-type assignments. Assignments can also be created, collected, corrected, commented on, and returned entirely electronically, saving paper, printing time and resources.

Keeping records. Computerized correction and collection facilitation utilities can automatically keep records of results for individual students. These records can be stored centrally and accessed by interested parties, such as staff and students.

Increasing convenience. Collection and (to a certain degree) correction of assessments can be automated, meaning that students can obtain instant feedback for some assessments. Students find assignments for which they can receive an instant correction more useful when assessing whether they have mastery over a particular topic and more convenient because they can do the assessment at any time and any number of times.

Increasing ease with which data can be used. Because the data from assignment corrections is stored in electronic form, it is easier to analyse and use the data in spreadsheets and other statistical packages.

The purposes of assessment

We can put some of these concerns in context and also be in a better position to identify the strengths and limitations of Web-based assessment if we step back for a moment to consider the purposes of assessment.

Rowntree (1990, p.302) sees the main purposes of assessment as:

> an attempt to gain knowledge of the learners' competences and in particular what competences did they bring to the learning and what competences they have acquired as a result of your teaching.

Assessment is a process through which learners gain an understanding of their own competencies and progress as well as a process by which they are graded. The development of appropriate assessment activities to aid mastery is, as we saw in Chapter 2, at the heart of our approach to RBL.

A useful distinction made in Chapter 2 is between formative assessment where students are able to monitor their own progress or receive feedback from a tutor in a developmental context, and summative assessment that also includes grading. The distinction is an important one where online assessment is concerned and may influence the choice of assessment tools. If the main aim is to provide immediate feedback to students for formative purposes, then you may not be so concerned about security or plagiarism. It may also be appropriate to encourage students to submit work to a bulletin board or other conferencing system and to share their results and comment on each other's work. Much can be gained from this. In other contexts, where the main purpose of the assessment activity is to grade individual students on the basis of work produced singly, a more controlled environment, with authentication procedures, may be required.

Suitability of CAA for different disciplines

CAA can be used across the full range of subjects taught in universities, but in some discipline areas objective tests are seen as more appropriate and have been used more extensively than others.

A national study by Stephens and Mascia of HE in the UK (reported in CAA, online) found the subjects with the highest numbers of CAA tests were:

- computing;
- biology;
- accounting, finance and information;
- medicine;
- mathematics;
- engineering;
- psychology;
- modern languages;
- chemistry;
- library and information studies;
- geography;
- human services.

Most of the above were using multiple choice questions or similar. The Web, however, can support a great range of assessment activities and as we review these it is clear the range of disciplines that can benefit is not restricted to the above.

The range and types of assessment

It is easy to assume that computers are appropriate for multiple choice type questions only, but computer-based assessment is far wider. Computers can support a number of assessment styles and offer a much wider range of opportunities from multiple choice and other objective tests, through short-answer questions to full-blown essay questions.

Short-answer and essay-type questions

At its simplest level, Internet-based systems can support the process of submission and commenting on assignments. E-mail, for example, can prove to be a simpler and more convenient method of submission than handing in printed or written text. Electronic submission also enables a richer variety of media forms such as pictures, sound or video files to be included. This submission may take place using conventional e-mail or be integrated into a virtual learning environment (VLE) such as MERLIN (online) or Colloquia (online).

A predefined cover sheet or attachment giving name, assignment number, etc, may be used. The student would fill in certain fields and submit it with the assignment. The grader may use this sheet for writing comments and grading the assignment before returning it electronically to the student. This approach is used by the Open University for the electronic submission of assignments on their FirstClass computer conferencing system.

Marking assistants

Marking assistants are pieces of software designed to speed up the marking of assignments by enabling predefined comments and annotations to be linked to a student's assignment that has been submitted electronically. The assignment plus annotations can then be returned electronically to the student. One example is Markin, by Holmes (online):

> Once you have loaded or pasted your student's text into the Markin program, you can mark it using a system of buttons and annotations which you can customize to meet your exact requirements. The marked work can then be automatically compiled into a World Wide Web page, in which highlighted points in the student's text are linked to annotations and comments entered by the teacher. Alternatively, the text can be saved as a printable file, or as an RTF file that can be loaded into a word-processor. In all cases, error statistics are automatically compiled and included in the text.

Figure 7.1 shows the program being used for correcting a piece of English Language text. The buttons can be customized to add comments appropriate to the subject matter under consideration.

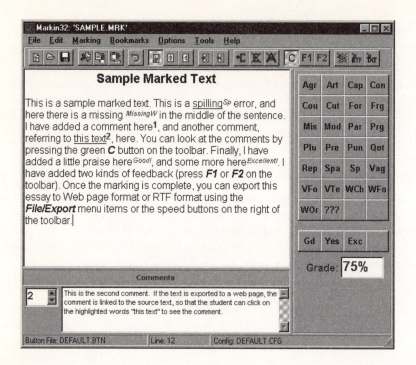

Figure 7.1 *The Markin program (http://www.cict.co.uk/software/markin)*

Using a bulletin board

A bulletin board or conferencing system may be used to provide general feedback, or for submitting short answers that are not part of the formal assessment. On a photography course at De Montfort University, students attach digital photographs they have taken. These photographs can then be viewed by other students as part of the process of peer learning. The tutor can post general comments to the bulletin board on the work submitted. An example of a bulletin board being used for peer learning is shown in Figure 7.2.

The student and the tutor are not restricted to making only one response each. An educational 'conversation' and 'teach back' (Chapter 2) can take place involving, in varying degrees, all those participating in the bulletin board. Students' contributions to the bulletin board as a whole can also be assessed. Marks may be awarded for the quality and regularity of a student's contribution.

Web pages

Students may also submit a Web page containing their material for assessment. This may be based on a predefined template developed by the tutor into which students place their content.

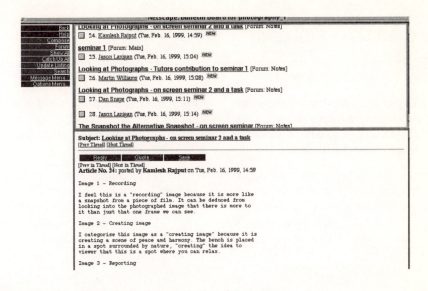

Figure 7.2   *A bulletin board being used for peer learning*

The Web page can potentially contain any of the media types and interactive features that we discussed in Chapter 3. There may be little point in students submitting a Web page containing only text, unless of course it also contains links to other Web-based supporting or contextual material, but the value in some disciplines of submitting assignments that contain 3-D models or photographs is great. Students studying Built Environment modules at De Montfort University are submitting Web pages including photographs, plans and CAD models.

This form of submission does raise important questions as to what is being assessed, particularly when Web-based submission is still fairly new for both students and teachers. The criteria for assessment need to be clear. Is the student being assessed on the content alone or on the content, design and structure of the Web pages as a whole? If the latter, what is the balance in terms of the assessment weighting between these components?

In design-based disciplines electronic portfolios of work can be submitted, replacing or supplementing traditional portfolios or presentations.

Automated marking of essays and short answers

Attempts have been made to develop systems that will automatically mark short answers and essays submitted electronically. Early systems tried to identify predetermined key words or phrases. Cox (online) wrote in his Web-based newsletter:

I thought that I would find a surfeit of information and many research projects about machine grading. I was surprised by the paucity of research and by the lack of wide spread use of machine assistance in marking essays.

I was unable to find any commercial products for machine marking of essays (or even of machine assistance).

He does identify some important developments. *The New York Times* (27 January 1999) reported that:

Beginning early in February, the two essay questions on the Graduate Management Admission Test, taken by about 200,000 business-school applicants every year, will be scored by both a human being and an electronic robot called the 'E-rater'.

In this case the computer will second-mark, and if the computer-marked score differs from the first by more than a fixed amount, a human second-grader will be used. Such systems use techniques known as 'latent semantic analysis' (LSA) and it is claimed that, 'over many diverse topics, LSA scores have agreed with human experts as well as expert scores agreed with each other'. Details of the work of the LSA group at Colorado University can be found at (http://lsa.colorado.edu/).

Computer programs

Systems have been developed to automatically mark computer programs written by students and submitted for grading as part of their assignments. Ceilidh (online) is an established system originally developed at the University of Nottingham. Ceilidh automatically marks students' programs interactively.

A typical use would be that a student would read online a set question, obtain a skeleton outline of the solution program, develop a solution program, and submit the program for marking. Ceilidh marks the work and provides feedback on the mark awarded and information on where marks were lost. The marks are also made available to the student's tutor, and are stored for future reference.

Using mathematical tools for assessment

A Computer Mathematics System (CMS) such as *Mathematica*, while not designed primarily for assessment and not currently a Web-based system, may point to the way assessment systems generally could develop in the future. Ramsden (online) suggests that:

the direct use of a CMS with students enables us to build elements of *self-assessment* into questioning strategies aimed primarily at *teaching*.

To expand on this: CMS-based courseware allows the user to compose her own input, possibly along lines different from those foreseen by the designers. In its scope for free experimentation, it resembles nothing so much as that archetypal piece of appropriate mathematical technology: the back of an envelope. The important difference, of course, is that the CMS user receives immediate feedback as she works, from which she can get many important clues about how her learning is progressing. It is in the way it combines these two elements – freedom of exploration and continual feedback – that *Mathematica* shows its most interesting face.

Objective tests

The most common form of assessment on the Web is the use of objective tests such as multiple choice questions.

The student will select from, or the responses will be compared to a set of predefined responses to that question. The marking of the responses is considered objective because no judgement has to be made on the correctness or otherwise of an answer at the time of marking.

Typically the student has to select one or more right answers from a range. The system will then 'mark' the attempt and provide feedback. Variations on this will include selecting objects, filling in blanks, matching pairs, etc. This form of assessment is often heavily based on tried and tested paper and pencil tests.

Storage and reporting of results

A key distinction when examining Web-based assessment systems is between those that use CGI applications to pass back student results to a server where they are stored and can be used for course management and monitoring, and those systems, usually based on Java and JavaScript, that do not record scores but only provide direct, immediate feedback. The latter systems are more appropriate for formative assessment. The distinction is not a completely hard and fast one. McCormack and Jones (1998, pp.284–5), for example, provide an illustration of JavaScript that will write the results from a quiz to an e-mail that is automatically sent to the tutor.

The two types of test may look the same to the student and appear to function in a similar manner, but for teaching purposes they can be very different.

The range of questioning styles supported

Objective tests can support a wide range of question styles. Flax, for example (Routen and Graves, online), currently supports the following:

- multiple choice – one item has to be selected from a range;
- type-in – a word or phrase has to be entered;
- text select – a word or phrase from a passage is selected;
- links – pairs of items have to be linked;
- select tree nodes – the correct node in a tree diagram has to be selected;
- checklist – all the correct items have to be selected;
- image map – an area on a picture or diagram is selected;

- order – a list of items has to be ordered correctly;
- numbers – numerical data is entered.

Figure 7.3 shows the links example from Flax. Students link the boxes on the left to what they believe to be the right answer in the box on the right by dragging the mouse. The response will be marked when the 'accept' button is clicked and feedback given.

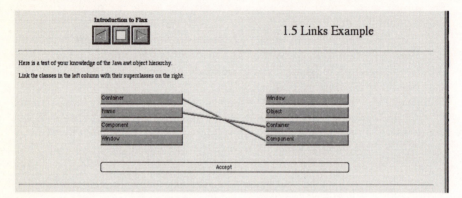

Figure 7.3 *Links example from Flax*

Hot potatoes (http://web.uvic.ca/hrd/halfbaked/) supports the following:

- multiple choice;
- fill in the gap;
- short answer;
- jumbled sentence;
- crossword puzzle.

The fill-in-the-gap option provides you with an online cloze test; see Figure 7.4. Hot potatoes is now well established, claiming to have over 3000 users in 70 countries.

One big advantage of tools like Flax and Hot potatoes is that, as they are using Java and JavaScript, they can be incorporated directly into your own Web page, enabling you to customize the surrounding text. Formative assessment can then be closely integrated with the course content.

Server/client-based systems

We noted a moment ago that a server needs to be running a CGI application so that information can be passed from the Web page back to the server, where it can be stored and aggregated, opening up a range of different assessment and monitoring options for both students and tutors.

Figure 7.5 shows an example from a course built using WebCT. It is a multiple-choice question that is made available for a fixed period of time so the student

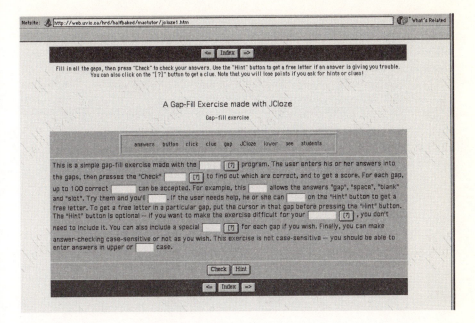

Figure 7.4   *Cloze test example from Hot potatoes (http://web.uvic.ca/hrd/halfbaked/)*

has to attempt it in that period. The scoring is weighted; in this example question 2 is worth one point. An indicator box shows whether the question has been attempted or not. The students' scores are tracked and held by the system and if permission is given, students may view their scores and any associated feedback comments made by the tutor.

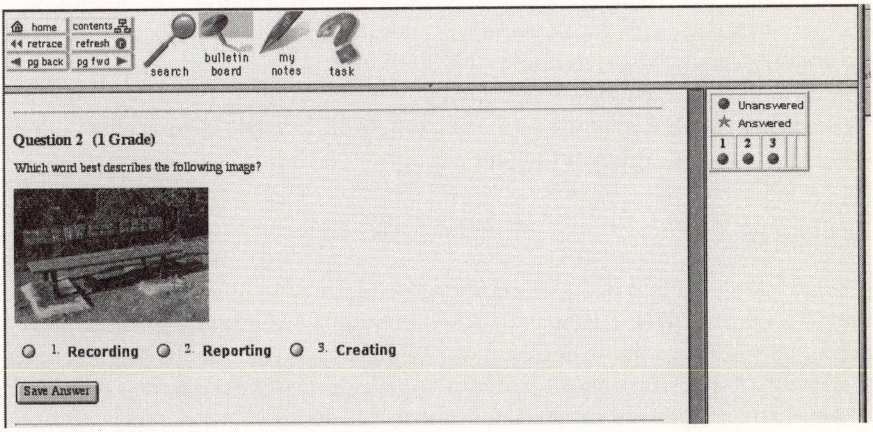

Figure 7.5   *A question from WebCT*

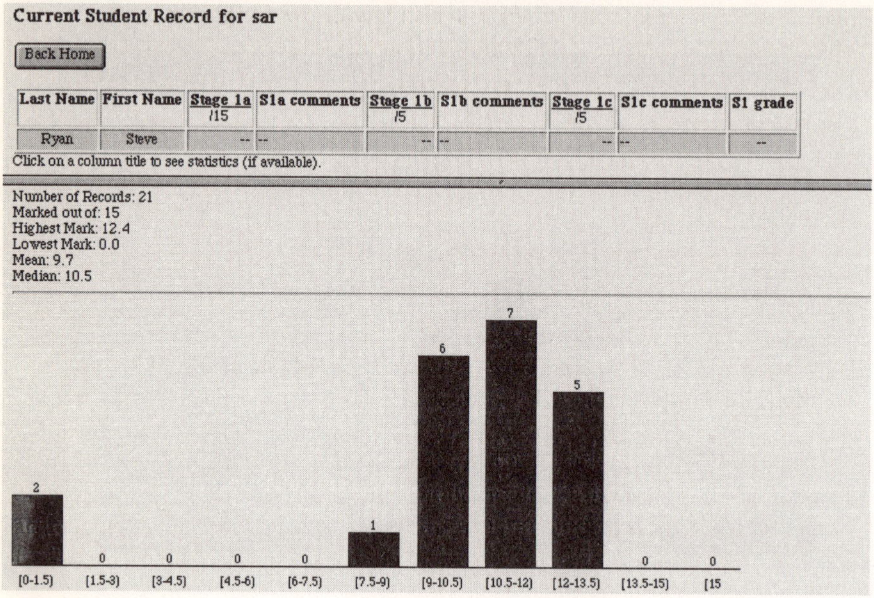

Current Student Record for sar

[Back Home]

Last Name	First Name	Stage 1a /15	S1a comments	Stage 1b /5	S1b comments	Stage 1c /5	S1c comments	S1 grade
Ryan	Steve	--	--	--	--	--	--	--

Click on a column title to see statistics (if available).

Number of Records: 21
Marked out of: 15
Highest Mark: 12.4
Lowest Mark: 0.0
Mean: 9.7
Median: 10.5

2	0	0	0	0	1	6	7	5	0	0
[0-1.5)	[1.5-3)	[3-4.5)	[4.5-6)	[6-7.5)	[7.5-9)	[9-10.5)	[10.5-12)	[12-13.5)	[13.5-15)	[15

Figure 7.6 *An example of mark distribution from a WebCT test (student view)*

Students' scores then become part of the course management system. Data such as when tests were attempted and the length of time a student spent completing the test can be tracked, and these can be viewed by the tutor either on an individual student basis or as whole class lists. Graphs of the distribution of marks can also be generated, providing data not only on class performance but also on the appropriateness of individual assessment elements. For example, questions that are answered badly by a significant number of students may indicate the inappropriateness of the question or some ambiguity in its wording. It may also indicate weaknesses in the teaching material being tested. An example of mark distribution from a WebCT test is show in Figure 7.6.

Adaptive tests

It could be argued that many of the above examples of testing can be carried out using pencil and paper. This may be true, although it would often be a lot slower and more resource-intensive. Computer-based testing can also be adaptive; that is, depending on a student's response to a question or set of questions, others of appropriate difficulty are selected to test that student.

The following description is from Educational Testing Services (online), a major developer of adaptive tests:

A computer-adaptive test is tailored to the individual test taker. Candidates receive a set of questions that meet test design specifications and generally are appropriate for their performance level. Test design determines the total number of and types of questions asked, as well as the subject matter presented.

The computer-adaptive test starts with questions of moderate difficulty. As the candidate answers each question, the computer scores the question and uses that information, as well as the candidate's responses to previous questions, to determine which question is presented next. As long as the test taker responds correctly, the computer typically selects a next question of greater difficulty. In contrast, if the test taker answers a question incorrectly, the computer typically selects a next question of lesser difficulty. Subsequent questions are presented based in part on the test taker's performance on previous questions and in part on the test design. In other words, the computer is programmed to fulfil the test design as it continuously adjusts to find questions of appropriate difficulty for test takers of all performance levels. This means that different test takers will be given different questions.

Plagiarism

An increasing concern is plagiarism. Is the submission of assignment by computer and the greater use of the Internet leading to more plagiarism? It is certainly true that the Internet increases opportunities for students to obtain work written by others that can be passed off as their own. Web sites supplying and selling material for this purpose have sprung up. E-mail also facilitates the unauthorized sharing of answers and work among students. In the UK the Joint Information Systems Committee (JISC) is funding investigations into this area; see for example (http://www.jisc.ac.uk/pub99/c05_99.html). Work is also being carried out into the use of 'smartcards' and other identification devices to help check on the identity of the student undertaking an assessment.

The future of online testing

In his report on the future of large-scale, computer-based educational testing, Bennett (online) identifies three stages or generations of tests (see Table 7.2). We are currently in the first generation of large scale electronic testing. The next generation of tests will be able to assess a wider range of competencies by incorporating multimedia elements and accepting longer written answers or oral responses, as well as traditional multiple choice questions.

His third generation, generation 'R' (for reinventing) will see 'instructional integration' – the assessment will be embedded seamlessly in the distance learning session:

Table 7.2 *Three generations of large scale assessment (Bennett, 1999). Reprinted with kind permission of Educational Testing Service*

Generation	Key characteristics
First-generation computer-based tests (infrastructure building)	1 Primarily serve institutional needs 2 Measure traditional skills and use test designs and item formats closely resembling paper-based tests with the exception that tests are given adoptively 3 Administered in dedicated test centres, as a one-time measurement 4 Take limited advantage of technology
Next-generation electronic tests	1 Primarily serve institutional needs 2 Use new item formats (including multimedia and constructed response), automatic item generation, automatic scoring, and electronic networks to make performance assessment an integral program component; measure some new constructs 3 Administered in dedicated test centres, as a one-time measurement 4 Allow customers to interact with testing companies entirely electronically
Generation 'R' test (evaluation)	1 Serve both institutional and individual needs 2 Integrated with instruction via electronic tools so that performance is sampled repeatedly over time; designed according to cognitive principles 3 Use complex simulations, including virtual reality, that model real environments and allow more natural interaction with computers 4 Administered at a distance 5 Assess new skills

Decisions like certification of course mastery, graduation eligibility, and school effectiveness will no longer be based largely on one examination given at a single time but will also incorporate information from a series of measurements... This merger of assessment and instruction will be realized in some significant part through the use of electronic learning tools. These tools will implement a range of instructional methods. For present purposes, however, their most salient characteristic will be in leaving an electronic record of student activity that might contribute almost incidentally to summative decision making. (Bennett, online)

The idea of generation R tests is an interesting and important one. Although Bennett is focusing on large-scale tests, the movement towards the integration of assessment and teaching applies across all forms of Web-based teaching and learning. We saw an example of this in Ramsden's discussion of CMS and *Mathematica*. His highlighting of the 'electronic record of student activity', or profiling, is also significant. The Instructional Management Systems project (IMS) will lead to the establishment of common standards for such student profiles that will be linked to the student as they move from one piece of courseware to another, even across different systems. We will explore these ideas further in Chapter 8.

Conclusion

Computer aided assessment covers far more than the traditional multiple choice test. Systems now in place support a variety of objective tests that can involve the manipulation of textual, graphical or mathematical elements; the submission and commenting on work; and automated marking of assignments. But perhaps, as Bennett suggests, we are still very much at the beginning of a process. The seamless integration of assessment with teaching, so that performance is continually monitored and adaptive, dialogic teaching and support is then provided, may well come about.

In the meantime, caution still needs to be exercised. Just as the World Wide Web may support flexible assessment, so too can it support ways of circumventing these systems. The trading online of essays and coursework is perhaps the most obvious example. A university's reputation for quality is bound up with the perception of the reliability and validity of its assessment procedures and moves towards online assessment need to take account of this.

Chapter 8

Integrated systems

Introduction

In this chapter we will examine developments towards integration and the creation of virtual learning environments (VLEs). This integration has a number of facets and in particular we will focus on:

- the growth of integrated course delivery systems;
- the development of standards to enable the exchange and integration of teaching material developed in a variety of contexts;
- the integration and reuse by teachers of educational objects developed by others and the development of an 'educational economy' to support this process.

Virtual learning environments

A recent feature of the Web has been the development and growth of VLEs or course delivery systems. Typically these systems will include course materials, assessment facilities, conferencing and chat software as well as management tools for student administration and monitoring. Some systems will also include authoring tools. These systems are known by a number of names, for example 'online delivery applications', or by their proprietary names such as WebCT, LearningSpaces or TopClass.

They are all relatively new but their popularity is increasing rapidly. WebCT, for example, claims that in February 2000 it had over 5.2 million student accounts in over 1150 institutions in 51 countries (http://www.webct.com).

Features of course delivery systems

Course delivery systems have a range of different features but the main ones can be grouped under the following headings:

- student features;
- tutor features;
- designer features.

Student features

When students log on to a course delivery system, typically they will have access to a range of different features. The following description is based on WebCT, but it is indicative of the range of features found in these systems.

Course content

This content will be presented in the form of Web pages. Usually there will be a built in navigation system that will take the student to the 'next' and 'previous' pages, the beginning and the start of a section. Other buttons will call up some of the features discussed below.

The course content pages are served as standard HTML pages and can usually contain all the elements that are found on a standard Web page, including video, audio plug-ins and JavaScript (see Chapter 3). This is an important feature as it means that content created elsewhere can be incorporated. The pages can also contain links to material held outside the system. This means that links can be made to any Web site, although when students visit the external Web site they will no longer be tracked by the system.

Course conferencing system or bulletin board

This allows communication among all course participants. The conferencing system will usually contain a range of different discussions running simultaneously and within these discussions a number of linked discussions or threads will take place. The conference may be linked to specific parts of the course so that, when a student sends a message from a specific Web page, that message will be sent to the appropriate conference.

Synchronous communication or chat

This enables real time communication among course participants. These will also be related to different topics or areas. The names of participants currently online will be shown. These chat areas may or may not be logged.

E-mail

An electronic mail facility allows one-to-one messaging among course participants. It also enables students to submit work directly to the tutor and that work will not be seen by other students. This is clearly important if the work is to be assessed.

Notebook

The notebook allows a student to take notes on any of the content that is being studied. The notebook is personal to that student and is also linked to the content that was being studied. When students return to that content, they can call up the notebook and see the notes they originally made.

White board

A white board is a shared work area allowing synchronous communication among course participants. A user draws on his or her white board and all other users see what has been drawn and can, if the tutor grants permission, add to or modify the content.

Objective tests

Students' responses are automatically marked correct or incorrect by the system. An explanation can accompany each answer saying why the chosen answer was correct or incorrect. Hints or extra information may also be provided.

Student presentation areas

This is an area where students can upload pre-prepared Web pages that can be seen by all course participants. This tool is useful for displaying course projects, group work and individual presentations.

Grading information

Students can view their own marks. They may also be given information about the distribution of marks on the course.

Calendar

A calendar can contain information for everyone on the course, such as assignment submissions, as well as private entries made by and visible only to the individual student who makes them.

Tutor features

VLEs will typically have a number of features to assist tutors when teaching online courses.

Progress tracking

This allows the tutor to monitor student progress on a course. A number of parameters may be tracked, including when an individual student accessed the system, what parts of the system were accessed and the time spent on it. Details may also be available about the frequency and extent of student use of bulletin boards or conferences.

Timed, automatically graded quizzes

Quizzes can be delivered online on a predetermined day. Tutors are provided with data on which students have attempted the quiz and the scores of individual students. This information may then be held in a student performance database.

Student management

Class lists and grade lists are produced by the system. These can be annotated by the tutor and printed out in various formats, eg, alphabetically or by performance.

Designer features

These are specific tools and features built into the VLE to assist the course designer when developing a course to be delivered via the VLE.

A standard interface

VLEs have their own standard interface that may allow customization by the designer. Navigation features are already built in. Levels of headings and sub-headings are already pre-set and contents pages may be generated automatically. These features may serve as a short cut in the assembly of a course but the price paid for this convenience may be high. An over-rigid system tempts tutors and developers to shoehorn their content into this predetermined format. The format itself will then be imposing the structure rather than the structure being determined by pedagogical considerations.

Customization

Courses can usually be customized in varying degrees. Background colour, font colour and font size can be changed and alternative graphical icons can be used, although their functionality will remain the same. Various features can be made available to the student or hidden, and the extent and type of feedback given can be controlled.

Site management features

This includes features to assist in the backup of materials, the uploading of files from tutors or designers and updating and version tracking facilities. All these 'hidden' activities can have a major impact on the robustness and usability of the VLE.

Comparative evaluation of systems

The growth of online education means that more and more universities are considering what system to invest in and support across the institution. Currently it is still common to find several different systems being used alongside each other. The emergence of agreed standards in the future will enable these systems to work more or less seamlessly together, but at present there is a desire to standardize on a particular system and thus simplify administration and support. McCormack and Jones (1998, p.343) point out that there is no one correct answer to the question of what system to use, rather a careful comparison and analyses of the various features of different systems can guide institutions in their choice.

McCormack and Jones carried out such an analysis. They selected four VLEs and built a dummy course with them. This enabled them to compare the ease of developing the course as well as examining the range of features available in the final product.

An interesting study has been undertaken at the University of Minnesota (University of Minnesota Digital Media Center, online). Here four systems were being used by different groups within the University while other departments were uncertain as to which system, if any, to adopt. This led senior management to commission a study of the four systems with a view to making recommendations for adoption. This study also built a course in the four systems and interviewed and surveyed users and developers on their experiences. The study concluded that, 'though functional, the first-generation tools have significant usability short-comings and present a number of technical and pedagogical support challenges for University faculty and staff'.

A number of recommendations were made. Two points of general relevance are: 1) college and university administrators review their technical, training, and design support plans to ensure that sufficient resources are devoted to providing staff to support faculty in their use of emerging technologies; 2) each of the four systems' designs move from the current restrictive paradigm of the 'lone developer' towards a more open, team-centred approach to course development.

A comparison system

An essential reference source for anyone considering the adoption of a VLE is Landon's (online) 'Online delivery applications: a Web tool for comparative analysis'. The site is designed to help educators evaluate and select online delivery applications. It contains detailed information on, and specifications of 14 such systems. It enables you to make a direct comparison of the feature sets of any two applications as well as providing a full comparison table of all applications. The various features of these systems are weighted so that the comparisons made are more useful than a simple counting up of ticks on a chart.

The Web-based tool for making these comparisons may be downloaded for personal or educational use. Institutions can therefore undertake their own evaluations of specific systems and compare their findings with those already published. In addition, the weightings for various elements can be changed so that institutions will be able to undertake evaluations using an instrument that reflects their own priorities.

The comparisons and the evaluation tool can be found at http://www.ctt.bc.ca/landonline/.

Case study: using WebCT

After examining a range of course delivery systems, De Montfort University decided to pilot online course material using WebCT.

Development

The courseware developers and systems administrators generally responded positively to the WebCT design and development environment. Some technical difficulties were encountered and inevitably some compromises were made in the design and structure of materials but overall, considering that we were working with a new (for us) system, problems were relatively few. The development in some cases took considerably longer than anticipated, but this was mainly due to factors not directly related to the system.

Using WebCT

Students log on to the system using their name and password. This gives them access to the course they are registered for as well as letting the system identify the user so that scores for assignments and tests can be logged and contributions to the bulletin board can be identified.

Students can now check timetables, review scores or proceed to the course material. These materials appear in the form of Web pages within the WebCT navigational framework. Sometimes a Web page format may not be appropriate, but a link can be made to another form of resource. In a module on photography, for example, links are made to chapters in a book that is held online in Acrobat PDF format. An example screen is shown in Figure 8.1. This format gives a designer far more control in laying out a page than is possible with conventional Web pages. The option is also available to print the material out at high resolution, something not currently possible from a standard Web page. These features were necessary on the photography module

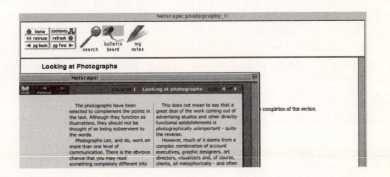

Figure 8.1   *A screen showing the navigation controls and an Acrobat file being viewed*

and it proved possible to integrate, in what appears to the student a seamless manner, elements that are held outside WebCT, such as the PDF files, with the rest of the system.

The e-mail and bulletin board features have proved particularly useful. The bulletin board has been integrated into the assessment components. Students are asked to undertake an activity and write a short response of, say, 100 words and submit this to the bulletin board. Students can then read each other's responses and the tutor can, on the bulletin board, make general comments on the activity and on the way students have attempted it.

Simulations

Courseware developers have produced a number of simulations for use on the course. These include an example on the effect of light shining from different sources on the appearance of an object. These simulations have been developed using JavaScript and, because they are designed to run in a conventional Web page, they run correctly when part of WebCT.

Student work

The tools that allow the uploading of student work are proving useful. On one course the tutor has developed a simple Web template for student projects. Students then 'load' the template with their work and submit it to an area of WebCT reserved for students' Web pages.

Students on the photography course are required to take photographs with a digital camera and these are either uploaded to the bulletin board where they can be seen by all course participants or e-mailed to the tutor, as an attachment, for comment and grading.

The facility to create image banks, where each image can have linked to it a description of the image, is also proving useful. Students can search the image bank, and thumbnail pictures of all the images matching their criteria are displayed.

Our experience to date has generally been positive in using the system. We are convinced that courseware delivery systems have an important role to play in the development of online learning. As these systems become more mature and robust, their value will increase. However, it must be remembered that these systems are only tools and their effectiveness will depend on the quality of the content, the learning activities and the structure of the courses that are delivered using them.

Integration between systems – the IMS project

A number of different course delivery systems are now available and are being used widely. The choice of an appropriate course delivery system is important, but it is not critical in the sense that the institution need be locked in to using that system or else starting again from scratch. Future developments mean that these systems will be able to work together. Initiatives such as the Instructional Management Systems project (IMS) are making this possible.

The importance of the 'knowledge industry' is now being increasingly recognized by business and governments. We saw in Chapter 1 that in the UK the government-sponsored National Grid for Learning was designed to not only stimulate developments within schools but also to encourage developments by the British software and computer industry. Similar developments are also taking place in the United States, through initiatives such as the Advanced Distributed Learning Initiative Partnership and the Instructional Management Systems Project. These developments have been supported and encouraged by government at the highest level.

A key element of these initiatives has been to encourage government departments to, 'Work with businesses, universities, and other appropriate entities to foster a competitive market for electronic instruction' (The White House, online). This is widely recognized as a major new market that industry and education and training organizations will be able to exploit. Some have approached it with almost a missionary zeal:

> Not since Copernicus convinced the scientific world that the Earth moved around the sun have world trade opportunities been so stupendous.
>
> The end of the Cold War, alone, created 3 billion new customers. Simultaneously, the Internet and the new technologies allow providers to affordably reach users worldwide. English became the planet's business language. And America became the headquarters to a revolution where obvious winners are those in the knowledge business. (Franklin Institute, online)

Part of the process of developing this competitive market is the creation of common standards that will facilitate the exchange and marketing of educational and training products. It is in this context that the IMS initiative is likely to be significant.

What is IMS?

> IMS is a global coalition of academic, commercial and government organizations, working together to define the Internet architecture for learning. The technical specifications we are creating will facilitate the growth and viability of learning on the Internet through assuring interoperability of instructional systems and learning content. (IMS, online a)

The IMS system is designed to be Web-based. It is built on the premise that the Internet will be used increasingly to deliver education and training worldwide and that the demand and market for educational and training products will continue to expand.

IMS is an initiative of EDUCAUSE (http://www.educause.edu/), an organization with membership from many leading US academic institutions and supported by many of the largest computer and software companies, publishers and other content providers, US government departments and international representatives. In the UK this representation is coordinated through the Joint Information Systems Committee (JISC) (http://www.jisc.ac.uk).

Currently we are seeing the development of a range of VLEs, but courses developed in one are unlikely to be usable in another without some considerable adaptation. This process is expensive and time-consuming and works against the trading or exchange of courseware.

IMS is not trying to develop one universal VLE; rather it is developing what are intended to become agreed standards that developers of VLEs will follow. If they conform to the standard, the systems will be able to work with each other. This standard will be aimed at all organizations involved in the development and delivery of education and training using Internet-based technology. This includes commercial and military training; primary and secondary education; universities; continuing education; and community, junior and vocational colleges.

Furthermore, the intention is that IMS will be used worldwide: organizations and educational institutions with differing structures, objectives and cultural perspectives will all be able to be accommodated. This is a tall order and whether this intention can be realized remains to be seen.

The project is focusing on resources, activities and integration:

- Resources are the learning materials or content that students interact with. IMS is developing specifications for searching, digital packaging, and modularizing content with the goal that any content can run on any learning server. Resources can be drawn from any developer and potentially reused in different learning activities.
- Activities that organizations provide for learners have their own set of specifications. These assure that learner progress through courses or in relation to learning goals can be tracked and recorded and can take advantage of the learner profile. Activities ranging from individual tutorials to collaborative projects can be managed in a standard way.
- Enterprise integration of learning servers, student record systems, content repositories and electronic commerce requires specifications for interchange of information among these systems. (IMS, online b)

IMS standards are being developed to cover the following areas:

- user profiles – personal, performance and preferences data;
- metadata – methods and terms for describing content;
- learning content – assessment, sequencing and reporting;
- management – content, course and collaboration;
- services – links to administrative records, billing and library systems.

User profiles are mobile, user-controlled collections of personal and educational data including personal, performance and preference information. This data represents a rich resource that users can draw on to facilitate, customize and manage their learning experience(s).

At the heart of the IMS project is the setting of a standard for metadata – data that describes other data. The overall goal of IMS metadata is to promote and facilitate the discovery and retrieval of appropriate learning resources. A Web page, for example, may contain hidden fields that contain descriptions of the content of that page as well as information on who 'owns' it, copyright information, charging details and suggestions on ways in which the content might be used. These fields can be searched by software, enabling pages to be found which match the specifications of that search. With the establishment of a widely supported standard, difficulties of 'finding' appropriate material on the Web will, in part, be overcome.

An example of IMS interoperability

We saw in Chapter 7 that computer aided assessment is growing rapidly. Currently a number of proprietary CAA systems are available and, in addition, many Web developers write their own multiple choice questions using CGI and PERL scripts. Multiple choice questions may also be written in Java.

IMS standards will enable a wide variety of multiple choice questions to be shared. The intention is to develop standards that will provide:

- the ability to issue question items/banks to users regardless of the VLE deployed by the user;
- the ability to use question items/banks from various sources within a single VLE;
- support for tools to develop new question items/banks in a consistent manner;
- the ability to report test results in a consistent manner. (IMS, online c)

Moreover, students' scores for different assessments will be tracked by the management and profiling software so that results from taking a test on a course in one VLE can be used to monitor progress or guide course selection in another.

IMS and UK higher education

The importance of the IMS system for UK HE has been recognized. The JISC has agreed to fund membership, at partner level, for the whole of UK HE as part of its standards work. This will enable UK HE to influence the development of IMS standards and will help make sure that issues relevant to the UK are considered. A UK IMS Centre has been established and is now influencing developments:

A key part of the UK IMS Centre's work is to represent the special needs of the UK HE community to the overall IMS project, in order to ensure that the IMS specification includes a response to these needs. An example where we have already been able to do this has been with regard to offline working. In the US, where local phone calls are free, the cost of Internet access is not time dependent. In the UK this is not the case, making offline working crucial… After raising this with the IMS project in the US, they have incorporated this into their specification. (UK IMS, online)

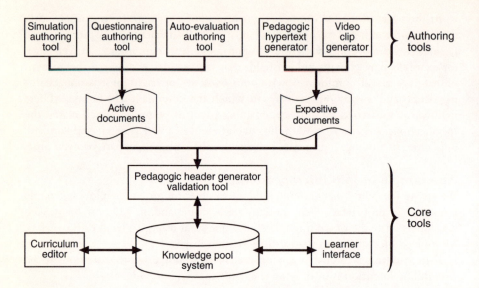

Figure 8.2 *Ariadne tools (http://ariadne.unil.ch/tools/). Reproduced from the Ariadne Web site with kind permission of the Ariadne Project*

Ariadne

The European Commission has funded an important project, Ariadne, involving a range of partners across Europe. 'The project focuses on the development of tools and methodologies for producing, managing and reusing computer-based pedagogical elements and telematics supported training curricula' (Ariadne, online).

This involves the development of an international system of interconnected knowledge pools (KPs) and producing tools and basic methodologies for maintaining and exploiting the KPs in a wide variety of educational and training contexts. The project is now in its second phase where the tools and methodologies are being refined, tested and evaluated. The main tools are illustrated in Figure 8.2.

Unlike IMS, Ariadne is concentrating on the development of a range of tools. These include core tools for accessing and managing the knowledge pool and a variety of authoring tools for developing content to be added to the knowledge pool. But in order for the system to work, for resources to be located from the knowledge pool, an agreed metadata system is required (see Forte *et al*, 1997 a and b).

IMS and Ariadne

Partners in Ariadne and IMS have recognized that it would be inappropriate to develop competing metadata systems; indeed, to do so would contradict the underlying principles of both projects. They have therefore agreed to cooperate under the auspices of the IEEE LTSC Committee (http://www.manta.ieee.org/p1484/). This will lead to the joint adoption of metadata standards while retaining the option of producing extensions to these standards that address the particular needs of the respective projects. This is particularly important in the case of Ariadne, where there is a requirement for a metadata system that supports a range of languages and differing cultural contexts. The statements of agreement to cooperate include the following:

> ARIADNE and IMS agree to collaborate on moving forward, on the basis of these and other existing results, towards a common structure and core of educational metadata descriptors and to propose them for international standardization... The proposed common core shall be designed in view of fostering the interchange and reuse of educational resources across linguistic and cultural barriers and shall strive to remain commercially, pedagogically and culturally neutral. (Ariadne, online – http://ariadne.unil.ch/metadata/agreement.content.html)

IMS and global universities

The IMS project is setting some bold and visionary objectives. It offers the possibility of establishing a standard that will enable the worldwide sharing of courseware with a real chance of being able to tailor courses to individual students' needs. The economies of scale that would be brought about by such a project may open up educational opportunities to locations and groups that are currently not able to benefit fully from them. It has the potential to make a major contribution to facilitating the development of lifelong learning in convenient and flexible ways that will meet the diverse needs of society.

However, one needs to question whether such a system could provide a common method for specifying the organization of content and whether these specifications will remain 'pedagogy neutral' (IMS, online b). Is it realistic to expect the standards and specifications to be sufficiently flexible to be able to effectively serve the needs of the whole range of educational and training systems? What of national and cultural differences? Can these be accommodated in such a system? Or will it lead to the globalization of a small number of courses and dominance of educational systems worldwide by a few powerful and influential providers?

Educational objects

A lot of interest has been aroused recently in 'reusable' educational objects or components. These are small applications or programs that can be incorporated into your Web page and then used by you in a variety of different contexts. They are often written in the Java programming language and are known as 'applets'. You may, for example, have a graphing applet into which you can input your own data and see the resulting graph. Another example may be from chemistry where you see 3-D presentations of molecules that can be manipulated on screen. An important feature of these applets is their emphasis on interactivity. Students are often required to manipulate them in some way and the applet will then provide feedback on their actions.

The emphasis of this approach is on reusability. It seeks to develop discrete elements or chunks that can then be reused by different teachers in different ways. One aim is to overcome resistance to using complete 'off the shelf' courses produced elsewhere. These chunks then support teaching materials produced by individual teachers, rather than seeking to replace their efforts.

Another advantage of this approach is the potential to achieve economies of scale and make effective use of scarce resources. It is, for example, a complex task to produce an applet that will draw graphs on screen. It requires programming skills that only specialists possess. If the completed applet is made widely available it may then justify the initial effort required to produce it.

Finding objects

How does a teacher find suitable educational objects? One approach is illustrated by the educational object economy (EOE). This approach, developed originally by Apple Computers and partners, has established a database of educational objects on the Web (Apple Computers, online) that can be searched by potential users in order to locate suitable objects.

The objects are initially classified following the Dewey classification system so that objects are grouped under familiar subject headings. Within these headings, the system provides a description of the object, ownership details, the location of the object, indications of the educational level it is aimed at, and ownership and copyright details.

One of the most interesting features of the EOE is that it is built around the idea of a community of users. It is seeking to encourage collaboration and cooperation. As part of this process, users of individual objects are encouraged to write a review of the object, describing how they used it. These comments may be educators' comments describing how the object was used with students, or technical comments focusing on particular features of the object. These comments are added to the database so that when potential users are browsing the database they can read the comments of other users before deciding to download and use the object.

The educational objects database also contains updates, news and features, and papers and reports relating to the use of the EOE. Madra *et al* (online) describe their use of objects in the classroom. They make some valuable points about the need to plan carefully how the objects are to be used and on the importance of integrating activities associated with the objects with other teaching activities.

EOE and IMS

The educational objects economy database is also being designed to be IMS-compliant. The object descriptions in the database will contain IMS metadata so that users of IMS-conforming systems will be able to search EOE's and where appropriate use objects as part of their learning environment.

Extending the EOE

One aspect of the concept of a community of users is that institutions are actively encouraged to take the basic EOE database shell and use it for their own purposes. The shell can be customized in order to meet different users' needs. It is hoped that a network of EOE will be developed on the Web, encouraging and extending the original concept. A copy of the database and instructions for use and customization can be downloaded from the main EOE Web site (http://www.eoe.org).

An example of an EOE database

At De Montfort University we have developed an Educational Objects Database focusing primarily on materials and resources produced as part of the Architecture and Urban Studies course.

The database contains materials produced by staff and project work produced by students. This material can be reused as part of other teaching projects. A key feature of the database is the ability for users to add comments on how they used it, particularly identifying teaching and learning issues. This includes rating the object, thereby providing useful information for future users. The database contains a range of objects, not in this case primarily applets, but Web materials, drawings, models and examples of computer aided design. Two examples are shown in Figure 8.3.

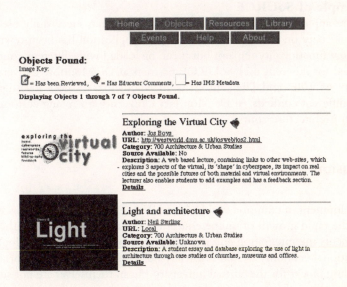

Figure 8.3 *A screenshot from the EOE database*

The database is now being extended and other Architecture and Built Environment departments in the UK are being asked to participate.

SoURCE

SoURCE, Software Use, Reuse and Customization in Education, is a project involving a consortium of universities led by the Open University. It is investigating reusability issues from a slightly different perspective.

SoURCE adopts the view that the transfer of educational software across institutions has, in the main, been unsuccessful because the perceived effort (or cost) of reusing applications has outweighed the perceived benefits. SoURCE is taking an integrated approach to reuse by looking at how to improve the cost/benefit ratio at both the institutional and individual level. This approach has two key innovative elements. It focuses on providing academics with customizable applications that enable them to retain control over content and teaching but do not require high levels of technical competence to reuse. These customizable applications are based on existing educational programs, which have been demonstrated to be educationally effective in one context and have the potential for wider utilization (Twining *et al,* 1998, p.54).

Another strand of SoURCE is a feasibility study into the requirements for a national library of reusable educational software for HE.

The process of customization and implementation is being carefully evaluated and the findings will be widely distributed. SoURCE serves as a model for the kind of collaborative partnerships that can lead to the efficient reuse of resources.

An example of SoURCE
A software application, The Elicitation Engine, has been successfully used at the Open University on an Education course. The application has been rewritten so that the key functionality remains but it can be loaded with different content and customized for different uses. SoURCE partners at De Montfort University, The University of Wales and The University of Middlesex are now investigating its usage in different contexts. At De Montfort University it is being customized for use on an Architecture course.

Conclusion

The development of common standards and Web-based delivery systems will help support the rapid growth of online education and training. Indeed, without such developments the integration and exchange of resources and the development of an 'educational economy' would not really be possible. These are important tools and building blocks for the 'virtual university' but in themselves are not sufficient. In order to achieve that we require the abilities, commitment, effort and imagination of faculty staff, educational technologists, librarians, courseware developers and others. The tools may appear to offer short cuts, and no doubt some will be tempted to take them, leading to the production of more poorly thought out and under-developed material.

It is well to remember the comment made by Downes (quoted in Freeman and Ryan, 1997, p.373) that:

> The really truly hard part to Web-based course design is in content design. Any reasonably competent computer professional can provide chat facilities, threaded discussion lists, Web pages, online registration, etc. But the core of online course materials will have to be determined by experts in the field working with experts in distance education delivery.

No one system, however good, can do that work for us.

Chapter 9

Changing cultures in HE

Introduction

By the culture of an educational institution we mean, as do social anthropologists, the shared beliefs, attitudes and ways of behaving that give a social group its identity. In traditional HEIs, there is a well-established culture. Roles are reasonably clearly defined. Participants in the community have strong expectations about how they and others should behave: students study, lecturers teach and do research, support staff support, administrators administrate and managers manage.

Under the impact of new technologies and other changes in HE roles, expectations and potentially whole cultures are changing and being re-engineered or reconfigured. As is to be expected from a move towards greater use of RBL (as defined in Chapter 2), both those who teach and those who are taught are likely to be greatly affected. Here we will examine these assumptions in a little more detail, drawing on evidence and examples. We also consider new roles that are evolving or are created *de novo* as processes and systems change and new needs have to be met.

The chapter is organized as follows:

- We review in fairly general terms the changes of role and expectation that are occurring for teaching staff, students, support staff, managers and administrators.
- We present brief case studies illustrating how RBL can be successfully 'embedded' as a significant component in traditional courses.
- We look in more detail at staff development needs, drawing on our own experiences of delivering courses about RBL to academic staff.

Those who teach

In HE, a majority of those who teach also carry out research. Here we focus on teaching but do so noting that there are possible pay-offs for staff active in research. Done well, the use of new technologies and RBL can mean that teaching, assessment and administration are all carried out more efficiently and effectively, leaving more time for research. We contend that the practice of being a teacher in HE is changing. What will the new forms of practice look like? What are the implications for staff development and support needs for teaching staff?

Probably the most significant change that is coming along is that teachers will no longer be the prime source of teaching content. It is already the case that to some extent teaching content is determined by committee and is planned ahead by teams, and that teachers are given syllabi and curricula they must follow. We referred in Chapter 1 to the example of the University of Phoenix where the typical online faculty member is part-time and earns only $2000 a course teaching from a standardized curriculum. However, where traditional forms of teaching are employed – those not involving an extensive use of RBL or new technologies – teachers in HE still have a great deal of control over the details of content and how that content is delivered. They may take a short description in a module handbook of a segment of a course and turn it into a lecture, choosing a sequence of topics and incorporating additional topics and references as they think fit. Much teaching is still face-to-face and didactic. In their own and students' eyes, teachers are authority figures in respect of content.

Traditional forms of teaching

It is perhaps worth reminding ourselves of the common patterns of teaching that occur in HE. Of course there are many variations but the following is fairly typical.

Over a 12-week seminar, students attend a series of lectures. Students may be part of a large group of up to 200 or more students. The timetable slot is perhaps up to 2 hours, but rarely will lecturers occupy the whole of that. They may leave some time for problems or questions at the end or they may just curtail the session after one to one and a half hours. Such lectures are typically presented on a weekly basis.

Associated with the lectures there may be smaller group sessions known as 'tutorials', 'lab sessions' or 'problem sessions'. A small group may well be as small as 15 or large as 30; they will be subsets of the larger group that attends the lectures. Typically these small groups come together on a fortnightly basis in sessions timetabled to last for 2 hours. Usually the same teacher who provided the lecture will provide support for the tutorial.

Work in the tutorial may take a variety of forms. There may be a review of important concepts from the lecture with practical and worked examples. Usually there is an opportunity for students to raise particular problems that they are experiencing and for them to receive some one-to-one tuition. In some discipline areas it is common practice to use the tutorial sessions for students to work through problems and other examples of the kind they may meet in a final exam, and for them to be able to request help with particular techniques or concepts.

Sometimes it is the case that the work carried out contributes towards summative assessment. This is a way of ensuring that students do indeed attend the sessions and give the problems posed due care and attention. Recall the discussion in Chapter 2 concerning principles of course design. There it is emphasized that, in good practice, summative assessment requirements match fairly the course content and stated learning outcomes. In the traditional mix of lectures and tutorials as just described, it is often quite difficult to ensure that summative assessment is fair and comprehensive in this manner. Some decisions about content may be taken informally as the course evolves. Summative assessment may be inflexibly tied into final exams or set projects.

Notice also the demands made upon the teacher if it is indeed the same one who gave a lecture to 200 students who is also providing fortnightly tutorials to smaller groups. He or she has to run several parallel sessions where essentially the same problems and issues are being covered. This is time-consuming for the individual and may be quite tedious. Furthermore, if summative and formative assessment is brought into the process, a very large amount of assessment work may be generated.

New forms of teaching

We will now contrast the traditional forms of teaching with the greater use of RBL and new technologies.

There are several ways in which the practice of being a teacher in HE is changing. Lecturing to groups (large and small) may be carried out at a distance using videoconferencing (as discussed in Chapter 6). Lectures may be recorded on video for repeat transmissions or for students to play back in their own time. Lectures may be enhanced by multimedia presentations or by accessing CAL, CD ROM and Web-based source materials.

Smaller group seminars and tutorials may take place in a variety of computer and IT mediated forms: video and audio-conferences; synchronous and asynchronous discussion groups, using mailing lists and 'threaded' discussions.

Using RBL means that teachers are no longer the prime source of content teaching. The content may be delivered synchronously or asynchronously using stand-alone packages or resources down loaded from the Web.

As described in Chapter 7, assessment may be delivered by computer, marked by computer and grades processed by computer to provide class lists and statistical summaries and to update individual student records. The teacher increasingly acts as learning coach or learning facilitator.

As a subject specialist, but no longer expected to be fully responsible for detailed teaching content, he or she becomes a learner too, as novel resources are explored. This may be done prior to tutorial sessions in order to identify and evaluate suitable resources. It may also happen as tutor and students learn together. As an extra pay-off, material being explored may have content relevant for research interests. We say more about the role of learning facilitator below.

Advantages to the teacher
With well-developed systems, a teacher might hope to find several advantages:

- After initial investment, preparation time is reduced.
- There is increased opportunity to engage with learners in one-to-one or small group dialogical encounters, ie, to really 'teach'.
- The chores of marking and administration are minimized.
- Staff meetings and administration-related queries from students are minimized by the judicious use of e-mail and electronic bulletin boards.
- Creating and adapting RBL materials may produce materials for multiple use and, potentially, for national and international distribution.
- Teaching staff may acquire new teaching and research related skills – information and instructional design, Web publishing, general Internet and digital archive searching skills, evaluation methodologies, team working, dialogical teaching.
- Developing and evaluating RBL may lead to publishable research.

Some disadvantages to the teacher
There are also some potential 'downsides' that may affect the successful introduction of these changes. Teaching staff may be:

- reluctant to give up their autonomy *vis-à-vis* teaching content and forms of delivery;
- reluctant to accept, without strong evidence and/or personal experience, that new methods and materials are effective;
- anxious about adopting teaching methods and materials that are much more open to peer examination and appraisal;
- anxious about having to work in teams;
- anxious about engaging in less formal, dialogical encounters with students;
- reluctant to acquire new RBL and IT-related skills.

For these reasons, there may be a fall in morale and even active resistance to change if it is not introduced in sensitive, participatory ways. It is a sociologist's truism that lack of opportunity to participate constructively in a community's workings leads to alienation.

The need for adequate resourcing and support
There may be a number of problems if adequate resources are not made available; this is especially so at the outset. Necessary 'front-loaded' investments are several:

- staff development (general awareness raising, specific training in RBL and IT-related skills);

- adequate support from technical staff for CIT aspects of teaching delivery;
- support from educational technologists, other media and design specialists;
- conscious efforts to facilitate team working;
- opportunities for staff to reflect on and develop dialogical teaching skills;
- periodic reviews of changes, with forums in which concerns can be raised.

It is important, too, that staff have confidence in their leaders. Senior management must not only seem to be responsible and caring, by introducing changes sensitively and supportively; they must also command the respect and confidence of those who are being led. Just as lack of participation leads to alienation, so lack of effective leadership leads to stress and anxiety. Staff need to be sure they are being asked to engage in well-justified pursuits and that their efforts will not be wasted for lack of planning and foresight.

New roles for the teacher

Teachers may be employed to create learning materials, to evaluate existing learning materials, or to adapt existing learning materials for particular purposes. A particular package of learning materials may be embedded in courses in a variety of ways to satisfy specified learning outcomes. Thus a teacher may act as an editor, an instructional designer or a course manager. None of these functions requires that a teacher has direct contact with students and all require new types of knowledge and skill. Teachers may also find themselves working as part of a team with instructional designers, courseware developers and others. Roles and responsibilities will need to be negotiated and new ways of working managed. The expertise of the teacher is one requirement for the development of good Web-based RBL materials, but the skills of the other members of the team are also essential for successful development.

However, as we note below, students being taught using RBL methods still require teaching support if their learning is to be successful. But this does not have to be provided by individuals responsible for course content. As with the case of the UK's Open University (described in Chapter 2), staff may be recruited specifically to fulfil support functions. Such staff may be expected to be subject specialists but may not themselves be familiar with the details of the learning materials and the learning experiences of the students. They are far more involved with commenting on particular course content, assessing and commenting on students' work, supporting the development of study skills or otherwise 'facilitating learning'.

The teacher as learning facilitator

Here we review some of the other activities a 'learning facilitator' may engage in. As noted above, instead of the traditional didactic lecture, one can envisage a variety of forms that might take its place or augment it. These include the video lecture, where a subject specialist with particularly good presentation skills may give a one-off presentation that is made available on video, rather like an Open

University television programme. Such videos might be delivered to students at a distance, on a one-to-one basis, or on campus they might be delivered to large groups of students. In the latter case there would be an additional role for a learning facilitator who could be available to introduce the video and to answer comments and queries afterwards.

Lectures may be made more interactive. Whether or not the main content was delivered by video or 'live', students' understanding of concepts is sampled using some kind of press button/voting type of technology. In the case of a live lecture, the outcome of the interactivity could inform the lecturer about what topics to elaborate upon and could even change the course of the lecture as a whole. In the case of a lecture presented by video, such interactive feedback could provide a learning facilitator with information about what topics to address in more detail.

For the smaller group tutorials or problem solving sessions where the brunt of the learning and teaching is carried by RBL materials, there will still be a role for the learning facilitator who is on hand to trouble-shoot students' problems and to answer their queries.

Those who are taught

How will students be affected by an increased use of CIT and RBL?

Younger persons may be expected to embrace 'the new' faster than older ones, but will still arrive at college or university tied to expectations and stereotypes, which can work for or against change. We can expect students to increasingly bring experiences of CIT or RBL from schools, FE colleges, homes, libraries, cybercafés and workplaces.

The impact of new technologies may lead to students having new expectations about the learning experience. They are likely to expect to have access to PCs and networks in a variety of locations and may well expect to be spending large amounts of time online. However, they may not be ready to accommodate themselves to new kinds of learning experience such as learning individually with PCs, using CAL packages and the Web, or participating in online conferences.

Some expected changes affecting the student experience

HE has always had a measure of RBL and 'student-centred' activities. Students have to work autonomously doing projects, assignments and research. They experience the need to be organized and to manage their time well.

In the terminology of Ford *et al* (1996), with RBL, students need to have access to 'learn places' and 'learning packs'. They may also need access to other resources. Students also often need access to teachers and to each other, for small-group discussion, peer collaboration, one-to-one tutoring, 'chat' and social life.

Some changes students are experiencing now include:

- increased use of computers and IT for word-processing, data-processing and library and bibliographic searching;
- use of CAL and multimedia resources;
- accessing the Web, e-mail and other CMC;
- increased use of different forms of RBL including CD ROM and Web-based materials, text-based distance learning type materials, and other text-based resources produced by on-demand printing;
- increased flexibility and less need to be on campus, blurring on-campus or distance learning, full- or part-time study.

Other changes being introduced or considered for introduction include modularization and credit transfer leading to individually tailored teaching programmes, and HE, FE, school and training distinctions being broken down, with short credit-bearing courses taken by 'capability' rather than by age or location.

In the future, with increasing flexibility of access, the distinction between being a student or teacher may become blurred. 'Students' may occupy a number of roles: engaging in peer–peer collaborations; supporting other learners at earlier stages (for reward or as necessary experience). They may make their own work available on the Web as putative RBL materials. They may access and contribute to 'serious' research and scholarship arenas via the Web, mailing lists, online conferences and electronic journals. Last but not least, there is potential for more access to and participation in institutional politics and decision making.

Student support needs

As well as the forms of teaching support discussed above, students will need and expect more detailed and readily accessible information about what programmes of study are available and how they are delivered. As an ideal, they should also receive in-depth assessment of aptitudes and key skills, with opportunities for individualized remediation, including opportunities to improve CIT and study skills.

As we note in Chapter 10, with seamless systems for delivering learning and teaching, the educational experience may be adapted to individuals at many different levels of resolution, from choice of programme and form of access down to choice of tutorial strategy for particular lessons, concepts and skills.

Support staff

Already we are seeing changes in roles and responsibilities and new career opportunities under the impact of new technologies. This is affecting technical staff who create and maintain the infrastructure of networks and computers. The production of RBL materials has implications for staff who work with media and information, graphic designers, desktop publishing and other lens media production staff, who may have new roles as Web master, instructional designer or learning technology support staff.

There is an already evident need for more staff to be deployed to carry out staff development work relating to CIT, RBL and learning and teaching.

There is an increased demand for librarians with CIT and related skills and educational technologists to carry out research and development. Such roles are beginning to overlap, as staff who previously may have had little contact now find themselves working as part of cooperative teams or, inadvertently, coming into conflict over roles and remits. Collis (1996) reviews the roles of those involved in 'tele-learning' with some thoroughness.

Administrators and managers

Other aspects of culture change in HEIs, driven by this move towards RBL and greater use of new technologies, are affecting administrators and managers involved with admissions and student data services, curriculum management, examinations, resource management, marketing intelligence, policy revision and strategy.

There are also implications for how HEIs are organized. New technologies can provide more opportunities for participation, allowing decision making to be more democratic. The converse is also possible. The need to respond quickly and flexibly to new markets may make institutions more management-driven. Wise leaders will be those who can strike a balance between the two sets of demands.

From a number of sources senior managers are being encouraged to contemplate whole-institution approaches. Ford *et al* (1996) present a complete 'learning environment architecture method' for transforming ('re-engineering') HEIs into institutions where the primary activities are the production of RBL materials ('learning chunks') and the delivery of 'learning functions' to students in designated 'learn places'. They note, in particular (as we do, above) the likely impact on the roles of academic staff: 'Academics… will be seen as developers of learning resources and managers of learning rather than the conduit through which knowledge flows to the student'.

Dolence and Norris (1995) present a similar 'vision for learning in the 21st century' and the ways in which HEIs should be transformed to address the needs of 'the Information Age learner'. Again, the emphasis is on increased and flexible use of RBL and the changing roles of academic staff.

Among other useful sources dealing with 'culture change' in HEIs, we particularly recommend the National Council for Open and Distance Education's (Australia) Website (http://cedir.uow.edu.au/NCODE/), the Node Web site Canada, (http://thenode.org/) and Erling Ljoså's (online) insightful article on 'The role of university teachers in a digital era'.

Case studies

Introduction

The following brief case studies are about embedding RBL and meeting staff development needs in a traditional university, De Montfort University (DMU) in Leicester, UK. Although only some of the learning materials were Internet-based (others were on CD ROM delivered over local networks), what is of particular interest are the lessons learnt about effecting 'culture change'. We give a summary of what we consider to be some of the necessary ingredients for success. None of these is likely to come as too much of a surprise. They largely correspond to what others recommend but they do have the merit of being grounded in practical experience. Shifts towards greater use of RBL and greater use of online delivery are overlapping trends but not fully synonymous. Our experience shows that, while many new courses are being developed for full online delivery, a very common pattern of change is that of the gradual transformation of existing courses. The case studies are representative of this latter sort of development.

Embedding RBL at DMU

The UK's Teaching and Learning Technology Programme (TLTP) was launched in 1992 by the Universities' Funding Council (UFC), with an eventual budget greater than £40 million. The aim of the project is 'to make teaching and learning more productive and efficient by harnessing modern technology' (TLTP Central Web site – http://www.ncteam.ac.uk/tltp/).

In its first two phases, some 76 projects were funded, the majority of which produced CAL and multimedia materials in a diverse range of subject areas, available to the UK HE sector at minimal cost. It was considered important that staff at DMU be given the opportunity to evaluate these materials, and where suitable embed the materials into their teaching. It was recognized that this process would not 'just happen'.

In order to effect significant change institutionally it was thought important that there should be central coordination. Accordingly, a centrally funded institution-wide project was set up with the aim of enabling staff to evaluate and embed TLTP and other RBL materials into the curriculum.

The following resources were made available:

- a budget for the purchase of software;
- funding for a dedicated educational technologist;
- a budget to buy out the time of faculty staff;
- an open access RBL multimedia demonstration facility;
- a project Web site and mailing list.

Workshops were held where staff were invited to consider if suitable materials could be identified for embedding into their courses. The basic idea was that participating staff should, minimally, be willing to evaluate some selected RBL materials by hands-on inspection and informal trials, with the view to possibly using the materials as part of their teaching. If it was decided to use the materials in particular courses, project staff would work with the academics to help ensure the materials were well integrated with course requirements, adapting and augmenting as necessary. Project staff also helped design and carry out evaluation exercises.

In 1997 the Embedding Project was absorbed into a larger initiative, the 'Electronic Campus' (still ongoing at the time of writing), which includes the in-house development of RBL materials for online delivery and institution-wide use of CAA and CMC. (See Brown, 1998, for more on this initiative.) The 'Electronic Campus' Web site, with descriptions of projects supported, is at http://www.ecampus.dmu.ac.uk.

The Faculty of Applied Sciences

At DMU, the Faculty of Applied Sciences has been using CAL as part of its teaching for some years, as optional backup for traditional teaching methods. There are several reasons why science subjects lend themselves to CAL, as indicated by the number of TLTP products that are science related. 'Sciences' tend to have a relatively stable factual and theoretical subject content, well-defined methodologies for empirical investigation, data analysis, formal modelling and theorem proving. There is a wealth of topics that benefit from multimedia presentation, structured exposition and being supported by simulations.

The aim of the DMU Applied Sciences project was to use CAL and other RBL as a substitute for staff-intensive tutorials, which traditionally are used to support didactic lectures. Whereas lectures may be readily delivered to as many as 100+ students, tutorials are delivered to, at most, 30 students at any one time. The hope was that the RBL substitute sessions could be offered with minimal academic and technical support. More information about the background to the project is given in Scott *et al* (1998).

As a first step, it was decided to concentrate on one particular course module, 'Cell Biology and Biochemistry'. The module had a large class size (n>120), requiring the running of seven tutorial sessions in parallel. Five different lecturers contributed to the running of the course.

A range of materials was obtained (TLTP and some commercial products). Additional materials were obtained for free from the Web. Evaluations of the form and content of the materials were carried out by academic staff and additional materials (worksheets, assessments) were created. In discussion with an educational technologist, principles of good course design were made explicit and used to map selected RBL materials onto learning outcomes and assessment.

In the end, around one-sixth of the materials selected were TLTP products, two-thirds were commercial products and one-sixth were accessed from the Web. In all cases, the students' learning experiences were similar. They were given access to the RBL materials as a resource which they had to explore and use selectively in order to carry out summatively assessed learning tasks. The tasks were introduced in tutorial sessions but students were also able to access the learning materials on other non-timetabled occasions. To ensure problems of access and navigation were kept to a minimum, the very first tutorial session was used to introduce students to the CAL and other RBL materials. Throughout all sessions, a CAL support officer was available to deal with technical problems. Academic teaching staff introduced the topics and remained on call in case of problems. To the staff's evident delight, this was an infrequent occurrence – they had no problem finding other productive uses for their time.

Evaluation studies were carried out, including structured interviews with staff, observations of students' ways of working, summative assessments of progress and a questionnaire assessing the students' specific experiences with each set of RBL materials and overall experiences of the course as a whole.

Findings showed that the use of RBL tutorials in combination with traditional lectures was a success. An additional indicator of this was that staff involved in the project went on to use similar approaches for other modules.

Psychology teaching

At DMU the Faculty of Health and Community Studies has been using CAL as part of its teaching for some years along with traditional methods. The desired aim is to use CAL and other RBL to complement and supplement staff intensive tutorials, which traditionally are used to support lectures. As a first step, it was decided to concentrate on two particular course modules delivered to second-year psychology students. The students were based within the Department of Human Communication which is part of the Faculty of Health and Community Studies. The module, 'Biological Bases of Behaviour' was taught starting in September 1997, and the module 'Neuropsychology' was taught starting February 1998, with lessons learnt from the first module being incorporated into the second. The project is described in more detail in Scase and Scott (in press).

As in the Applied Sciences project, a range of materials were obtained and evaluated, and principles of good course design were made explicit and used to map selected RBL materials onto learning outcomes and assessment.

An evaluation questionnaire was used. Questions were asked comparing the usefulness of RBL and the usefulness of lectures. Students were asked general questions about RBL: whether they thought it was better for learning and more enjoyable than traditional tutorials; whether the support for RBL was adequate; and whether they thought the RBL integrated well into lectures.

Additional evaluation was performed by having small discussion groups with students and informal contact with individual students throughout the academic year.

Interesting results were obtained from those parts of the questionnaire focusing on RBL in general. Students were asked first whether they thought that computer-based RBL was better than traditional tutorials and second, whether RBL was more enjoyable than traditional tutorials. The results appeared bimodal, with one group of students disliking the RBL sessions and another group in favour. The students who did not like RBL were almost always mature students. These students said that they had the impression that they were using computers for the sake of it and not as a tool to aid learning of academic subjects. As a result, initial induction and training in the use of IT and computer-based RBL has been intensified to ensure that this group of students are more positively motivated.

The use of RBL in the Psychology Department has gone from strength to strength. Delivery has been augmented by the use of CAA and online conferencing. The model of delivery has been adopted for other modules taught by the Department's staff and the Department's Web site affords a uniform environment in which course materials and activities can be accessed. Further evaluation (in progress) indicates favourable responses from both students and staff.

Summary findings from the DMU Embedding Project

DMU's experience of embedding RBL shows:

- staff may make significant savings of time because aspects of delivering teaching, assessment and module administration are carried out more efficiently;
- students' learning experiences are enhanced:
  - objective measures show their learning is at least as good as by traditional methods and
  - subjective measures show that, for a majority of students, the learning experiences are enjoyable and motivating and preferred to traditional methods;
- programme managers report a willingness by staff to extend the RBL approach to other modules.

Our experiences with the Embedding Project have made clear that there are a number of issues that have to be addressed if RBL is to be successfully embedded.

These include the need for:

- staff time to be committed for the evaluation, adaptation and creation of resources, including issues of costs and licensing;
- staff to be aware of clear pay-offs for investing in the use of RBL;
- staff development, particularly re pedagogy and course design as well as the use of particular 'learning technologies';
- clear rationales as to why particular aspects of a module's teaching and learning (lectures, seminars, lab sessions, projects, etc) merit conversion to an RBL format;
- having enthusiasts in faculties and departments;
- having a central proactive team (educational technologists, media designers, etc);
- the use of explicit principles of course design to map RBL materials onto learning outcomes and assessment;
- student preparation, both general IT skills and the use of CAL and Web-based materials;
- ensuring RBL packages are of good quality both for content and ease of use;
- setting activities and formative assessment to support learning, where RBL materials serve as a resource, rather than being used as stand-alone packages;
- using summative assessments, rather than relying on RBL materials to be intrinsically motivating;
- ensuring infrastructure resources (networking, computer nodes, technical support) are adequate to meet expected demands.

Using RBL to teach about RBL

As educational technologists, we are frequently called upon to mount a variety of short courses and workshops, often on quite specific topics: course design, creating distance learning materials, using CAA, writing multiple choice questions, and using various forms of conferencing.

In 1999 we had the opportunity to run a full module on RBL as part of an MA programme in Learning and Teaching. Although DMU staff are encouraged to take the course, it is open to academics in other institutions actively engaged in teaching.

An early decision was taken to deliver the RBL module in RBL format. Essentially, this meant providing learning resources and appropriate support. Learning resources are accessible on a Web site. They include a study guide and six units to be viewed on screen or downloaded as PDF files, together with a range of links to Web-based resources at other sites.

In addition, the FirstClass conferencing system (described in Chapter 6) was used to support students as they worked through the units or addressed a special seminar topic. Two members of the team that developed the module acted as tutors, contributing to discussions and commenting on contributions.

The intention was to raise awareness of issues rather than provide 'vocational' type skills for producing RBL. We felt very strongly that teaching staff in HE (and, we suspect, in other sectors) are best won over to 'culture change' if they are given the opportunity to thoroughly reflect on and discuss issues concerning the advantages and disadvantages of using RBL. We also thought it was particularly important that attention was paid to sound pedagogy: understanding theories of learning and teaching and principles of course design (essentially the same themes that are overviewed in Chapter 2).

At the time of writing, we are evaluating the RBL module. Thus far, our findings are very positive. We believe we have given the MA students what they needed and have done so reasonably effectively. Certainly, having students experience working through RBL materials and conferencing directly have been vital components of the experience. A more comprehensive programme would include the explicit development of practitioner skills involved in producing and delivering RBL-based courses, including setting up and facilitating an online conference.

Concluding comments

A major theme of this book is that, under the impact of new technologies, educational systems and processes are being transformed. In this chapter we have paid particular attention to what is happening and is likely to happen in traditional institutions, where the bulk of the teaching is on campus, face-to-face and aimed at undergraduates, chiefly in the 18–25 age range.

We have argued that a 'culture change' is under way. Our expectation is that in the course of the next five to ten years a majority of such institutions will develop a number of 'hybrid' approaches to learning and teaching. Much emphasis will still be placed on supporting students, with some institutions taking pains to emphasize the quality of teaching support and the general quality of life on campus and in the local community. In addition, many will have specialized niche markets, for example, short courses and postgraduate professional development.

New technologies will play an increased role, partly driven by students' expectations, but also because they demonstrably do improve the quality of teaching and learning and represent an efficient use of resources. It is possible there will be a greater differentiation between institutions, with richer ones providing 'deluxe' services, poorer ones offering more basic provision and some facing closure or takeover in the face of increased competition in the HE market place.

We engage in more 'future gazing' in Chapter 10.

Chapter 10

Around the corner

Introduction

Throughout this book we have mainly been surveying the current scene with a view to what's likely to happen over the next five years or so. What about the next 10, 15 and 25 years? Here, we look ahead to the brave new world of education in the 21st century.

First we consider the likely impact of a number of technological developments. The ideas are presented as brief notes with some references that are very suggestive of how things might progress. We conclude by highlighting the interrelated 'great debates' that are the current concerns of the educated world and whose outcomes will help shape the coming world of education.

The technological developments we look at include:

- the creation of seamless systems;
- intelligent agents;
- electronic publishing;
- universal systems for 'managing knowledge';
- virtual reality and virtual presencing.

The great debates we look at are concerned with the role and form of HEIs in the context of globalization and the need for sustainable development.

Technological developments

The creation of seamless systems

In Chapter 8 we looked at integrated systems for course development, delivery and management. There are other ways in which educational systems are likely to become integrated and seamless in operation. The 'trick' involved in achieving this is sharing databases through the use of metadata descriptions and allowing different users selective access to those databases depending on their needs and their authority. Thus databases to do with curricula may be accessed by:

- students wishing to know about courses and to access resources;
- academic staff wishing to develop courses;
- senior management responsible for curriculum oversight, quality checks, timetabling and resource allocation;
- visitors to the university wishing to know what is on offer;
- other managers concerned with knowing what particular courses a student or cohort of students is following;
- other institutions involved in collaborative projects.

Another significant database, or set of databases, is concerned with monitoring and managing student admissions and progression. This may be selectively accessed by:

- students themselves who wish to peruse their own records;
- course managers and tutors who wish to know about the students for whom they are responsible or to record assessment details;
- senior managers who wish to monitor admissions, failure and drop-out rates;
- those wishing to investigate in-depth student demographics and possible relations with progress and drop-out.

See Figure 10.1 for a summary of these functions.

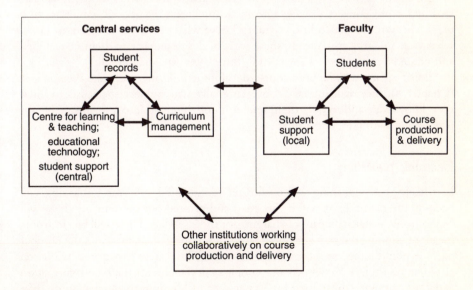

Figure 10.1 *'Seamless' systems*

Existing student data services already support many of these functions and have the capability of doing more. IBM, with its 'global campus' concept, is an example of a commercial organization which very much has its eye on developing software that will support the management functions of a university, as well as course development and delivery functions, in a seamless manner. The LearningSpaces virtual learning environment (VLE) would be one component of such a system.

IBM itself is a member of the IMS metadata standards steering group and has particular responsibility for advising on the metadata standards that would be used for curriculum management and student data systems. See IBM's HE Web site, http://www.hied.ibm.com/.

These seamless systems will enable course materials developed by a range of different providers to be integrated. A university may, for example, 'buy in' parts of a course developed by another university or commercial company and it will then be fully functional running in the VLE of the purchasing university. The assessments, activities and student monitoring features contained in the bought-in material will be integrated with the purchasing university's system. Issues such as copyright, intellectual property rights and charges for using the bought-in material will also be dealt with by the system.

Intelligent agents

It is likely that we will see increased use of artificial intelligence in educational systems and Web-based applications. This will come in a variety of forms. We will have intelligent agents helping to search and filter resources, abstract information, summarize and translate.

'Intelligent tutoring' will develop so that instruction becomes more individualized and more conversationally informed. Intelligent agents will converse with users who wish to get to know you, to know what you want to learn, to know what your interests are. Already these sorts of developments are being developed and piloted by the Media Lab at MIT (http://www.media.mit.edu/).

Similar agents will support course development. Using tools like Webmapper (Chapter 4), they will interact conversationally with subject specialists to elicit their knowledge and to help them render it coherent and into a form suitable for positioning within a course shell.

Electronic publishing

It is likely that publishing will be further transformed and Web publishing will become the norm. Texts will be accessed and printed out on demand; there will be electronic metadata means of charging for these services. There will be electronic means of assessing research activity in terms of numbers of citations and the number of times publications are accessed. All these possibilities were anticipated by Nelson (1990) in his Project Xanadu. As an example of developments, the Bath Information and Data Services (Bids), used by 70 per cent of UK universities, has more than

1000 journal titles online from Elsevier Science, along with titles from OUP, Blackwell's, Academic Press and John Wiley; see http://www.ingenta.com.

We may well soon be in the age of 'paperless paper'. We will be using thin plastic sheeting that electronically displays text and graphics in an interactive manner. Whole books will be downloadable onto such sheets, which will have the ergonomic advantages of paper books, together with the advantages of digital storage and retrieval of information. Electronic paper (e-paper) has been developed by Xerox (http://www.parc.xerox.com/epaper).

We will be seeing an increasing range of wireless devices that can interact with the Internet. Small, handheld devices, telephones with data screens and a whole range of 'digital assistants' will increasingly be able to send and receive data over the Internet, enabling new and exciting possibilities for learning and professional training without the need for a fixed network connection.

Universal systems for 'managing knowledge'

As well as intelligent agents there will be a number of tools and systems developed to support what is now known in the business world as 'knowledge management'. There will be the development of increasingly sophisticated metadata systems, offering multi-faceted views of data and data about data.

There will be increasingly sophisticated ways of visualizing and mining data, including ways of exploring the 'cyberspace' of the Internet. See, for example, Martin Dodge's Web site, 'The geography of cyberspace', http://www.geog.ucl.ac.uk/casa/martin/geography_of_cyberspace.html.

The European Commission has established the 5th Framework Programme for research and development concerning Information Society Technologies (http://www.cordis.lu/ist). Within the documentation for the 1999 Work programme, there is an item (Action Line VI.2.2, p. 39) whose objective is:

> to explore means of creating a 'universal information ecosystem' in which every single knowledge entity (whether a person, organization or entity acting on their behalf) can be globally, yet selectively, aware of the opportunities afforded by all others at any point in time. 'Knowledge entities' will seek to achieve their objectives by identifying those most appropriate to collaborate with and the most effective ways in which to do so, dynamically self-organizing and establishing new organizational structures as needed. This initiative will explore novel scenarios, techniques and environments in a context where more and more people and organizations need to communicate, cooperate and trade with each other in a truly open and global environment.

Visions of such a universal information ecosystem have been round for many years. Perhaps the most famous forerunner is to be found in the writings of H G Wells who promulgated the concept of world brain or world mind (Wells, 1938). In the 1970s, von Foerster et al (1972) proposed to the American government the development of an 'individual–society cognitive interface'. They submitted their proposal five times before it was finally rejected.

We have already made reference to Nelson's Project Xanadu, and to Bush's (1945) pioneering thinking. More recently we have a number of thinkers considering ways in which the Web itself will become more organized and possibly self-organizing as a coherent repository of knowledge; see, for example, Heylighen *et al* (online). See also Rossman's (1993) book, *The Emerging World-Wide Electronic University*, in which he discusses the concepts of a 'global encyclopaedia' and 'world brain'.

Pask was prepared to consider the possibility that our current generation of computing devices might one day metamorphose into a system 'like a brain and carry out operations that are mindful'. Pask asked, 'How do we view ourselves and our society, confronted with the prospect of being transformed beyond our imaginations? Have we wit enough to fear the future? Have we wit enough to overcome that fear?' (Pask and Curran, 1982, Chapter 12). See also the Pask memorial Web site (http://www.venus.co.uk/gordonpask/).

Certainly, the technological infrastructure for a universal information ecosystem continues to be developed. The company Teledisc is building a global, broadband 'Internet-in-the-Sky'. On its Web site, Teledisc states:

> Using a constellation of low-Earth-orbit satellites, Teledisc and its partners will create the world's first network to provide affordable, world-wide, 'fibre-like' access to telecommunications services such as broadband Internet access, videoconferencing, high-quality voice and other digital data needs. On day one of service, Teledisc will enable broadband telecommunications access for businesses, schools and individuals everywhere on the planet. (http://www.teledesic.com/)

The service is targeted to begin in 2003.

Virtual reality and virtual presencing

The use of 3-D visualization where people represent themselves and others as avatars is already being explored in gaming and socializing in MUDs (Multi-User Dungeons). See, for example, the Web site for 'Worlds Ultimate 3-D Chat Plus' (http://www.worlds.net/3dcd/index.html).

It is possible with other technologies such as laser holographic projections and immersive virtual reality to achieve full virtual presencing. For example, one might attend a committee meeting and experience sitting at a table with colleagues when, in fact, one is sitting with holographic projections, and colleagues elsewhere are experiencing a similar phenomenon. Such developments are already being explored at MIT's Media Lab (http://www.media.mit.edu/).

The European Commission's 5th Framework Programme, referred to above, calls for work on advanced training systems where:

the focus will be on the application of simulation and animation, 3-D visualization and immersive virtual reality, and virtual presence for collaborative learning, knowledge management, group interaction and personal tutoring and evaluation. (Key Action III.3.3, p. 24 of the 1999 Work programme)

The role and form of HEIs in the information age

Introduction

Throughout the world, educational, political and other social systems are in transition under the combined impact of demographic, cultural and technological changes. Arguably there is a special role for HEIs, not only to accommodate themselves to these changes, but also to lead the way in understanding them and to help avoid or ameliorate the painful consequences of change and contribute to the practical achievement of sustainable development. In order to move towards these goals, it is worthwhile, if not essential, for there to be a reappraisal of the roles and functioning of HEIs.

Some of the current great debates and issues within and about HEIs include the following, several of which have already been mentioned (in particular in Chapters 1, 8 and 9):

- the breaking down of the distinction between traditional forms of education and distance learning;
- the breaking down of the distinction between private and publicly funded institutions;
- the call for one or more global world university systems;
- as steps towards this latter, the call for more cohesion amongst educational institutions at state and nation state levels, with universal transferability of credits and shared curricular structure (see, for example, Green et al, 1999);
- tensions over who are the real power brokers in higher education: academics, student customers or managerial teams engaged in business re-engineering and forms of entrepreneurship;
- tensions over the forms of partnership which should be established between HEIs and business corporations.

At the time of writing, it is not obvious how the various tensions and issues will be resolved. We highlight them because we see them as becoming increasingly important, impinging more and more on those who work and study in HE.

Globalization and related issues

At the transnational level the great debates about the future of higher education inevitably overlap with other great debates, such as how to address world poverty and the need for sustainable development. Associated with the problem of world poverty, there is the issue of world literacy levels. When as many as 80 per cent of the world's population cannot read or write, how are educational opportunities to be delivered? What is the role for HEIs and a (possible) virtual, global university in all this? There are at least two main ways in which the Internet may be expected to play a significant role: 1) it may serve as the key medium for delivering quality information and educational materials to the parts of the world where they are most needed; 2) it may provide the forum for planetary conversation to take place, a medium for supporting political debate locally, nationally and internationally.

Examples of current developments in the latter can be found at Democracies Online (http://www.e-democracy.org/do/). Regarding the former, in a 'vision statement' discussion of trends and directions in open and distance education, Professor David Hawkridge of the UK's Open University distinguishes five major issues that are now 'firmly on the agenda' (Hawkridge, 1995b). These are:

- globalization, with the possibility that students may 'vote with their feet' and sign up to their institution of choice, possibly a foreign one;
- electronification – this is Hawkridge's own term for capturing the impact of CIT developments such as the Internet and digitization of media;
- commodification – Hawkridge asks if HE is likely to become 'big business' as educational resources become increasingly available as 'packages' to be bought and sold;
- domination – globalization and commodification may lead to further cultural and commercial domination by the 'first world';
- liberation – globalization and commodification may lead to students' needs being met worldwide.

Hawkridge notes that 'liberation' is the opposite of 'domination' and asks these questions. Will barriers of access be removed for the disabled and the poor? Can open and distance education increase international understanding, give greater esteem to minority cultures and spread knowledge among the dispossessed? Hawkridge believes these are 'all ideals worth striving for'.

The need for sustainable development

Introduction

The concept of sustainable development is not well defined. Rather than denoting well understood and agreed scientific, technical criteria the term appears to serve as a useful way of referring to overlapping and possibly contradictory sets of aspirations.

The term itself embodies contradictions: development implies change, sustainability implies conservation of some sort. Sometimes what is to be sustained is set against a world of limited resources; sometimes what is sustained is set against systemic damage to ecosystems or the biosphere as a whole. It seems that either of these may lead to direct conflicts between aspirations for improved standards of living (for example, supplying drinking water or electricity) or aspirations concerned with conserving resources or limiting the damage to particular ecologies. One thing that is generally agreed is that any agreements about what is meant by sustainable development should include aspirations and criteria concerning social justice (see Bossel, 1999, for more on defining and measuring sustainable development).

Education for sustainability

Of particular interest for the HE sector is Second Nature:

> a non-profit organization working to help colleges and universities expand their efforts to make environmentally sustainable and just action a foundation of learning and practice. Education for Sustainability (EFS) is a lifelong learning process that leads to an informed and involved citizenry having the creative problem-solving skills, scientific and social literacy, and commitment to engage in responsible individual and cooperative actions. Second Nature focuses on colleges and universities because they educate our future teachers, leaders, managers, policy makers and other professionals. (http://www.2nature.org/)

Governance and sustainability

Of more general interest is the United Nations Development Programme (UNDP), which has a Management Development and Governance Division (MGDG) with the aim of 'sharing knowledge for good governance'.

The UNDP has a vision of development 'that centres on people's choices and capabilities and that does not undermine the well-being of present or future generations'. The UNDP has called this approach 'sustainable human development', meaning:

> development that not only generates economic growth but distributes its benefits equitably, that regenerates the environment rather than destroys it and that empowers men and women rather than marginalizes them... Such development depends on good governance, including the empowerment of individuals and communities. The challenge for all societies is thus to create a system of governance that promotes, supports and sustains human development – especially for the poorest. (http://magnet.undp.org/)

Global knowledge development

In the early summer of 1997 there was a conference in Toronto entitled 'Global Knowledge Development 1997'. The conference was supported by the World Bank and other institutions. As part of the lead up to the conference and as a follow on, a mailing list discussion group was formed (gkd97). A number of issues associated with globalization, sustainable development and the impact of new technologies have been discussed. Discussions are archived at the Global Knowledge Partnership Web site (http://www.globalknowledge.org/), which describes itself as:

> The home of a growing partnership and dialogue focused on harnessing knowledge and information as tools of sustainable and equitable development and mobilizing the innovations and resources of the information revolution as tools to empower the world's poor. This partnership and dialogue have

their roots in an international conference on Knowledge for Development in the Information Age co-hosted by the World Bank and the Government of Canada in June 1997 in Toronto, in cooperation with a broad range of public and private partners. This site serves as the venue for an ongoing Global Knowledge Virtual Conference; an information resource on tools, partnerships and best practices related to harnessing knowledge and information for development; and the virtual meeting place for a growing network of partnerships linking development agencies, non-governmental organizations, the private sector, foundations, universities and other organizations and individuals committed to assuring that the world's poor are full partners both in the benefits of the information age and in building and sharing knowledge that contributes to sustainable and equitable development.

A particularly clear and focused voice in the gkd97 discussions is that of Michael Lootes. Lootes has developed the Humanity Libraries Project (formerly known as the Humanity CD ROM Project). The project aims to achieve 'massive information diffusion to developing countries to help solve poverty, to increase human potential, and to provide education to all' (http://www.oneworld.org/global projects/humcdrom/).

A role for HEIs

Ashby (1956) points out that any complex system, whose range of possible behaviours is not yet exhausted and that is subject to a constraint (any 'lawful' or regular occurrence that has the power to affect the system), will become informed of that constraint.

By Ashby's dictum, like it or not, we are in the process of becoming more informed of the constraints (the 'laws') of our world. We fail to become well-informed at our peril. In Ashby's terms, there is a need to 'amplify intelligence', to improve the second order, self-organizing processes of 'controlling control', of 'regulating regulation'.

HEIs have a role to play in amplifying intelligence, understanding and awareness (see Scott, 1998, for more on this theme). Here the Internet may well prove extraordinarily important for the delivery of information and education to members of the world's communities at all ages, levels and stages. It behoves the academic community to accept reflexive responsibility for its key role of both defining and promoting the 'good'.

We are not the only ones with these concerns. In his review of Hazemi *et al's* (1999) *The Digital University: Reinventing the academy,* which he summarizes as being a 'look at a variety of experimental and introductory usages of internet and intranet around UK universities and colleges', Anthony Smith, President of Magdalen College, Oxford, complains that the authors 'infuriatingly shy away from any consideration of the role of the university as an institution through which society forms itself' (Smith, 1999).

Concluding comments

In this book we have explored the impact of CIT on HE. Our major theme has been that CIT enables an increased use of RBL but that, to be effective and of good quality, RBL requires the explicit adherence to strong principles of course design and good pedagogy.

We have considered developments as they affect course delivery, assessment and communications systems. We have reviewed the range of resources made available by growth of the Internet and the World Wide Web. We have looked at integrated 'virtual learning environments' and metadata systems that promise to revolutionize educational publishing and course delivery.

In this final chapter we have looked ahead to what is 'around the corner' in terms of further ways CIT may impact on educational systems. We have also raised – but not answered – questions about the role of HEIs in a global context where there is the pressing need to achieve sustainable development.

As educational technologists, we like to fit media to purposes. In this instance, we have produced a book. We approve of I A Richards' (1943) definition that 'a book is a machine to think with'. We hope our book has managed to provoke constructive thought in our readers.

Glossary

Terms in *italics* are cross-references to other definitions in the Glossary.

Acrobat   A product from Adobe that enables high-quality text and graphics to be displayed on screen and printed. A *plug-in* enables Acrobat files to appear within a browser. Acrobat files are also known as PDF files (Portable Document Format).

ActiveX   A brand name of technologies from Microsoft that form a group of conventions and supporting libraries that allow interaction between different pieces of software in a consistent, object-oriented way.

Advance organizers   (Ausubel, 1968) help a learner anticipate what is to come. They may take the form of a listing of learning outcomes, textual introductions, explicit course shells or other maps of course content. Icons or other devices may be used to clearly signpost to students where they are within course materials and to aid cross-referencing.

Aims and objectives   We place the terms 'aims' and 'objectives' together as they are often used in association. A distinction is implied. Aims are usually broad statements of intent used as a way of framing the activities of a course team. Objectives are more specific statements of desired *learning outcomes.*

Applet   A stand-alone application written in the *Java* programming language. An applet is a piece of software code that runs under the control of a Web *browser* and is commonly used to enhance the interactivity of a Web page and to deliver client-side content. Applets run in their own frame, and can display graphics, accept input and even open network connections.

Applications sharing   A way for two or more people to work cooperatively while in different locations: all group members can simultaneously view and edit the same file over a computer network.

Approaches to learning   A term used by Biggs (1987) and others to refer to the different goals that learners may set themselves when studying learning materials or working through courses. Biggs distinguishes deep, surface and achieving approaches:

- Deep approach to learning. Learners who adopt a deep approach to learning set themselves the goal of developing a good understanding of the material in question. They will focus on relating knowledge to personal experience, and actively organizing and structuring knowledge and content.
- Surface approach to learning. Learners who adopt a surface approach to learning set themselves the goal of completing a set task and will focus on content items, and memorize facts and procedures for requirements of assessment.
- Achieving approach. Learners who adopt an achieving approach to learning set themselves the goal of maximizing attainments and will analyse course requirements in the light of resources and commitments, and use a mix of deep and surface approaches.

Asynchronous communication   This is communication over time. Typically it will be via a bulletin board or conferencing system where text messages are sent to be read later.

ATM   Asynchronous Transfer Mode – a high-speed transport technology for communications networks.

Audio-conference   A meeting held over a telephone between two or more locations.

Bandwidth   The width of the frequency spectrum (Hz) used for transmission. The size determines the rate at which information can be transmitted across a medium, measured in bits per second (bps).

Bridge   A device that interconnects several telecommunications channels.

Broadband   High-bandwidth (high-capacity) communications conduit.

Browser   An application that lets you look at and interact with information on the Web. The two main ones are Microsoft Internet Explorer and Netscape Navigator.

CAL   Computer Aided Learning or Computer Assisted Learning. A CAL package is usually a relatively stand-alone set of learning materials delivered by computer and distributed over local networks, on floppy disks or by CD ROM. Learning materials are usually quite clearly structured and sequenced.

CGI   Common Gateway Interface permits interactivity between a client and a host operating system through the Web via the *Hypertext Transfer Protocol (HTTP)*. It's a standard for external gateway programs to interface with information servers, such as HTTP or Web servers. A CGI program is executed in real time, so that it can output dynamic information – perhaps a weather reading, or the latest results from a database query. CGI allows someone visiting your Web site to run a program on your machine that performs a specified task.

Client   A computer or program that accesses services provided by a *server* over a computer network.

Cloze   The name of a test procedure where respondents are required to read a passage of prose with words deleted and fill in the gaps.

Codec   COder-DECoder – hardware that codes and decodes signals. In video-conferencing, the codec converts analogue signals to digital signals and compresses the output before transmission and decompresses the incoming signals and converts them back to analogue form.

Comprehension learning   Pask's term for that aspect of the learning process concerned with 'knowing why'.

Compression   Reduces the amount of data units required to represent information, necessary especially when transmitting video. Decompression reverses the process.

Computer mediated communication (CMC)   This refers to the ability to communicate via computer. It includes text-based communication, audio-conferencing and videoconferencing. The communication may be one-to-one but often in an educational context it will be group communication. CMC may be *synchronous* or *asynchronous*.

Constructivist theories of learning   These assert that 'learning' implies that new cognitive structures are acquired only as a consequence of adaptation. Such theories also assert some cognitive structures and processes (learning strategies) may actively guide these constructive activities.

Conversation theory   An approach to the understanding of the processes of learning and teaching developed principally by Gordon Pask. The key idea is that learning takes place through learner and teacher being in conversation, exchanging conceptions and misconceptions of topics in the form of verbal explanations and non-verbal modelling or demonstrations.

Course shell   A way of pre-specifying the structure and sequencing of topics within a course in terms of particular kinds of *learning chunk*.

CSS   Cascading style sheets, which allow the Web designer to control the fonts, colours, leading, margins and typefaces of a Web document without compromising its structure. CSS is a simple style sheet mechanism that allows authors and readers to attach style to *HTML* documents. Visual design issues, such as page layout, can be addressed separately from the Web page logical structure.

CU–SeeME   A system that enables videoconferencing over the Internet.

DHTML   Dynamic HTML – used to describe the combination of *HTML*, style sheets and scripts that combine to make a Web page animated or interactive. A typical example might be for a button to change shape or position on a Web page, without the need for a new download.

Digital   Information represented as discrete numeric values, eg binary format.

Discussion lists   See *Mailing list*.

Downloading Copying data to your computer from another, over a computer network.

Dublin Core A *metadata* element set intended to facilitate discovery of electronic resources. The Dublin Core is intended to be usable by non-cataloguers as well as resource description specialists. Most of the elements have commonly understood semantics of roughly the complexity of a library catalogue card. See http://purl.oclc.org/dc/.

Educational object A small piece of educational material that forms a self-contained *learning chunk*. This object can be incorporated and reused in different educational contexts. An example might be a *Java applet* showing an interactive graph of a chemical reaction. This applet can then be displayed on different Web pages with differing contextual materials allowing it to be used for a range of educational purposes.

E-mail E-mail messages are text messages sent between computers anywhere in the world. It is now possible to include images, sounds and other file types in or with e-mail messages.

Embedding This refers to the process of incorporating *RBL* materials into traditional courses.

Entailment structure As part of a *knowledge and task analysis* of course content, an entailment structure is a form of concept map showing how topics may be derived from one another or explained in terms of one another.

EOE Educational Object Economy – a Web site containing a database of *educational objects* that can be downloaded. Users can add their comments on the objects to the site. See http://www.eoe.org.

E-zine An electronic magazine, distinguished from a journal by the absence of peer review.

Formative assessment Assessment carried out to obtain information about a student's progress in order to provide feedback for that student and his or her teachers. This feedback may provide motivational reinforcement. It will also provide knowledge of results, so that learning and teaching strategies may be adapted or modified to be more effective, including implementing remediation programmes.

Frame A frame in a web *browser* is an area of a screen where a separate file can be viewed. A common example of the use of frames is to have a browser with two frames. One on the left side is narrow and has navigation controls. The larger frame on the right has the main content. When a navigation button in the left frame is pressed, the content in the right frame is changed. The navigation frame remains the same.

FTP A protocol used to transfer files from one computer to another.

GIF   Graphics Interchange Format – a proprietary image specification of Compuserve Information Services. GIF was intended to be a platform-independent format with which users could transfer files over modem lines at low speeds. It is a compressed format using 8 bits, giving between 1 to 256 colours. See http://wdvl.com/Graphics/Formats/GIF.html for more detail on this and other graphics formats.

Globetrotting   (Also vacuous globetrotting.) Comprehension learning without complementary operation learning may lead to globetrotting, possibly vacuous globetrotting, where similarities and differences between subject areas are cited but the concepts referred to lack operational content, that is they cannot be performed or demonstrated. The risk then is that the learner engages in mere 'talk'.

Gopher   Gopher is an *Internet* protocol in which hierarchically-organized file structures are kept on *servers* that themselves are part of an overall information structure. Gopher was a step toward the Web's *HTTP* that has been overtaken by the *browser*. It was developed at the University of Minnesota, whose sports teams are called 'The Golden Gophers'.

HEI   Higher Education Institution.

Holist learning strategy   A learning strategy that adopts a many-steps-at-once approach. (See also *serialist*.)

Hotspot   A place within a *node* (eg, a Web page) which, when clicked, causes another page to open and replace the current one.

HTML   A way of describing how text should look in a *browser*. Commands are inserted between brackets like this <H1>. The browser interprets them and the text is given properties. <H1> will make the text a heading. HTML can also be used to bring images, sound files, *Java applets,* etc onto the page.

HTTP   Hypertext Transfer Protocol – a set of rules for exchanging files (text, graphics, sound and video) on the Web. An essential part of the protocol is that HTTP files contain references to other files whose selection leads to new transfer requests across the *Internet*.

Hypertext   A way of presenting information with connections between one piece of information and another. In a Web *browser* these connections are known as 'links'.

Improvidence   Operation learning without complementary comprehension learning may lead to improvidence – the failure to see similarities between knowledge domains. The learner is obliged to learn the 'same' things over and over again.

Instructional Management Systems (IMS) project   The IMS project is developing *metadata* standards so that educational and training materials on the *Internet* can be described in a way that will allow them to be easily identified. It is also producing a range of standards so that data and information can be exchanged between *virtual learning environments,* student record systems and other databases. This will, for example, enable assessment activities produced in one system to be used in another, or student profile information to be exchanged between institutions.

Internet   An interlinked network of networks that allows any computer in the world connected to it to exchange data with any other computer in the world.

IRC   Internet Relay Chat – one of the most popular and most interactive services on the *Internet.* It is the Net's equivalent of CB radio, using real-time chat as a means of communicating between members of both private and public groups. It is text-based real-time group discussion over a computer network.

ISDN   Integrated Services Digital Network – a telecommunication technology for digitally transmitting different types of information. Each ISDN channel is 64 kilobytes in *bandwidth* and several can be combined to increase the available bandwidth.

ISP   Internet Service Provider – an ISP will connect a user from home to the Internet via a telephone line.

Java   A programming language that is intended to work on almost any computer, and which could change the *Internet* from being an information delivery system to a truly interactive computing environment. *Applets* are small Java programs. They can be run within Web *browsers.* See *educational object.*

JavaScript   A programming language whose code sits within *HTML* documents and enables some degree of interaction between users and the Web page. This interaction can range from buttons changing when a mouse is moved over them to more complex simulations.

Knowing why and knowing how   We use the terminology 'knowing why' and ''knowing how' to distinguish between theoretical, conceptual knowledge and practical, performance knowledge.

Knowledge and task analysis   The process of analyzing and characterizing the structure of course content. (See also *task structure.*)

Learning chunk   A term used by Ford *et al* (1996) to refer to the different groupings of learning material that make up a course or *learning pack.* Typical learning chunks are module, unit, lesson, book and chapter. (See also *course shell.*)

Learning conversation or 'full' learning conversation   According to Harri-Augstien and Thomas (1991), a learning conversation or full learning conversation involves not only learning about the why and how of a topic but also discussion about the how and why of the learning process itself.

Learning outcome   A term now commonly used as an alternative to 'objective', since it lacks the narrow behaviourist connotations of the latter and also reminds us that the outcomes belong to the learner, not to the teacher or course team. In the text, we distinguish between three kinds of learning outcomes:

cognitive – the acquisition of 'knowing why', acquiring conceptual knowledge;

performance – the acquisition of 'knowing how', mastering operations and procedures;

attitudinal – the acquisition of the beliefs and values appropriate for a particular vocation or profession.

Learning pack   A relatively self-contained set of learning materials (see Ford *et al*, 1996).

Learning strategy or approach to learning   These terms refer to descriptions or models of what learners may do or actually do as learners.

Learning style   A fairly enduring characteristic of a learner that biases him or her to adopt a particular strategy or approach.

Learnplace   A term used by Ford *et al* (1996) to designate any location where learning may occur. The emphasis is on flexibility of access.

Mailing list   A list of *e-mail* addresses of people interested in the same subject. When a list subscriber sends a message it goes to everyone on the list. You can reply to the messages, send new messages, or just 'lurk', reading the messages without participating. The key advantage of a mailing list over a newsgroup (see *Usenet*) is messages are automatically delivered to your e-mail box.

MAN   Metropolitan Area Network – a high-*bandwidth* communications network that normally covers a geographic region, such as a large city.

Metadata   Data about data. Metadata describes how, when and by whom a particular set of data was collected, who it belongs to, what it contains, and how the data is formatted. Systems such as *IMS* use metadata to 'find' educational resources that have the specified characteristics.

Modelling facility   Pask's general term for the 'world' in which teachers and learners construct models or problems or otherwise exemplify a particular topic.

MOOS   *MUDS* that are built on Object Oriented Principles.

MP3 (MPEG 1 layer 3)   A protocol for audio compression with very little loss in sound quality. The compression up to 12:1 produces very little degradation. The advantage of MP3 is that it can be broken up into pieces, and each piece is still playable, making it possible for MP3 files to stream across the *Internet* in real time.

MUDS   Multi User Dungeons or Dimensions – text-based virtual reality environments.

Node   A place within a *hypertext*. On the Web, a node is a Web page.

Objectives   See *Aims and Objectives.*

Operation learning   Pask's term for that aspect of the learning process which is concerned with 'knowing how'.

PDF   See *Acrobat*.

PERL   Practical Extraction and Report Language –a programming language often used to build *CGI* applications, with many applications far beyond the needs of CGI.

Plug-in   Additional software for a *browser* that enables, for example, audio or video to play within the browser. There are plug-ins for *QuickTime* and *Acrobat* PDF files as well as many others. Two important plug-ins that enable interaction and animation to take place within a browser are Shockwave and Flash.

QuestionMark   A commercial computer aided assessment product. It is widely used in HE in the UK.

QuickTime, QuickTime VR or VRML (virtual reality modelling language)   A product from Apple Computers that runs on both Apple and Windows PCs. It is very widely used to display digital video, audio and virtual reality products. A *plug-in* enables QuickTime to run inside a *browser* window.

RBL   Resource-based learning. A useful summary definition is provided by the Australian National Council of Open and Distance Learning (online): 'an integrated set of strategies to promote student-centred learning in a mass education context, through a combination of especially designed learning resources and interactive media and technologies'.

RTF   Rich Text Format – a format for exchanging word-processing files. RTF files can be opened by many different word-processors on a range of computer platforms.

Serialist   A learner with a bias to work locally, serially, on one topic at a time. A serialist learning strategy is one that adopts a one-step-at-once approach. (See also *holist learning strategy*.)

Server   A computer or program that allows other computers and clients to access information stored on it over a computer network.

SMIL   Synchronized Multimedia Integration Language (pronounced 'smile') – a way to describe the behaviour of temporal data, such as video, text and sound, on the Web. It is a subset of *XML*.

Summative assessment   Assessment carried out in order to award a mark or grade that indicates how a particular student's performance compares with that of his or her peers or set criteria. (See also *formative assessment*.)

Synchronous communication   Communication in real time, for example a videoconference where all the participants are taking part at the same time.

Task structure   As part of *knowledge and task analysis* of course content, a task structure is description of the procedures that constitute satisfactory performance. Task structures are often conveniently displayed using graphical techniques and conventions such as precedence charts and flow charts.

TCP/IP Transmission Control Protocol/Internet Protocol – a set of rules for sending and receiving data across networks. The *Internet* is based on TCP/IP. The IP envelopes and addresses the data and defines how much information can be put into the package. TCP breaks the data into packets, makes sure that they arrive at their destination and controls the reassembly of the data into the whole that was sent.

Teach back A term used by Pask and Scott (1972) to refer to assessment procedures where students' understanding of a topic is assessed by asking them to teach back what they have learnt. For performance outcomes, this means carrying out tasks to demonstrate *knowing how* skill. For cognitive outcomes this entails giving a narrative account of *knowing why*.

Teaching and Learning Technology Programme (TLTP) Launched in 1992 by the UK University Funding Council with an initial budget of more than £40 million. The aim of the project is 'to make teaching and learning more productive and efficient by harnessing modern technology'. See http://www.ncteam.ac. uk/tltp/.

Telnet An application program that allows users to conduct interactive sessions with computers elsewhere on the *Internet* by providing a character-based (ie, non-graphical) connection.

Tutorial in print A term used extensively by Rowntree and others (see Rowntree, 1990) to emphasize the supportive, friendly nature of the writing style used in distance learning and other *RBL* materials, which typically include activities with formative feedback and commentaries on how to learn.

URL Uniform Resource Locator – a way of addressing a 'thing' on the Web. Typing a URL into your browser is a way of asking for that document.

Usenet (News groups) A worldwide distributed discussion system that consists of a set of 'newsgroups' with names that are classified hierarchically by subject. Messages are posted to these newsgroups and can be read and responded to by anyone else. Messages are distributed using NNTP (Network News Transfer Protocol).

Vacuous globetrotting See *Globetrotting*.

VBScript A script language, like *JavaScript,* that is written in text within an *HTML* document. It is used to enable interaction between the user and the Web page being browsed. VBScript is used to control and communicate with compiled *ActiveX* objects.

Versatile learner One who can adopt either a *holist* learning strategy or a *serialist* learning strategy to fit task demands.

Videoconferencing An interactive two- or more-way teleconferencing between people at remote locations by means of audio and video transmission.

Virtual Learning Environment (VLE) A term used to describe learning systems that have a wide range of features and attempt to provide a 'total' environment for study. This will include resource materials, assessment activities, communication and support systems as well as course management and monitoring tools. An example of such a system is *WebCT*.

VRML Virtual Reality Modelling Language – a standard language for the animation and 3-D modelling of geometric shapes. It allows for 3-D scenes to be viewed and manipulated over the Internet in an interactive environment. Using a special VRML *browser*, the user can connect to an online VRML site, choose a 3-D environment to explore and move around the '3-D world'. It is possible to zoom in and out, move around and interact with the virtual environment.

WebCT The brand name of a *virtual learning environment* widely used in HE. Details can be found at http://www.webct.com.

XML Extensible Markup Language – a way to define and share document information over the Web.

References

The African Virtual University (online) http://www.avu.org

Ambrose, T and Paine, J (1993) *Museum Basics*, Routledge, London

Anon (online) Elissa's Essay About Zines, http://members.aol.com/erickalyn/elissa.html

Anon (online) We can learn from newspapers, http://www.gooddocuments.com/philosophy/newspapers_m.htm

Apple Computers (online) EOE: a global community for web based learning tools, http://www.eoe.org

Ariadne (online) http://ariadne.unil.ch/project/main.content.html

Arvan, L *et al* (1998) 'The scale efficiency projects', *JALN*, **2**, 2, and http://www.aln.org/alnweb/journal/vol2_issue2/arvan2.htm

Ashby, W R (1956) *Introduction to Cybernetics*, Wiley, New York

Ausubel, D P (1968) *Educational Psychology*, Holt, Rinehart and Winston, New York

Ballantine, R (1990) *Richard's New Bicycle Book,* Pan Books, London

Bangemann, M (online) Europe and the Global Information Society: Recommendations to the European Council, http://www.echo.lu/eudocs/en/report.html

Bates A (1995) 'Creating the future', in ed F Lockwood, *Open and Distance Learning Today*, Routledge, London

Bennett, R (online) Reinventing assessment: speculations on the future of large-scale educational testing, http://www.ets.org/research/pic/bennett.html

Berge, Z L and Collins, M P (online) 'Facilitating interaction in computer mediated online courses', background paper for FSU/AECT Distance Education Conference, Tallahassee FL, http://star.ucc.nau.edu/~mauri/moderate/flcc.html

Biggs, J B (1987) *Student Approaches to Learning and Studying,* ACER, Melbourne

Birkbeck College (online) The principles of protein structure using the Internet, http://www.cryst.bbk.ac.uk/PPS/

Blair, A (1998) Forward to *Connecting the Learning Society: The National Grid for Learning,* The Government's Consultation Paper, HMSO, London

Block, J H (1971) *Mastery Learning: Theory and Practice,* Holt, Rinehart and Winston, New York

Bloom, B S (1956) *Taxonomy of Educational Objectives: The classification of educational goals*, David McKay, New York

Bosak, J (online) XML, Java, and the future of the Web, http://metalab.unc.edu/pub/sun-info/standards/xml/why/xmlapps.htm

Bossel, H (1999) *Indicators for Sustainable Development: Theory, method, applications,* International Institute for Sustainable Development, Winnipeg

Boyd, G (1993) 'Educating symbiotic P-individuals through multi-level conversations', *Systems Research,* **10**, 3, pp 113–28

Brin, S and Page, L (online) The anatomy of a large scale hypertextual Web search engine, http://www7.conf.au/programme/fullpapers/1921/com1921.htm

Brochet, M G (1989) *'Effective moderation of computer conferences: Notes and suggestions',* in ed M G Brochet, *Moderating Conferences,* University of Guelph, Guelph, Ont, pp 6.01–6.08

Brown, S (1998) 'Reinventing the university', *ALT-J,* **6**, 3, pp 30–37

Burns, J, Lander, R, Ryan, S and Wragg, W (online) Practical guidelines for teaching with video conferencing JTAP publication, http://www.jtap.ac.uk/reports/htm/jtap-037.html

Bush, V (1945) 'As we may think', *Atlantic Monthly,* 176, 1, reprinted in I Greif (1988) *Computer-Supported Co-operative Work: A book of readings,* Morgan Kaufmann Publishers, San Mateo, CA

CAA Centre (online) http://caacentre.ac.uk/home.html

Calder, J (1994) *Programme Quality and Evaluation,* Kogan Page, London

Canole, G and Oliver, M (1998) 'A pedagogical framework for embedding C&IT in the curriculum', *The Association for Learning Technology Journal,* **6**, 2

Ceilidh (online) http://www.cs.nott.ac.uk/~ceilidh/papers/Overview.html

Center for Next Generation Internet (online) Trends in Internet growth, http://www.ngi.org/trends/TrendsPR0002.txt

Chickering, A and Ehrmann, S (online) Implementing the seven principles: technology as lever, http://www.aahe.org/technology/ehrmann.htm

Ciolek, M T and Goltz, I M (online) The internet guide to construction of quality online resources, http://www.ciolek.com/WWWVL-InfoQuality.html

Clarke, J (1982) *Resource-based Learning for Higher and Continuing Education,* Wiley, Chichester

Collis, B (1996) *Tele-learning in a Digital World. The future of distance learning,* International Thomson Computer Press, London

Colloquia (online) http://toomol.bangor.ac.uk/ll/readme.html

Connolly, D (online) XML, http://helix.nature.com/webmatters/xml.html

Coopers and Lybrand (1996) *Evaluation of the Teaching and Learning Technology Programme, Final Report,* HEFCE, London

Coopers and Lybrand (online) Transformation of higher education in a digital age, proceedings of the Coopers and Lybrand Learning Partnership Round Table, Aspen, http://consulting.us.coopers.com/cicsite/cicpress.nst/ef404ae1aac513e7802564db007a9625/

Cox, K (online) http://edutools.cityu.edu.hk/wwwtools/grading.htm

Cyberatlas (online) http://www.cyberatlas.com/big_picture/demographics/ovum.html

Daniel, J (1996) 'New technology: killer applications at the Open University', keynote paper presented at On-Line Educa, Berlin: International Conference on Technology Supported Learning

Daniel, J (1998) 'VC's view', *Sesame,* April/May, p 12

Dearing, R (online) *Higher Education in the Learning Society,* Report of The National Committee of Inquiry into Higher Education, http://www.leeds.ac.uk/educol/ncihe/appendic.htm

Delong, S (1997) 'The shroud of lecturing', *First Monday,* **2**, 5, and http://www.firstmonday.dk/issues/issue2_5/delong/index.html

DiPaolo, A (1999) 'Online education: myth or reality? The Stanford online experience', keynote paper presented at On-Line Educa, Berlin: International Conference on

Technology Supported Learning

Dolence, M G and Norris, D M (1995) *Transforming Higher Education: A vision for learning in the 21st century,* Society for College and University Planning, Ann Arbor, Michigan

Donovan, J (1991) 'Solutions anticipating a market', *Byte*, December, p 151

Educational Testing Services (online) Frequently asked questions, http://www.ets.org/cbt/edans1fq.html#eq4

Edwards, J (online) Electronic journals – problem or panacea, http://www.ariadne.ac.uk/issue10/journals/

Ed/x (online) http://www.ed-x.com

Farrell, G (online) The development of virtual education: a global perspective, The Commonwealth of Learning, Vancouver Canada, http://www.col.org/virtualed/index.htm

Feenberg, A (1989) 'The written world: on the theory and practice of computer conferencing', in eds Mason and Kaye, *Mindweave: Communication, computers and distance education,* Pergamon Press, Oxford, pp 22–39

Feldman, S (online) The Internet search-off, http://www.infotoday.com/searcher/feb/story1.htm

FlyLab Addison Wesley Longman and California State University (online) http://www.cdl.edu/FlyLab/

Ford, R *et al* (1996) *Managing Change in Higher Education: A learning environment architecture,* SRHE and OU Press, Buckingham

Forte, E, Forte, M and Duval, E (1997a) 'The Ariadne Project (part I) – Knowledge Pools for Computer Based and Telematics Supported Classical, Open and Distance Education', *European Journal of Engineering Education,* **22** (1), pp 61–74

Forte, E, Forte, M and Duval, E (1997b) 'The Ariadne Project (part II) – Knowledge Pools for Computer Based and Telematics Supported Classical, Open and Distance Education', *European Journal of Engineering Education,* **22** (2), pp 153–166

Fraeters, H, Reynolds, S and Vanbuel, M (1997) *Learning about videoconferencing* Leuven University Press, Leuven, and http://www.savie.com

Franklin Institute (online) About us, http://www.bfranklin.edu/about.html

Freeman, H and Ryan, S (1995) 'From concept to delivery a new tool for courseware developers', in eds J Tinsley and T van Weert, *Education World Conference in Computers in Education VI,* Chapman and Hall, London

Freeman, H and Ryan, S (1997) 'Webmapping: planning, structuring and delivering courseware on the internet', in eds T Muldner and T C Reeves, *Educational Multimedia/Hypermedia and Telecommunications,* Association for the Advancement of Computing in Education, London, pp 372–7

Gagné, R, Briggs, L and Wager, W (1992) *Principles of Instructional Design*, Harcourt Brace Javanovich, Orlando, Fl

Gahran, A (online) Cut the fluff! A contentious 'case in point' exploration, http://www.contentious.com/articles/1-1/cip1-1/cip1-1-p.html

Gates, D (online) The library of Babel, Pretext Magazine, http://www.pretext.com/oct97/features/story1.htm

Gilster, P (1994) *The Internet Navigator,* 2nd edn, Wiley, Chichester

Green, A, Wolf, A and Leney, T (1999) *Convergence and Divergence in European Education and Training Systems,* Institute of Education, London

Gubernick, L and Ebeling, A (1997) 'I got my degree through E-mail', *Forbes* Magazine, 16 June, and http://www.forbes.com/forbes/97/0616/5912084a.htm

Gunawardena, C N (1992) 'Changing faculty roles for audiographics and online teaching', *American Journal of Distance Education,* **6,** 3, pp 58–71

Harasim, L M (1989) 'On-line education: a new domain', in eds Mason and Kaye, *Mindweave: Communication, computers and distance education,* Pergamon Press, Oxford, pp 50–62

Harnad, S (online) The hundred years war started today: an exploration of electronic peer review, Electronic Peer Review Conference, http://www.mcb.co.uk/literati/articles/hundred.htm

Harri-Augstein, S and Thomas, L F (1991) *Learning Conversations,* Routledge, London

Harris, R (online) Evaluating Internet Research Sources – CARS: Credibility, Accuracy, Reasonableness and Support, http://www.sccu.edu/faculty/R_Harris/evalu8it.htm

Harter, S P (online) *Journal of Digital Information,* **1,** 1, http://jodi.ecs.soton.ac.uk/Articles/v01/i01/Harter/

Hatvany, B (online) Archiving the Electronic Journal, 61st IFLA General Conference, http://www.nlc-bnc.ca/ifla/IV/ifla61/61-hatb.htm

Hawkridge, D (1995a) 'The big bang theory in distance education' in ed F Lockwood, *Open and Distance Learning Today,* Routledge, London

Hawkridge, D (1995b) 'Trends and directions', in *Research and Developments in Open and Distance Learning Vision Statements,* Post ODLAA Conference Workshop, audiotape and pamphlet, Deakin University

Hazemi, R, Hailes, S and Wilbur, S (1999) *The Digital University: Reinventing the academy,* Springer, New York

HEFCE (online) The 'e-University' Project, Higher Education Funding Council Circular 04/00, http://www.hefce.ac.uk/Pubs/Circlets/2000/cl04_00.htm

Hegarty, M, Phelan, A and Kilbride, L (1998) *Classrooms for Distance Teaching and Learning: A Blueprint,* Leuven University Press, Leuven, and http://wwwlinov.kuleuven.ac.be/BIC

Heppell, S and Ramondt, L (1998) 'Online learning – implications for the University for Industry. A preliminary case study report', *Journal of Education through Partnership,* **2,** 2, pp 7–28

Heylighen, F, Joslyn, C and Turchin, V (online) Principia Cybernetica Web, http://pespmc1.vub.ac.be/

Hobbs, J M (online) Synchronised multimedia integration language specification 1.0, http://www.developer.com/journal/techfocus/091498_smil.html

Holderness, M (online) The librarian of Babel. The key to the stacks, Ariadne, http://www.ariadne.ac.uk/issue9/babel/

Holmberg, B (1998) 'What is new and what is important in Distance Education?', *Open Praxis,* **1,** p 32

Holmes, M (online) http://www.netshopper.co.uk/creative/education/languages/martin/markin.htm

Holoviak, J and Seitter, K L (1997) 'Transcending the limitations of the printed page', *Journal of Electronic Publishing,* **3,** 1, and http://www.press.umich.edu/jep/

HotBot, Altavista (online) HotBot: http://www.hotbot.com/super.html; Altavista: http://www.altavista.com/ http://www.ets.org/cbt/edans1fq.html#eq4

Huber, P (1997) 'The rise of the Internet', *Inside Multimedia,* 167, 11 May, p.12

Instructional Management Systems Project (IMS) (online a) http://www.imsproject.org/)

Instructional Management Systems Project (IMS) (online b) Content and management systems interoperability scope for version 1.0 specifications, http://www.imsproject.org/work_public/content_scope.html

Instructional Management Systems Project (IMS) (online c) Question and test interoperability scope for version 1.0 specifications, http://www.imsproject.org/work_public/question-test_scope.html

JISC (online) Joint Information Systems Committee: Five Year Strategy 1996–2001, http://www.jisc.ac.uk/pub/strategy.html#sec7

Johnson, G and Chatterton, P (1996) 'Technology enhanced flexible learning within Ford of Europe', paper presented at On-Line Educa, Berlin: International Conference on Technology Supported Learning

Jonassen, D H and Grabowski, B L (1993) *Handbook of Individual Differences, Learning and Instruction,* LEA Associates, New Jersey

Kaye, A R (1989) 'Computer mediated communication and distance education', in eds Mason and Kaye, *Mindweave: Communication, computers and distance education,* Pergamon Press, Oxford, pp 50–62

Kaye, A R (1992) 'Learning together apart', in ed A R Kaye, *Collaborative Learning Through Computer Conferencing: The Najaden Papers,* Springer Verlag, Berlin

Kleeman, J (online) Now is the time to computerize pen and paper tests, http://www.qmark.com/company/1998paper.html

Klevan, D and Kramer, A (online) Creating an interactive student medium for learning about the Holocaust Museums on the Web 1999 (Conference Proceedings), http://www.archimuse.com/mw99/papers/klevan/klevan.html

Kolb, D A (1984*) Experiential Learning: Experience as the source of learning and development*, Prentice-Hall, Englewood Cliffs, NJ

Landon, B (online) Online educational delivery applications: a web tool for comparative analysis, http://www.ctt.bc.ca/landonline/

Laurillard, D (1993) *Rethinking University Teaching*, Routledge, London

Leonard, A (1998) *Bots,* Penguin (for Hardwired), Harmondsworth

Lewis, L *et al* (1997) *Distance Education in Higher Education Institutions,* National Center for Educational Statistics, US Department of Education Office of Educational Research and Improvement, NCES 98-062

Lin, E (online) Musical offerings, http://www.developer.com/journal/staffpicks/071598_picks.html

Ljoså, E (online) The role of teachers in a digital era, Eden Conference, Bologna, http://kurs.nks.no/eurodl/shoen/eden98/Ljosa.html

Lockwood, F (1998) *The Design and Production of Self-instructional Materials,* Kogan Page, London

Lottor, M (online) Internet Software Consortium, http://www.isc.org/ISC/news/pr2-10-2000.html

Mace, U *et al* (1998) 'Weaving a better Web', *Byte*, March

Madra, J and Rudolph, S (online) Steps to using Java applets in the classroom in the 'papers' section of the EOE website, http://www.eoe.org

Marcel, J (1805) *Conversations on Chemistry,* Longmans, London

Marchal, B (online) The two faces of XML, http://www.developer.com/news/techfocus/050498_xmlupdate.html

Marton, F, Hounsell, D and Entwistle, N (1984) *The Experience of Learning,* Scottish Academic Press, Edinburgh

Mason, R (1991) 'Moderating educational computer conferencing', *DEOSNEWS,* **1**, 19

Mason, R (1992) 'Introduction: written interactions', in ed R Mason, *Computer Conferencing: The last word,* Beach Holme, Victoria, BC

McCormack, C and Jones, D (1998) *Building a Web-based Education System,* Wiley Computer Publishing, New York, pp 236–7

Merlin (online) http://www.hull.ac.uk/merlin/

Meta-Center (online) http://www.archimuse.com/mw98/papers

Michalski, J (online) Metaphors and the net, http://www.edventire.com/pods

Miles, J (1987) *Design for Desktop Publishing*, Gordon Fraser, London

Morgan, A (1993) *Improving Your Students' Learning,* Kogan Page, London

Morkes, J and Nielsen, J (online) Concise, SCANNABLE, and objective: how to write for the Web, http://www.useit.com/papers/webwriting/writing.html

Naido, V and Schutte, S (1999) 'Virtual institutions on the African Continent', in ed G Farrell, *The Development of Virtual Education: A global perspective,* The Commonwealth of Learning, Vancouver, Canada, and http://www.col.org/virtualed/index.htm

National Research Council (1993) *National Collaboratories – Applying information technology for scientific research, Committee on a National Collaboratory,* National Research Council, National Academy Press, London

NCODE (online) Quality guidelines for resource based learning. Report to NCODE 11 from RBL working party, http://cedir.uow.edu.au/NCODE/info/definitions.html

Negroponte, N (1996) *Being Digital,* MIT Press, Cambridge, MA

Neimanis, K and Geber, E (1998) From 'Come and Get It' to 'Seek and You Shall Find': Transition from a central resource to an information meta-center, http://www.archimuse.com/mw98/papers/neimanis/neimanis_paper.html

Nelson, T H (1990) *Literary Machines,* Version 901, Mindful Press, New York

Newby, H (1999) 'Higher education in the twenty-first century', *New Reporter,* **16,** 22 March, and The University of Southampton, http://www.soton.ac.uk/%7einfoserv/pubaff/newrep/vol16/no14future.html

New York Public Library (online) Schomburg Center for Research in Black Culture, Louis Armstrong Jazz Oral History Project, http://www.nypl.org/research/sc/scl/MULTIMED/JAZZHIST/jazzhist.html

Nielsen, J (online a) Trying to kill a meme for the growth of the Web, http://www.useit.com/alertbox/9509.html

Nielsen, J (online b) The telephone is the best metaphor for the Web, http://www.useit.com/alertbox/9705.html

Nielsen, J (online c) Does Internet = Web?, http://www.useit.com/alertbox/9809.html

Nielsen, J (online d) Differences between print design and Web design, http://www.useit.com/alertbox/990124.html

Noble, D (1997) 'Digital diploma mills: the automation of higher education', *First Monday,* **3,** 1, and http://www.firstmonday.dk/issues/issue3_1/noble/index.html

Pask, G (1975) *Conversation, Cognition and Learning,* Elsevier, Amsterdam

Pask, G (1976) *Conversation Theory: Applications in education and epistemology,* Elsevier, Amsterdam

Pask, G (1988) 'Learning strategies, teaching strategies and conceptual or teaching style', in ed R R Schmeck, *Learning Strategies and Learning Styles,* Plenum Press, New York

Pask, G (1990) 'Correspondence, consensus, coherence and the rape of democracy', *Journal of Communication and Cognition,* **23,** 2-3, pp 217–28

Pask, G and Curran, S (1982) *Microman: Computers and the evolution of consciousness,* Macmillan, New York

Pask, G and Scott, B (1972) 'Learning strategies and individual competence', *International Journal of Man-Machine Studies,* **4,** pp 217–53

Pask, G and Scott, B (1973) 'CASTE: a system for exhibiting learning strategies and regulating uncertainty', *International Journal of Man-Machine Studies,* **5,** pp 17–52

Pask, G, Kallikourdis, G and Scott, B (1975) 'The representation of knowables', *International Journal of Man-Machine Studies,* **7,** pp 15–134

Paulsen, M F (1995) 'Moderating educational computer conferences', in eds Z L Berge and M P Collins, *Computer-Mediated Communication and the Online Classroom Volume 3: Distance learning,* Hampton Press, Cresskill, NJ, pp 81–90

Perry, W G (1970) *Forms of Intellectual and Ethical Development in the College Years*, Holt, Rinehart and Winston, New York

Peters, J (online) The Hundred Years War Started Today: an exploration of electronic peer review, Electronic Peer Review Conference, http://www.mcb.co.uk/literati/articles/hundred.htm

Porter, L (1997) *Creating the Virtual Classroom: Distance learning with the Internet*, Wiley, New York

Prendagast, G A (1996) 'Using computer supported coorperative learning to deliver cost effective training', paper presented at On-Line Educa, Berlin: International Conference on Technology Supported Learning

Pullinger, D (online) http://www.nextwave.org/pullinger.htm

Ramsden, P (online) Linking assessment to learning: what a computer mathematics system has to offer, http://othello.ma.ic.ac.uk/articles/Brunel-Assessment-Conference.html

Rescher, N (1973) *Conceptual Idealism*, Blackwell, Oxford

Rescher, N (1977) *Methodological Pragmatism*, Blackwell, Oxford

Rhiengold, H (1992) 'Virtual communities', in ed R Mason, *Computer Conferencing: The last word,* Beach Holme, Victoria, BC

Richards, I A (1943) *How to Read a Page*, Routledge and Kegan Paul, London

Romiszowski, A J (1984) *Producing Educational Systems*, Kogan Page London

Rossman, P (1993) *The Emerging Worldwide Electronic University,* Praeger, Westport, CT

Routen, T and Graves, A (online) Flax, http://www.cms.dmu.ac.uk/coursebook/flax

Rowntree, D (1981) *Developing Courses for Students,* Paul Chapman, London

Rowntree, D (1985) *Developing Courses for Students,* Paul Chapman, London

Rowntree, D (1990) *Teaching Through Self-instruction*, Kogan Page, London

Rumble, G (1997) *The Costs and Economics of Open and Distance Learning,* Kogan Page, London

Saglamer, E (online) Tufte's Napoleon map, http://www.ddg.com/LIS/InfoDesignF96/Emin/napoleon/textindex.html

Salmon, G (1998) 'Developing learning through effective online moderation', *Active Learning,* **9,** December

Salmon, G (2000) *E-Moderating: The key to teaching and learning online*, Kogan Page, London

Scase, M and Scott, B (in press) 'Embedding resource based learning materials in psychology teaching', in ed N Hammond, *International Handbook of Learning Technology in Psychology,* Psychology Press, London

Schmeck, R R (ed) (1988) *Learning Strategies and Learning Styles,* Plenum Press, New York

Schultz, S, Klar, R, Auhuber, T, Schrader, U, Koop, A, Kreutz, R, Opperman, R and Simm, H (online) Quality Criteria for Electronic Publications in Medicine, GMDS, Freiburg, http://www.imbi.uni-freiberg.de/medinf/gmdsqc/e

Scott, B (1998) 'The role of higher education in understanding and achieving sustainable development: lessons from sociocybernetics', presented at the Congress of the International Sociological Association, Montreal, July. Extended abstract in the proceedings (online) http://www.dmu.ac.uk/~bscott

Scott, B (1999) 'Knowledge content and narrative structures', in ed L Pemberton, *Words on the Web: Language aspects of computer mediated communication,* Intellect Books, Exeter (pp 13–24)

Scott, B (in press a) 'CASTE revisited: principles of course design in a hypertext environment', in ed N Hammond, *International Handbook of Learning Technology in Psychology,* Psychology Press, London

Scott, B, Ravat, H, Ryan, S and Patel, D (1998) 'Embedding TLTP and other resource based learning materials into the curriculum', *Active Learning,* **8,** pp 41–4

Scott, P and Eisenstadt, M (1998) 'Exploring telepresence on the Internet: the Kmi Stadium Webcast experience', in eds M Eisenstadt and T Vincent, *The Knowledge Web: Learning and collaborating on the Net,* Kogan Page, London

Smith, A (1999) Review of Hazemi *et al's* 'The Digital University. Reinventing the academy', *Times Higher Education Supplement,* 2 April, p 27

Smith, J (online) Digitising collections: the redefining of museums, http://www.archimuse.com/mw98

Soby, M (1992) 'Waiting for Electropolis', in ed A R Kaye, *Collaborative Learning Through Computer Conferencing: The Najaden Papers,* Springer Verlag, Berlin

Stam, D (1993) 'The informed muse: the implications of "new museology" for museum practice', *Museum Management and Curatorship,* **12**

Teather, D (online) Exploring museology and the Web, http://www.archimuse.com/mw98

Tiffin, J W and Rajasingham, L (1995) *In Search of the Virtual Class: Education for the information society,* Routledge, London

Tufte, E (1983) *The Visual Display of Quantitative Information,* Graphics Press, Connecticut

Twining, P, Stratfold, M, Kukulska-Hulme, A and Tosunogla Blake, C (1998) 'SoURCE: Software use re-use and customisation in education', *Active Learning,* 9 December

UK IMS (online) http://www.imsproject.org.uk

University for Industry (online) A new way of learning: the UFI network – developing the University for Industry concept, http://www.lifelonglearning.co.uk/ufi/dev103.htm

University of Minnesota Digital Media Center (online) http://www1.umn.edu/dmc/portfolio/comparison/exec-summ.shtml

von Foerster, H, Brun, H, Easley, J A Jr, Lehman, F K, Weston, P E and Witz, K G (1972) 'Cognitive technology: A citizen-society problem solving interface', research proposal submitted to the National Science Foundation, Biological Computer Laboratory, Urbana, Ill

WDVL The Web Developer's Virtual Library (online) http://WDVL.Internet.com/Internet/Web/About.html

WebCT (online) http://homebrew1.cs.ubc.ca/webct/WhyUseWebCT.html

Wells, H G (1938) *World Brain,* Doubleday Doran, Garden City, NJ

The White House (online) Press release, http://www.adlnet.org/documents/pres-exec.htm

Wiener, N (1948) *Cybernetics,* Wiley, New York

Wiener, N (1954) *The Human Use of Human Beings,* Houghton Mifflin, Boston, MA

Williams, M (online) A primer for a good Web page, Seattle Times Company, http://www.seattletimes.com/news/technology/html98/issu_032998.html

Yager, T (1991) 'Information's human dimension', *Byte,* December, p.153

Subject Index

Author Index

Visit Kogan Page on-line

Comprehensive information on
Kogan Page titles

Features include

- complete catalogue listings,
  including book reviews and
  descriptions

- special monthly promotions

- information on NEW titles and
  BESTSELLING titles

- a secure shopping basket facility
  for on-line ordering

PLUS everything you need to know
about KOGAN PAGE

http://www.kogan-page.co.uk